DISCERNMENT IN THE EARLY CHURCH AND TODAY

Reclaiming Paul's Vision for Formation and Community Building

JOHN G. LEWIS

Seabury Books
NEW YORK

Copyright © 2025 John G. Lewis

All rights reserved. No part of this book may be reproduced, stored in a retrieval system, or transmitted in any form or by any means, electronic or mechanical, including photocopying, recording, or otherwise, without the written permission of the publisher.

Unless otherwise noted, the Scripture quotations are from New Revised Standard Version Bible, copyright © 1989 National Council of the Churches of Christ in the United States of America. Used by permission. All rights reserved worldwide.

Seabury Books
19 East 34th Street
New York, NY 10016
www.churchpublishing.org

Seabury Books is an imprint of Church Publishing Incorporated.

Cover design by Newgen
Typeset by Nord Compo

ISBN 978-1-64065-774-8 (paperback)
ISBN 978-1-64065-773-1 (hardback)
ISBN 978-1-64065-775-5 (eBook)

Library of Congress Control Number: 2024947637

TABLE OF CONTENTS

Foreword... v
Introduction: An Invitation to Pilgrimage 1

1. Experiencing Resurrection Power on the Road to Damascus 15
2. Christ-Patterned Moral Reasoning in Philippi.............. 43
3. Pastoral Care as Formation in Holiness at Thessalonica...... 71
4. Formation and Discernment Gone Awry in Corinth........ 105
5. Discernment in Rome: Under Grace, Not Under Torah..... 155
6. Discernment in Christ Jesus Today 209

Epilogue: Where Have We Been? Where Are We Going?..... 227
Bibliography.. 237
Acknowledgments 245
Notes.. 249
Index.. 273

FOREWORD

Discernment in the Early Church and Today is written for anyone seeking to follow Jesus as a faithful disciple. This includes individual congregants pursuing practices of faithful discipleship; clergy persons or church leaders involved in pastoral ministry or Christian formation; any person or group focused on discerning how their local church can thrive as a vibrant Body of Christ in their local context; and those who teach Christian formation and ministry in seminaries, colleges, and local schools of formation for ministry.

Throughout this book, I demonstrate ways to reclaim from the early church its wisdom in formation, community building, and the practice of communal discernment. For more than twenty-five years of leading St. Benedict's Workshop, or simply the Workshop, I have experienced the amazing fruits of communal discernment. I am confident that learning this practice of discernment can effectively shape Christian life, leadership, discipleship, and moral transformation in local churches today. It's this practice, adapted from Scripture, distilled from the process developed for use in the Workshop, that I want to share with you in this book.

What is discernment? Simply stated, discernment is determining the best course of action, given the situation. It informs the choices to be made concerning how to act. For our purposes, discernment is also a theological process for gaining insight on the will of God in particular circumstances. The practice involves reflecting on actions and their consequences. It means distinguishing God's influence and work in the world from the influence and work of competing forces. For this reason, discernment requires the counsel and wisdom of others. Discernment is a way of life for a community to stay connected to the work of the living God in today's world.

The process of discernment at the Workshop was born when I was working with a committee to develop the ministry that would become the Workshop. A committee member offered this suggestion.

> John, your New Testament doctoral work is focused on your interpretation of the apostle Paul's pastoral theology and ministry, and the role of discernment in his churches. Why don't you use your understanding of Paul as the framework for replicating his pastoral ministry and practice of discernment by analogy in our twenty-first-century Christian context?

This prophetic insight was at once both energizing and evocative. We started to look for ways to reclaim the wisdom and practice from the early church to reimagine Christian formation and the practice of discernment for today. We recognized that, by doing so, we might help to transform life in local workplaces and today's church.

The committee member's suggestion affirmed important aspects of my doctoral work on ministry and discernment in Paul's churches. Revelation happens when we listen patiently to one another as we try to discern God's will for our lives. "Aha moments" take place during a community's patient, deliberative conversations, just as Paul described in 1 Corinthians 14:29–31. Discerning God's will—whether for an individual or for a church—is *collective* and *deliberative* work in the community that gathers for that purpose.[1]

This revelatory moment in the life of the Workshop energized me to adapt for use by contemporary Christians the practice of discernment that Paul taught all his churches. It gave me confidence that people would recognize their experiences of resurrection power more often if we gave them tools to use Scripture to inform their discipleship and a process for reasoning together to discern God's will for their lives. Today's disciples now have access to the entire New Testament canon. These scriptural narratives and stories about Jesus and his powerful ministry give disciples countless resources for stimulating their moral imaginations and shaping their practices of discipleship in the diverse contexts of modern life.

The Workshop's practice of discernment had a humble beginning. Only two people responded to my first invitation to encounter this adapted practice of discernment in community. As word spread about the practice, new members trickled into this first small group. By the end of the Workshop's first year, the group had grown to eight participants. But the group members were actively evangelizing others to join this weekly practice. Several other groups began to form and meet on other days at different times and locations.

The momentum and excitement grew as participants discovered how God was knitting them together into communities committed to Christlike care for one another and ministry in the wider world. When these folks first joined a group, they were often strangers to one another, or at best mere acquaintances. But over time they became devoted friends in Christ. They shared their stories of joy and sorrow, and fruit and failure, in their active discipleship. They also began to recognize more and more experiences of God's resurrection power at work in their lives through the ordinariness of their Christlike discipleship in daily life.

This early experience probably mirrored Paul's own humble experience when he first arrived in a new city. He would set up shop and introduce visitors to Jesus, the crucified and resurrected Jewish Messiah. He worked long hours with his hands, probably as a tentmaker (Acts 18:2–3). He did not want to become a financial burden to his new congregations (1 Thessalonians 2:9). Paul's manual labor and refusal to accept payment for his teaching was central to his Gospel of Christlike self-giving for others, but it was disdained by his culture that promoted self-advancement and material success.

Paul's early churches started in each city as a small group of mostly curious Gentile visitors to his artisan shop. They would slowly grow into larger groups through Paul's pastoral ministry and his vision for a flourishing community where all the members shared the same Christlike care for one another (1 Corinthians 12:25–26). If one member suffered, all suffered together. If one member was honored, they all rejoiced together. At some point, as Paul's churches grew, they began meeting weekly in someone's home to share a common meal followed by a practice of discernment they learned from Paul.

As word spread slowly about the Workshop's weekly practice, people began asking what it was all about. In response, I simply referred to it as a "reflection group" and didn't give people any more details. There was a good reason for my brevity. I knew that if I responded by using well-worn church words and phrases such as Bible study, discernment, God's will, discipleship, worship, or Christian moral formation, people would immediately think they knew exactly what the group was doing.

In fact, through our weekly reflection-group practice, participants reimagined their understanding of these and other words that were so familiar to them. They were learning that in the early church these words had multi-layered meanings and applications to life in Christ—well beyond their superficial uses in churches today. In the Workshop's reflection groups, we use the entire canon of Scripture and our own transformed moral imaginations to discern together our practices of Christlike discipleship in the myriad contexts of daily life.

The Workshop's practice of discernment in community, adapted from the discipline Paul taught each of his churches, now shapes the work of many different groups. The practice guides conversations for individuals discerning Christlike actions in their practice of discipleship; conversations in decision-making processes for church leadership groups and committees; ecumenical associations; and it even informs the life and practice of leaders and employees in some small businesses.

During these twenty-five years, I have seen the difference that discernment in community makes in the lives of individual followers of Jesus and in the church.

The Way Forward in this Book

Discernment in the Early Church and Today invites readers to participate in a journey across time and space. We travel back and forth in time between the first-century world of the early church and the twenty-first-century world of modern life. Our time travel seeks to reclaim early church wisdom associated with formation, community building, and the practice of discernment that fueled their common life.

Our travel across time and space will be much like that of Jacob and Jesus. Jacob dreamed that there was a ladder set up on the earth, with the top of it reaching up into heaven. He saw the angels of God ascending and descending on the ladder. God promised to remain with Jacob, guiding him, protecting him, and giving that land to him and his descendants to be a blessing to all the families of the earth. Jesus draws on this same imagery in his response to Nathaniel. When Nathaniel proclaimed Jesus as the Son of God and King of Israel simply because Jesus saw him under a fig tree, Jesus responded, "Do you believe because I told you that I saw you under the fig tree? You will see greater things than these…very truly, I tell you, you will see heaven opened and the angels of God ascending and descending upon the Son of Man."

It is my hope that during our travel together over time and space that you, too, will see the heaven opened and the angels of God descending. They will show you how the wisdom of the early church's focus on formation and community building in the practice of discernment can bring new life to you, your church, and to your wider community.

Pentecost 2025

INTRODUCTION
An Invitation to Pilgrimage

Join Me on a Pilgrimage to Change Your Life as a Christ-Follower

I invite you to join me on a pilgrimage back to the earliest decades of the church. The journey takes us to holy places—small churches with a big vision—where many of the earliest followers of Jesus gathered. They came together as the Body of Christ to discern how to serve the living God and to be transformed into the image of their Lord Jesus Christ.

This pilgrimage takes us to churches either founded or served by the apostle Paul. His letters to these churches are the earliest Christian writings. They tell us all we know about the Christian movement in the first few decades after the death and resurrection of Jesus. Paul's letters are the only texts in the New Testament that give us insights to the format of worship in the early church. He wrote his letters explicitly to be read after the congregation finished eating their shared meal. The letters demonstrate the crucial role of discernment for formation and community building in their worship. "Paul is the New Testament writer who most explicitly and extensively speaks of discernment, and most emphatically places it at the heart of Christian moral life."[1]

Why Was Discernment So Important to Paul?

What made Paul's ministry so dynamic was his insistence that God's resurrection power, encountered in the risen Christ, could be experienced and recognized daily. Christ-patterned human choices and actions became channels for experiences of new life in the community. Each time a community gathered for worship, discernment was the key practice for identifying Christlike actions and connecting them with experiences of resurrection power. Discernment guided the quest to do God's will and to fulfill the desire to know Christ intimately through embodied discipleship.

The distinctive structure for worship in Paul's churches promoted discernment focused on community building, the formation of Christlike character, and the development, over time, of Christian practical wisdom. Their worship mirrored the structure of the two-stage dinner party well known in antiquity.[2] Meetings began with an actual, shared meal. The dinner had not yet become the later sacramental meal known as the Eucharist. After dinner, worshipers deliberated on their lives of faithfulness as followers of Jesus Christ. During these conversations in discernment, the early Christ-followers reflected on actions and their consequences. Through this lively, interactive, improvisational process, they learned from one another how to live Christ's way of life and recognize experiences of resurrection power.

This practice of discernment helped Christ-followers make sense of the moral life in Christ. Through the leading of the Spirit, they learned how God was building them up as a community grounded in Christ's way of life—his love embodied in acts of self-giving for others.[3] Christlike self-giving means putting the interests of other people ahead of one's own interests. Self-giving includes making sacrifices for others—including sacrifices of resources and time. It also involves willingly choosing not to exercise a right to something to which one is entitled. Christ served others sacrificially, even to the point of giving his own life on behalf of those he served. Spiritually enlightened in discernment, his followers sought to be transformed over time into this same self-giving image and shaped by God through their Christlike actions into countercultural communities called the Body of Christ.

Discernment was the heartbeat of formation and community building in Paul's churches. It was one of Paul's most crucial "ways in Christ Jesus" that he taught "everywhere in every church."[4]

Why Should We Reclaim This Practice of Discernment for Today?

Discernment in the early church was grounded in the role of personal witness to the experiences of resurrection power for new life in Christ-communities. Paul and the early Christ-followers believed that the resurrection of Jesus Christ wasn't just an event of the past, wasn't just a foretaste of the future to come, but actual, living, real experiences that impacted their day-to-day lives now. These experiences of resurrection power persuaded them to entrust their lives to this life-giving power of God at work in Jesus Christ. They remained steadfast in their commitment to walk the path of Jesus, even though it alienated them from family, friends, and neighbors, and, at times, led to their persecution and even martyrdom.

Between that first-century world and today, many Christian interpreters moved away from this experiential grounding in resurrection power and Christlike faithfulness. They began to focus on the biblical texts more as theological treatises. They often emphasized right belief *about* God, Jesus, salvation, resurrection, the church, and many other categories from the field of systematic theology. These interpreters downplayed the Christian practice and experiences of resurrection power that inspired the church to grow in its early years. In the case of Paul's letters, interpreters often emphasize Paul's thinking and oral preaching, rather than the Christ-patterned moral reasoning and embodiment of Jesus Christ that grounded his proclamation of the Gospel and pastoral ministry. This unfortunate interpretive strategy obscures the crucial role of discernment in Paul's churches.

Models of worship in the church today do not adequately prioritize Christian formation or experiences of resurrection power that lead to maturity in Christ. Most church communities are not built to practice discernment, which requires moral deliberation and experiential learning. The failure to form disciples through experiential learning in community contributes to the reign of individualism, political partisanship, and moral certainty in our culture. It leads to impaired relationships in families, churches, workplaces, and local communities, and disrupts a search for the common good. We are not building communities of care and trust as Paul envisioned.

Reclaiming this crucial practice of communal discernment is essential for building communities of resurrection life and forming disciples who actively participate in God's mission to reconcile a broken world.[5] In the opinion of biblical scholar Luke Timothy Johnson:

> The church needs to recover the distinctive importance of personal witness, above all the witness to God's working in human lives. Hearing personal witness to the power of God in individuals' lives increases the hearers' willingness to perceive the same power at work in their own lives.[6]

Whether in the early church or today, personal witness to the resurrection power of God is an essential aspect of the practice of discernment.

My goal on this pilgrimage is straightforward: to persuade pilgrims and readers to reclaim discernment as a group practice—the key discipline in Paul's vision for formation and community building in the Body of Christ.

The Format for This Pilgrimage

This imaginative pilgrimage has been organized by St. Benedict's Workshop (the Workshop), a nonprofit ministry in San Antonio, Texas. Our mission is to strengthen Christian communities by equipping them to use the Bible in their practices of discernment and discipleship in daily life.

The contemporary practice of discernment at St. Benedict's Workshop reclaims the role of personal witness to experiences of God's work in human lives. Our practice of communal discernment links these experiences of resurrection power with Christlike acts of self-giving for others. With my colleague at the Workshop, Jane Lancaster Patterson, I have led pilgrimages to Christian holy sites in Greece, Turkey, Israel, and the West Bank. In these holy places, we read ancient Christian biblical texts *in situ*. This practice opens the minds of our pilgrims to imagine the real-life events happening there 2,000 years ago. Pilgrims never read or hear the Bible the same way again after visiting these holy places where world-changing events took place.

On this pilgrimage, of course, we won't travel physically to these places. Instead, at each stop, we will imaginatively join an assembly of Christ-followers as they listen to the reading of Paul's letter to them. We will metaphorically sit in the balcony, watching but not participating in what transpires below.

Listening to Paul's letters in this way gives us a deeper and richer experience than what is available on actual pilgrimages to holy sites. On a typical pilgrimage today, we read a few biblical passages at one site and then move on to the next stop. On this imaginative pilgrimage, however, we will hear major portions of what Paul wrote to the churches we visit. We will experience the reading of the letter as Paul tries to persuade his congregation to act or refrain from acting in certain ways. We will hear how he tries to influence their after-dinner moral deliberations in discernment that will follow the reading of his letter. This format also allows me, as your pilgrimage guide, to identify and comment on some of the issues and challenges associated with formation, community building, and discernment in these churches and in Paul's letters.

Walking is another essential element of most pilgrimages. Traveling by foot is the only way pilgrims can still access certain holy places like the Temple Mount in Jerusalem, the Galilean hillside on the Mount of Beatitudes, or the Via Egnatia on which Paul walked into the ancient cities of Philippi and Thessalonica. If you ask anyone about their experiences on the Camino de Santiago in Spain, they will mention not only their physical challenges on the trail, but also the importance of proper care for one's feet at the close of each day.

Though it may sound ironic or even nonsensical, walking and foot care are essential parts of our pilgrimage in this book, too! In the early church, formation was focused on helping Christ-followers learn how to walk in the ways of Jesus to experience God's resurrection power. Unfortunately, the Greek verb *peripateō* ("to walk") in the New Testament is variously translated into English as "live," "conduct yourselves," or "act," which hides "the dynamic image of walking that is both more Pauline"[7] and more Jewish.

On this pilgrimage we examine how the practice of discernment empowered the early Christians to walk faithfully as followers of Jesus. Discernment was metaphorically the means of proper foot care in the early church. The practice of foot-washing, modeled by Jesus at the Last Supper, was probably part of the church's process for confirming or correcting the practice of Christlike faithfulness in daily life.

Spiritual transformation is always a goal of pilgrimage. I am persuaded that hearing and reflecting on these Scriptures in this way will spark your imaginations. You will begin to see ways to reclaim Paul's vision for discernment, formation, and community building in your own contexts.

We will be joined on this imaginative journey by a diverse group of twelve fictional pilgrims who have responded positively to the Workshop's invitation to participate in this pilgrimage. These pilgrims are Christ-followers who figuratively represent various folks who have accompanied us on earlier Workshop pilgrimages. They are active lay members from various Protestant and Roman Catholic congregations. They have expressed an interest in learning more about how discernment in the early church might inform their practice today. They have also heard about the Workshop's contemporary practice of discernment. They hope to see how the Workshop has incorporated some of the early church's wisdom gleaned from Paul's letters into its contemporary practice over these past twenty-five years.

Preparing for Pilgrimage

Pilgrimages to holy places do not start when the plane lands, pilgrims step off a bus, or even when they start reading a book like this one. One of the most important aspects of any pilgrimage is preparing in advance so that pilgrims open themselves to new experiences.

We take our cue from Jesus. He gave the following instructions to prepare his disciples for being sent out to turn their world upside down:

> Carry no purse, no bag, no sandals; and greet no one on the way. Whatever house you enter, first say, "Peace to this house!"...Remain in the same house, eating and drinking whatever they provide, for the laborer deserves to be paid. Do not move about from house to house. Whenever you enter a town and its people welcome you,

eat what is set before you; serve the weak who are there, and say to them, "The kingdom of God has come near to you."[8]

Pilgrims travel lightly, leaving behind both literal and metaphorical baggage. Taking too many clothes and heavy suitcases makes moving from place to place physically burdensome. Disciples unduly complicate their pilgrimage by bringing preformed expectations about who and what they will encounter on the journey. As Jesus warns twice in the passage above, good guests on pilgrimage do not expect or insist on things being the way they are back home. Faithful pilgrims leave behind what is familiar and comfortable. This opens us to change through our new experiences.

This book's imaginative pilgrimage is no different. Pilgrims must leave behind treasured Christian beliefs, practices, and traditions. We must be open to encounter fully what might be new and unsettling in the Scriptures we hear. By leaving these behind, we invite revelation and change to happen. This pilgrimage might turn us in a new direction in our understanding and practice of worship, discernment, discipleship, and Christian formation. Or the journey might simply affirm or even strengthen what we currently believe and do. Either way, our lives will be enriched by joining this pilgrimage. At the end of our journey together, we are free to reclaim the convictions and practices that give us life, comfort, and peace.

We also need to leave behind our current understanding of many "churchy" words. This may even come as a welcome relief. We hear many of these words so often we no longer pause to consider what they mean or how they shape our belief and practice.

In many cases these words meant something different in the early church from what many of us think today. As your guide on this pilgrimage, I will point out how these words and phrases were probably understood by Paul and his churches. The list includes familiar words and phrases such as gospel, church, worship, holiness, faith, grace, resurrection, salvation, and "in Christ Jesus," just to name a few. If we can hear these words and phrases in their first-century contexts, we can begin to understand more clearly Paul's vision for discernment, formation, and building communities of resurrection life.

On this pilgrimage we also leave behind many of the important historical and scholarly questions regarding Paul and his letters. For instance, we don't need to know the dating and sequence of Paul's visits to these cities or the dates of his letters to hear his vision for formation, community building, and discernment. Similarly, for simplicity I refer only to Paul as the author of each letter, knowing that most of his letters have other coauthors or may even be authored by those who learned from Paul. We can also leave behind the historical question of which coworker Paul sent to deliver each letter. In this book, I use my historical imagination to identify Paul's emissary in each city, with the goal of bringing to life the reading of each letter.

Where Are We Going?

Every pilgrimage needs a travel itinerary. We, too, have an itinerary, even though this is only an imaginative pilgrimage across time and space. We'll make stops on the road to Damascus, and in the cities of Philippi, Thessalonica, Corinth, and Rome. From time to time, I will also cross-reference what we hear at these stops with passages from Paul's letters to Galatia, Ephesus, and Colossae.

Now, for our pilgrimage travel brochure. Chapter 1, "Experiencing Resurrection Power on the Road to Damascus," presents Paul's transformative encounter with the risen Christ. After briefly comparing the story told in the Acts of the Apostles with Paul's own words describing the same event, we consider the revelation of the gospel and the risen Christ "in" Paul. The chapter explores some of that event's major implications for Paul's apocalyptic gospel and how the experience of resurrection power shaped his ministry among the Gentiles.

Chapter 2, "Christ-Patterned Moral Reasoning in Philippi," takes us to one of our two stops in Macedonia. Paul highlights the role of Christ's pattern of moral reasoning for the practice of discernment. We explore the ways he focuses on the story of Christ as the lens for interpreting the community's experiences of partnership in the gospel, grace, and the suffering of Jesus Christ.

We continue our time in Macedonia in chapter 3, "Pastoral Care as Formation in Holiness at Thessalonica." We explore the gospel's theme of mutual encouragement through pastoral care for one another. The chapter also examines the important role of experience, as Paul repeatedly invites the Thessalonians to recall specific experiences to encourage their steadfast faithfulness, despite persecution and setbacks. We also consider Paul's use of holiness as a synonym for the embodied faithfulness of Jesus Christ.

Chapter 4, "Formation and Discernment Gone Awry in Corinth," finds Paul employing the logic of the cross to address the church's serious divisions and broken relationships. Considered to be Paul's most practical letter, we see him exhaustively demonstrate how to reason with the logic of the cross in a myriad of situations from daily life. The letter provides a clear view of the two-stage structure of worship in Paul's churches and sets out a prescribed order for the practice of discernment.

Chapter 5, "Discernment in Rome: Under Grace, Not Under Torah," examines Paul's only letter written to a Christ-community he didn't start. He lays out his apocalyptic gospel to a group of Gentile and Jewish Christ-followers. They are primarily Torah-observant, but deeply divided over how to apply Torah to their common life. The chapter highlights two major sections of the letter. The first, in Romans 5–8, focuses on Paul's vision for formation. We take a close look at living "under grace" rather than "under Torah" by "walking in newness of life" according to the Spirit. In Romans 12–15, Paul presents the practice of discernment, including its key component of "proof through testing." We see how Paul provides numerous suggestions for concrete, Christlike actions through which he believes God will work to reconcile their relational alienation.

In chapter 6, "Discernment in Christ Jesus Today," our fictional pilgrims return from our imaginative journey to the early church. They assemble as a group in Christ Jesus and begin to practice discernment as part of St. Benedict's Workshop. We imaginatively enter their meetings to hear how they use Scripture and moral deliberations to imagine Christlike ways to engage the complexities of daily life.

The epilogue explores "Where Have We Been? Where Are We Going?" This section looks back and summarizes what we learned about formation, community building, and discernment in the early church from hearing some of Paul's letters. This review also suggests a few reasons why Paul's emphatic focus on discernment in worship receded over the next hundred years in the life of the church. The epilogue then looks forward to some ways the contemporary church might reclaim Paul's vision for formation and community building through the crucial practice of communal discernment in church plants, smaller churches, larger churches, and seminaries and local schools of formation.

The Structure of Each Chapter

The structure of each chapter follows a similar pattern. The first section, "Where Are We?" introduces pilgrims and readers to the specific location of the visit. The section provides some historical and geographic background that may affect the shape of the issues and conflicts in the church there and how Paul responds. In some chapters this section will include a historical topic required as background for understanding the specific letter being read. For instance, at our stop in Corinth, we will read more about the formal, two-stage dinner party structure of worship in Paul's churches. When we visit Rome, we'll read about the vast differences between worship then and now.

The section titled "Why Are We Here?" provides more details about the issues in the church to which Paul is writing and some of his concerns for why he is corresponding with them. Next comes the section called "What Words Matter?" This section simply introduces some of the most important Greek words Paul uses in the letter. Details about translations and meanings are covered throughout the chapter. Translations of passages from the New Testament are my own, unless otherwise noted.

Finally, before we enter each assembly to hear a letter, I encourage you to put down this book and reread or at least review the specific letter we're about to hear. This is not essential for understanding what we'll discuss, but it may be helpful. Keep the specific letter close at hand and refer to it from time to time as I offer my comments and insights at each stop.

Even before we depart, there a few other words and phrases I need to introduce. I will use these words consistently from this point forward.

I use the distinctive title "Christ-follower" to characterize anyone involved in the early church. I don't use the word "disciple" because Paul never uses the word. I also don't use the word "believer," often used to describe congregants in Paul's communities. The word implies a mental conviction rather than an embodied response to their encounters with the risen Christ. I also use the title "Christ-movement" to describe the early years when Christ-followers were still part of Judaism. It was nearly a hundred years later that the title "Christians" first emerged to describe participants in the Christ-movement. I avoid anachronistically calling Paul and the earliest Christ-followers by the title Christians. Similarly, I sometimes characterize one of Paul's congregations as a "Christ-community." The word "church" is also highly anachronistic. It leads readers to misinterpret dramatically what was happening in the worship of those early Christ-communities.

The final section of each chapter is called "Pilgrims Reflect on Their Experience." Readers get to listen to the comments, questions, concerns, and learnings of the twelve pilgrims who are imaginatively entering the assembly at each location where we stop.

Who Should Read This Book and Why?

This book focuses on ministry in the church and world. It is written to support Christian formation and the Christlike ministries of *every* member of the church. It is not just a book for ordained ministers, nor is it intended primarily for people in leadership positions in the church. It's written for anyone who wants to know Christ more intimately through Christlike practice.

The book challenges readers to reimagine Christian formation and opportunities for experiential learning together. Intended readers include Christians pursuing practices of faithful discipleship; clergy persons or church leaders involved in pastoral ministry or Christian formation; persons or groups focused on discerning how their local small group can thrive as a vibrant Body of Christ; and those who teach Christian formation and ministry in seminaries, colleges, and local schools of formation for ministry.

For those who want to go deeper, I include endnotes that engage some theological and practice-oriented issues and identify sources for quotations or distinctive positions I cite. Although not written for biblical scholars, the book is grounded in solid biblical scholarship as detailed throughout the text and endnotes.

My goal is straightforward: to persuade readers to reclaim the practice of discernment as a group practice. This was the crucial practice in Paul's vision for formation and community building "in Christ Jesus." To persuade readers, I walk along two related paths. First, at each stop on the pilgrimage, we will hear portions of Paul's letter read to that congregation. As your guide on this pilgrimage, at each stop I will offer insights on the letter grounded in my experience as a Christian pastor and biblical scholar. I will highlight Paul's vision for formation, community building, and discernment in connection with each letter.

Second, at each stop, the twelve figurative pilgrims offer their insights on what they heard in Paul's letter. Their experiences build momentum in their desire to reclaim this practice of discernment for today. In chapter 6, readers imaginatively join the first few gatherings of the pilgrims after their return from this pilgrimage. We watch what happens as they engage the practice of small group discernment adapted by St. Benedict's Workshop from the practice Paul taught to his churches. We see how discernment empowers their Christlike walks and forms them as more mature disciples of Jesus Christ.

Preparing for Departure

Before we depart on this pilgrimage, let's summarize our preparations. This pilgrimage highlights the early church's wisdom regarding Christian formation and community building through the practice of communal discernment. They emphasized the transformation of Christ-followers into the image of Jesus Christ. This took place through embodied acts of Christlike ministry and experiences of resurrection power, as discerned in the community's moral deliberations. Through their discernment,

Christ-followers learned how to partner with God in Christ, pursuing God's dream for a flourishing world filled with communities of resurrection life.

In this book, I draw from more than thirty years of experience in pastoral ministry, Christian formation, leading pilgrimages, and teaching the Bible in churches, universities, and seminaries. I am persuaded that today's Christ-followers must reclaim Paul's vision for formation and community building through the practice of discernment. Discernment leads to Christlike actions through which God works for healing, peace, and reconciliation, not only in churches, but in our local communities, workplaces, and the wider world.

But let me be clear. I am not suggesting a return to some imagined, idyllic time in the early history of the Christ-movement. Or that their approach to formation and community building through discernment brought peace and harmony. Far from it. The writings of the New Testament, including Paul's letters, bear witness to the many complexities, challenges, misunderstandings, and conflicts that beset the Christ-movement. These difficulties impacted the movement and its attempt to reflect and expand the powerful, life-giving reign of God through the life, death, and resurrection of Jesus Christ. We will encounter some of these challenging complexities and conflicts on this pilgrimage.

Instead, I offer this pilgrimage as a path to reimagine and reclaim the priority they placed on formation and community building through communal discernment. With a return to this practice, local churches today learn to recognize more easily their experiences of resurrection power through acts of Christlike self-giving by every member of the church. They shift the burden of decision-making and pastoral ministry from individual leaders to the shared practical wisdom and ministry that emerges from the "collaborative enterprise" that is their practice of discernment.[9] By reimagining and reclaiming this wisdom, today's churches can become flourishing communities of resurrection life in God's inbreaking kingdom, just as God in Christ and those early Christ-followers envisioned!

It's time to get on the road. Our pilgrimage begins with a journey back to the earliest days of the Christ-movement. Our first stop is the road to Damascus, where Paul's journey to become an apostle of Jesus Christ among the Gentiles first began.

CHAPTER ONE

Experiencing Resurrection Power on the Road to Damascus

"I Am No Longer Living, but Christ Is Living in Me" (Galatians 2:20)

The road to Damascus is our first stop on this imaginative pilgrimage to the early Christ-movement. This will be an unusual stop. We are not entering one of Paul's congregations to hear the reading of his letter to that community. Instead, we gather beside the road to Damascus to hear Paul's own words describing his first experience of the risen Christ.

According to the Acts of the Apostles, the risen Jesus confronted Saul the Pharisee on his way to persecute the Christ-followers in Damascus. In that moment, the creative power of God shockingly disrupted Saul's life and ignited his influential ministry to Gentiles. For the next thirty years Saul, also called Paul,[1] passionately carried out his divine calling as a prophet, teacher, and pastor among the Gentiles. Paul's experience of the risen Christ redirected the path he walked in Judaism and grounded how he modeled and taught Christ's way of life to Gentiles.

As pilgrims rather than tourists, we examine some implications of this event for the early Christ-movement. We will also evaluate its significance for Paul and his ministry. As pilgrims, we invest ourselves in this experience to be changed by it. Our goal is to reclaim Paul's vision for formation arising from this event and how that can become a catalyst for new life in the church and world.

Where Are We?

We are on the road that leads from Jerusalem to Damascus. We are getting close to this large and important urban center. Throughout its long history, Damascus has been a crucial crossroads on an important trade route from the Far East to the Mediterranean basin. The city is located sixty miles east of the Mediterranean Sea and 140 miles north of Jerusalem. It's situated on a plateau about 2,300 feet above sea level and surrounded by a large, fertile plain.

Damascus is one of the oldest, continuously inhabited sites known to archaeologists. Excavations suggest the city was inhabited as early as 8,000 to 10,000 BCE. Because of its cultural and historical significance, UNESCO designates the city as a World Heritage Site.

The city has a long history in biblical literature. It was conquered by the Assyrians around 732 BCE as reported in 2 Kings 16:9. Many of its Israelite inhabitants were carried away into captivity. By the first-century world of Jesus and Paul, Damascus has been dominated by the Romans since 64 BCE.

Why Are We Here?

The story of Saul's encounter with Christ in the Acts of the Apostles is well-known. His transformation from persecutor to apostle was so important to the early Christ-movement that three different reports of it appear in Acts.[2] Paintings by the Italian masters Caravaggio and Michelangelo have for centuries filled our imaginations with visual images of Paul being knocked off his horse to the ground. According to Acts, Saul was blinded by a bright light. He heard a voice from heaven asking "Saul, Saul, why do you persecute me?...I am Jesus, whom you are persecuting" (Acts 9:4-5 NRSV). Jesus then sends the blinded Saul to Damascus where, three days later, he regains his sight and is baptized. This dramatic encounter shapes most people's understanding of this momentous event.

Paul's encounter with the risen Christ occurred shortly after the death of Jesus.[3] Acts was probably written seventy-five years later and encouraged readers to interpret the event as Paul's conversion from the religion of Judaism to Christianity. By then, Christianity was emerging as a separate religion comprised primarily of Gentiles. This was not Paul's perception of the event. Paul's Jewish experience of the risen Christ was more multifaceted than what is reported in Acts.

Also, in Acts' vivid portrayal of Paul's subsequent ministry, he becomes the church's preeminent *preacher* of the good news of Jesus Christ to Gentiles. This impressive account of Paul as a supremely effective orator molds most people's perception of him as a persuasive oral advocate for Jesus Christ.

The Acts narrative tells only part of the story. This interpretation of his ministry emphasizes Paul's gift for *oral* persuasion that was a respected dimension of political and public discourse in the Roman Empire. Acts virtually ignores Paul's previous experience and expertise as a Jewish Pharisee. Paul *lived* and *taught* holiness in daily life through the application of Torah—the Jewish Law—to everyday situations. In Paul's encounter with the risen Christ, God called him to *continue* his fruitful ministry as a Jewish moral teacher. But this life-changing experience shifted the foundation of his moral teaching from Torah to the crucified and risen Jesus Christ.

To fill out this story of Paul's encounter with the risen Christ, we will hear Paul's own words describing the experience and explore how the event shaped his future ministry among the Gentiles.

What Words Matter?

This chapter introduces some key Greek words that matter in Paul's vocabulary of formation, community building, and discernment. They are words we will encounter again on our pilgrimage. I have placed these key words in brackets in the passages quoted or in parentheses in my explanatory sentences. At this stop on the road to Damascus, we will introduce:

- the verb *agapaō* ("to love");
- the noun *euanggelion* ("gospel" or "good news") and its related verb *euanggelizomai* ("to gospel");
- the noun *ekklēsia* ("deliberative assembly");
- the noun *apokalypsis* ("revelation") and its related verb *apokalyptō* ("to reveal");

- the noun *pistis* ("trust"/"faithfulness"/"faith"/"belief"/"trustworthiness"), its related verb *pisteuō* ("to trust"/"to believe"/or "to have faith") and the adjective *pistos* ("faithful"); and
- the verb *eudokeō* ("to be well-pleased").

These words and word-groups also form part of Paul's Jewish apocalyptic perspective. They shape how he sees and interprets what God is doing in the world in and through Jesus Christ. They also support Paul's vision for formation, community building, and discernment. By considering how he uses these words, we begin the process of reclaiming his vision for new life in the church and world.

We Settle in Beside the Road to Damascus

According to Acts 9:3 and 22:6, Saul encountered the risen Christ as he grew near to Damascus. In his own letters, Paul never mentions the location of this event or who was present. By then, all that mattered to Paul were the consequences of this event that reshaped his own religious life and vocation to ministry.

We choose a rest stop where we hope to find some shade and a breeze to get some respite from the intense heat. Maybe Paul was nearby this very spot. Pollen drifts in the air from the nearby grain fields and tickles our noses. We're getting no relief from the heat... We sit in a circle so we can hear some of our pilgrims read Paul's words about his encounter with the risen Christ.

We have only just arrived in the Middle East. This is our very first stop on the pilgrimage. We are having a little troubled getting settled. Droopy eyelids on a few people betray the lingering effects of jet lag. Several others are complaining about being hungry, even though it's the middle of the afternoon. A couple of other pilgrims are fussing with their cell phones, trying to activate their international cell phone coverage and locate local cellular service. Typical issues for pilgrims who have just landed in this time zone that is eight hours ahead of the time back home.

We will first hear Paul's own, brief description of his experience of the risen Christ and his interpretation of the event from his letter to the Galatians. Then, we'll explore how the encounter shaped his vision for formation, community building, and discernment. This will include a look at Paul's only other mention of this life-changing event in Philippians 3:2–11. He presents there his personal mission statement that also informs his ministry among the Gentiles.

God Reveals the Risen Christ in Paul (Galatians 1:11–17; 2:19–20)

Our first reader is Dante. He's an insightful, lifelong Roman Catholic, originally from New Jersey. He practices law in a small firm, always has a smile on his face, and has very good listening skills. He begins to read Paul's only written description of his actual experience with the risen Christ.

Galatians 1:11 I want you to know, brothers and sisters, that the gospel [*euanggelion*] that was gospeled [*euanggelizomai*] by me is not of human origin; **12** for I neither received it from, nor was I taught it by a human source, but I received it through a revelation [*apokalypsis*] of Jesus Christ.

13 You have heard, no doubt, of my former way of life in Judaism. I was violently persecuting the deliberative assembly [*ekklēsia*] of God and destroying it. **14** I advanced in Judaism beyond many contemporaries among my people, for I was far more zealous for the traditions of my ancestors.

15 But when God, who set me apart in my mother's womb and called me through his grace, was well-pleased [*eudokeō*] **16** to reveal [*apokalyptō*] his Son in [*en*] me, so that I might gospel [*euanggelizomai*] him among the Gentiles, I did not confer with any human being, **17** nor did I go up to Jerusalem to those who were already apostles before me, but I went away immediately into Arabia, and afterwards I returned to Damascus.

2:19 For through the Torah, I died to the Torah, so that I might live to God. I have been crucified with Christ; **20** "I am no longer living, but

Christ is living in me." And the life I now live in the flesh, I live by the faithfulness [*pistis*] of the Son of God, who loved [*agapaō*] me, indeed, who gave himself for me.[4]

Paul is responding to conflict with Jewish Christ-followers who have come into his congregations in Galatia and convinced some Gentiles to fully convert to Judaism. He distinguishes the divine source and authority of his gospel from the merely human source and authority of the Torah-observant gospel taught by these outsiders.

The Greek preposition *en* (1:16) reflects that this revelation of Christ took place *in* Paul. He came to know Christ intimately.[5] Paul experienced the crucified and risen Christ deeply *within* his own body. This experience differs sharply from the portrayal of the event in Acts, where a bright light and voice come *to* Paul *from outside* of him.

This revelation of Christ in Paul was not a one-time occurrence. It continued throughout his life and ministry. Paul confirms the enduring impact of this experience in Galatians 2:20: "I am no longer living, but Christ is living *in me*." In that first moment of revelation, Paul came to know the risen Christ living in him.

This experience persuaded Paul that God had placed a divine stamp of approval on Christ's pattern of life. Resurrection established Jesus as God's definitive revelation of what it means to be human and the one who empowers humans to participate in the life and character of God.[6] As a result of this experience, Paul entrusted himself to Christ's pattern of life and the resurrection power of God working in and through Christ.

Christ's pattern of life thereafter became the exclusive foundation for how Paul walked his own path of earthly life in Judaism: "the life I now live in the flesh, I live by the faithfulness [*pistis*] of the Son of God, who loved [*agapaō*] me, indeed, who gave himself for me" (2:20). Paul introduced Christ's act of self-giving for others in Galatians 1:4. The Lord Jesus Christ "gave himself for our sins to set us free from the present evil age." In 2:20 Paul connects Christ's love for him with Christ's act of self-giving for Paul.

Based on his experience of the risen Lord, Paul exchanged his zealous Pharisaic commitment to live exclusively by the Torah for walking according to the pattern of Christ's faithfulness. Paul does this by embodying Christ's love through his own acts of self-giving for others.⁷ Paul walked this path of Christ's faithfulness by analogy in the contexts of his own life. His actions demonstrate for others the risen Christ now living in Paul.

Paul was deliberate in using the phrase "in me" to describe this revelation. It is, as Morna Hooker observed, "stamped on him, so that he himself, by his life as well as his words, becomes the means by whom Christ is revealed to the Gentiles."⁸ Christ's pattern of faithfulness established the new moral norm for Paul's life and ministry. From this encounter he shifted the grounding of his moral teaching from Torah to Christ. Thereafter, his embodied proclamation of Christ not only revealed the crucified and risen Christ *to* others, but it also became the catalyst for the revelation of the risen Christ in and among his Gentile congregants.

Pistis—the Faithfulness of Jesus Christ (Galatians 2:20)

Most Bibles now translate Galatians 2:20 this way: "the life I now live in the flesh I live by faith [*pistis*] *in* the Son of God." My alternative translation throughout this book ("the faithfulness of Jesus Christ") reflects my conclusions derived from an extended scholarly debate concerning Paul's use of the *pistis* word-group and a grammatical issue associated with the genitive case in Greek.⁹ Much of the debate focuses on whether Paul and Christ-followers live by their own "faith *in* Jesus Christ" or by the pattern of Christ's life, translated as "the faithfulness *of* Jesus Christ."

Paul's texts are filled with variations from the *pistis* word-group, which has a wide range of meanings that include "trust," "faith," "faithfulness," "belief," and "trustworthiness." The New Testament texts almost always use this word-group to refer to relationships of trust, trustworthiness, and faithfulness, mostly between God and/or Jesus Christ and human beings.¹⁰

The now-traditional translation of 2:20 as "faith in Jesus Christ"¹¹ points mostly to a cognitive attitude on the part of Paul or Christ-followers. Their faith or belief affirms the factual existence of Jesus Christ and the various theological doctrines associated with him. People often approach this affirmation by learning more *about* Jesus and his teaching. This overlooks the corresponding expectation in the early Christ-movement that baptism into Christ anticipated embodied, Christlike acts of faithfulness on the part of his followers. Thus, as Teresa Morgan notes, "[t]here are good reasons, both within the texts and in the social context in which they were written, to think that this kind of commitment demands more than belief."[12]

Paul demands more than belief. He emphasizes the crucial role of *entrusting* oneself to Christ's pattern of faithfulness and the resurrection power of God working through it. Paul entrusted his own earthly life to this pattern after he experienced the risen Christ in him.[13] Because Christ is now living in Paul, he embodies daily the pattern of the faithfulness of the Son of God, "who loved me, indeed, who gave himself for me" (Galatians 2:20).

In Paul's congregations, Gentiles formalize their own commitment to entrust themselves to Christ's pattern of faithfulness through the ritual of baptism. "As many of you as were baptized into Christ have clothed yourselves with Christ" (Galatians 3:27).[14] Jesus Christ lives in Gentile converts as they, too, embody Christ's faithfulness and love through their own acts of self-giving for others. All that matters, says Paul, is "faithfulness working through love" (Galatians 5:6). To empower and guide this life of Christlike faithfulness working through love, God dispatched the Spirit of God's Son into the hearts of those who entrusted themselves to Christ's pattern of life (Galatians 4:6). It is this Spirit of Jesus Christ, poured into the hearts of Paul's converts, that inspires them to say, with Paul, "I am no longer living, but Christ is living in me" (see Galatians 2:20).[15]

On this pilgrimage, we explore the pivotal role of what it means for the early Christ-followers to entrust themselves to Christ's pattern of faithfulness. This is our focus, since "it is not belief per se that leads to righteousness or salvation,"[16] but Christlike daily living. "[T]he point to which everything in the Pauline letters themselves is directed lies not in believing (taking certain particular things to be in certain ways), but in living."[17] For Paul, Christ-followers experience righteousness and salvation through Christlike love, embodied in acts of self-giving for others in their daily living.

Paul's Gospel Is a Series of Gospel-Events (Galatians 1:11–16)

English translations typically render the singular noun *euanggelion* as "gospel" or "good news." But what is the *euanggelion*? Is it a written narrative of Jesus's ministry? What is the "good news"? Is it delivered orally in preaching? Is there something more?

Paul tells the Galatians that he received the *euanggelion* through a revelation of Jesus Christ (Galatians 1:11–12). Paul uses the word *euanggelion* throughout his letters. It appears three times in the first sixteen verses of Galatians (1:6, 7, 11) and four more times in one of the letter's other significant passages (2:2, 5, 7, 14). The letters attributed to Paul account for sixty of the seventy-six appearances of *euanggelion* in the New Testament.

The word *euanggelion* never appears in the Septuagint (LXX), the Greek translation of the Hebrew Bible used by Paul and most Jewish people in the first-century world.[18] This suggests that Paul did not derive its use from Jewish Scriptures.

When most people at the time heard the word *euanggelion*, they thought first of the Roman emperor, who was venerated as a god. Caesar, as J. Louis Martyn observed, "was heralded as the divine, salvific figure who provided deliverance and thus peace, joy, and wholeness for the entire civilized world."[19] Inscriptions on buildings unearthed through archaeological excavations refer to the good news (*euanggelion*) of *events* taking place in the life of the emperor, particularly military victories or the birth of a successor.

These inscriptions provide important clues to Paul's use of *euanggelion*. The word was familiar to his Gentile converts. Imagine the contrast between Paul proclaiming the good news of Israel's God with the good news associated with the Roman emperor! Paul used the word provocatively in a seditious, anti-Roman way. It characterizes the good news of the powerful, victorious *events* wrought by Israel's God through God's Son, Jesus Christ, bringing peace, joy, and ongoing salvation to God's people.

Paul's good news of God's victories started with the resurrection of Jesus Christ. This was the inaugural gospel-event.[20] It revealed God's power over death. This was God's ultimate victory over the powers of evil and death that oppose God's will for the world.[21] Paul's good news does not take the form of information *about* Jesus but points to *power* shown by God.[22] "What has happened…in the death and resurrection of Jesus reveals the very character of God…God's will [is] to 'do justice' on the earth by intervening actively in human affairs to establish right relationships where they do not yet exist because of human sin or folly."[23]

This revelation of resurrection power began a new history of God's power and kingdom breaking into earthly existence in a never-ending series of gospel-events.²⁴ Paul states this understanding clearly in First Corinthians: "The kingdom of God does not emerge by talk but by power [*dynamis*]" (1 Corinthians 4:20). The power of God that raised Jesus from the dead continues to create gospel-events—experiences of new life in God's kingdom—through Christlike acts of faithfulness.

How should we understand this divine power of resurrection? The Greek word *dynamis* is the source of our English word "dynamite." Paul might smile at the connection. He certainly thought of the gospel as "God's explosive world-changing power."²⁵

God's *dynamis* is "power as life," rather than "power as control," which is the cultural norm and expectation for how power works.²⁶ The genesis of Paul's understanding of power is God's creative act of raising Jesus to new life after death.²⁷ In Romans 4:17, without using the word *dynamis*, Paul characterizes God even more broadly as the one "who is creating life from death and calling into existence the things that do not exist." God's life-giving power not only raises the dead to new life, but also energizes people's earthly existence, enabling them to turn away from powerless, earthly idols to serve the living God in Christ Jesus.

Paul's experience of God's resurrection power in the risen Christ constituted yet another gospel-event. It was a vital and generative moment in the unfolding history of God's triumph over evil and transformation of life on earth. From the moment of his encounter with the risen Christ, Paul consistently bore witness to God's powerful activity in the world. He "offers himself as a paradigm of the work of the gospel."²⁸ Paul lives to God in Christ, grounded in his experience of the gospel of resurrection power.

Throughout his letters, Paul does not waver in presenting *euanggelion* as divine power experienced in human relationships.²⁹ "[T]he fundamental reality of the resurrection serves as an experiential foundation for all of Paul's teaching."³⁰ Paul teaches his congregations how to recognize these gospel-events of God's power as a crucial aspect of discernment. He seeks to ground their trust and practice of Christlike faithfulness in the same resurrection power of God that raised Jesus from the dead.³¹ Paul wants his congregants to entrust their lives to this power of God in the same way he did when God revealed the risen Christ in him. As we will see on each of our stops on this pilgrimage, these gospel-events continue to take place each time members of the Christ-community experience resurrection power for new life through Christlike acts of faithfulness.

Paul Embodies the Good News That God Reigns in Power! (Galatians 1:16)

Paul discerned his calling from God when the risen Christ was revealed in him. This revelatory gospel-event of resurrection power happened for a purpose: so that Paul might gospel (*euanggelizomai*) Christ among the Gentiles (1:16). Paul regularly employs the verb *euanggelizomai* to denote the activity of proclaiming the gospel.[32] The verb appears twenty-one times in Paul's letters (out of fifty-three appearances in the New Testament). The verb is translated into English in a variety of ways that include "preaching." As I suggested earlier, however, preaching is only part of the story—it is only the *oral* dimension of Paul's holistic, embodied proclamation of the gospel.

In the wider Greek world, *euanggelizomai* was often used as the proclamation of a victory. This included the announcement of liberation from enemies and deliverance from demonic powers.[33] The verb was often linked to salvation (*sōtēria*), since victory over enemies was understood to be the salvation of a city.[34]

The verb also appears twenty-three times in the LXX, with none more important for interpreting Paul than Isaiah's three uses of the verb (Isaiah 40:9; 52:7; 60:6). In Isaiah, *euanggelizomai* describes the activity of the herald who proclaims God's victories of deliverance and salvation to God's people. In this proclamation of God's victory, the herald climactically announces "Zion, your God reigns!" (52:7) Paul was aware of Isaiah's use of *euanggelizomai*. He quotes a version of Isaiah 52:7 in Romans 10:15. His frequent use of *euanggelizomai* is almost certainly grounded in the herald's announcement that "your God reigns!"

Paul's gospel distinctively proclaims that the resurrection power of God now reigns for new life in and through Christlike love embodied in acts of self-giving for others. Thus, through Paul's own embodiment of the faithfulness of Jesus Christ, Paul proclaims that "your God reigns!" Paul is the herald who is not just *orally* announcing God's victory and reign. He *demonstrates* God's powerful reign in and through his own body.[35] His persecuted body, bearing the marks of the crucified Jesus, serves as a public portrayal of Christ crucified and raised to new life (Galatians 3:1; 6:17).

In other words, Paul employs *euanggelizomai* to highlight how he heralds the good news of God's powerful reign through his words *and* Christlike ministry. He announces to everyone by his words and his actions, "your God reigns" in my life, and can also reign for new life in yours, too.[36] Paul's actions, and the experiences of power that follow from them, contribute to the never-ending history of gospel-events in which God is prevailing over the spiritual forces of evil.

Following his experience of the risen Christ, Paul began to gospel Christ crucified and raised among the Gentiles. Just as Jesus's acts of earthly ministry were conduits for experiences of God's life-giving power in the lives of others, Paul's Christ-patterned acts of ministry also facilitate new gospel-events for others. Through the risen Christ, living in Paul, God continued to channel resurrection power into the world through Paul's Christlike acts of ministry. "I will not venture to speak of anything except *what Christ has worked through me* to win obedience from the Gentiles, by word and deed, by the power of signs and wonders, by the power of the Spirit of God, so that from Jerusalem and as far around as Illyricum I have fully lived out the gospel of Christ" (Romans 15:18–19).

Paul's use of the verb *eudokeō* ("to be well-pleased") in Galatians 1:16 confirms his embodied proclamation of Jesus Christ and the good news of God's powerful reign in his body. In the New Testament, the verb is *always* associated with human actions,[37] often describing God's response to human behavior. The verb appears in the story of the baptism of Jesus in Matthew, Mark, and Luke, where the voice from heaven proclaims, "this is my Son...with whom I am well-pleased."[38] In Matthew, at the transfiguration of Jesus, the voice from heaven once again proclaims, "this is my Son...with whom I am well-pleased."[39] As we will see at later stops on this pilgrimage, Paul regularly encourages his congregations to discern actions that are pleasing to God.

Paul's use of *eudokeō* in 1:16 is a crucial key for better understanding the revelation of the risen Christ in Paul. His use of the verb indicates that this revelatory event happened at a time when God was well-pleased with Paul. I don't think God was well-pleased with Paul's active persecution of the early Christ-communities. So, where does that leave us?

I suggest that this revelation happened when God was well-pleased with some particular action being taken by Paul. In that revelatory moment, Paul recognized the risen Christ living in him, just as Christ was revealed to others through Paul's Christlike action. This revelatory moment happened so that Paul might gospel (*euanggelizomai*) Christ among the Gentiles (1:16) in word and embodied action.

This still leaves us with a pressing question. Is Paul referring to a revelation that happened when someone else recognized and called to his attention that he had taken some Christlike action? Is he referring to God being well-pleased with Paul's moral teaching as a Pharisee and desiring that Paul use these gifts to embody Christ rather than Torah? Did this revelation take place after God had already called Paul to proclaim Christ (see 1:15)? Is he talking about a moment of revelation during one of his mystical ascents into heaven?[40] We will never have satisfactory answers to these questions.

What we do know is this: Paul concluded that the purpose of the revelation of Christ in him was for him to gospel (*euanggelizomai*) Christ among the Gentiles (1:16). By embodying the faithfulness of Jesus Christ in his own life, and channeling God's life-giving power to others, Paul proclaimed to Gentiles in words and actions, "your God reigns!"

Paul's Gospel Is Grounded in a Jewish Apocalyptic Perspective (Galatians 1:12, 16)

Paul's theological and practical interpretations of his experience of the risen Christ were shaped in large part by his apocalyptic Jewish expectations. The Greek noun *apokalypsis* in Galatians 1:12 literally means a "lifting of the veil" or a "revelation."[41] Paul uses the active verb *apokalyptō* in 1:16. It denotes the divine act of revealing a reality in heaven "not normally visible on earth" and a temporal reality "not normally visible in the present moment."[42]

In first-century Judaism, these two words frequently characterized a "lifting of the veil" that allowed a Jewish mystic to catch glimpses of God's active reign for peace, justice, and life in the spiritual realm called heaven. The revelation is given so that God's heavenly action or will might be replicated by analogy on earth, so that what is happening in the heavenly realm is mirrored on earth.

The word *apocalyptic* also characterizes a theological perspective in Judaism. It developed over time from the Maccabean Revolt in the 160s BCE to the first-century world of Jesus and Paul. It was a theological framework used by some Jewish groups to explain why suffering, death, and oppression continued to be the experience of Jewish people who were faithful to God, the covenant, and Torah. These groups determined that their ongoing, unjust oppression was not punishment from God for unfaithfulness, as it had been during the Babylonian exile. Instead, they concluded that there were spiritual forces of evil actively working to oppose God's will for peace, justice, and life on earth.

Over time these Jewish apocalyptic groups also concluded that the situation was so dire that it would take God's active intervention in the world to set things right. They began to expect divine action to liberate the Jewish people from oppression and to inaugurate God's anticipated reign on earth. Some of these Jewish apocalyptic sects imagined that God would intervene in the form of a messiah, an anointed one (Greek: *Christos*). This messiah would deliver them from oppression, defeat the spiritual forces of evil once and for all time, and reign eternally in God's earthly kingdom. This divine intervention would begin God's "new age" or "new creation" on earth (see Galatians 6:15; 2 Corinthians 5:17). It would transform what Paul calls the "present evil age" (Galatians 1:4) into the time of God's complete and life-giving reign on earth.

The earliest followers of Jesus, including Paul, shared this Jewish apocalyptic perspective. They interpreted the death and resurrection of Jesus as God's intervention in the world to defeat the spiritual forces of evil and death. By raising Jesus from the dead, God inaugurated the new age with the inbreaking of new and eternal life in God's kingdom. This event delivered the followers of Jesus out of the present evil age (Galatians 1:4), where the spiritual forces of evil still opposed God's reign through their influence on human actions, including the actions of pagan leaders.[43]

Paul expresses his apocalyptic point of view in various ways. He occasionally personifies these spiritual forces of evil, giving them names such as "Flesh" (Galatians 5:16, 19), "Sin" (Romans 6:12–14), "this world"

(Romans 12:2), and "the spirit of the world" (1 Corinthians 2:12). In 1 Corinthians 10:11 he describes himself and his Christ-communities as people "upon whom the ends of the ages have descended." Heaven has metaphorically descended upon the earth, such that heaven and earth now overlap. In Philippians Paul tells the congregation that their citizenship is in heaven, and it is from there that they expect a savior, the Lord Jesus Christ (Philippians 3:20–21).

The early Christ-followers recognized, of course, that this new age of God's reign was not yet complete. Although the ultimate defeat of evil and death had been revealed when God raised Jesus from the dead, the completion and fulfillment of God's kingdom awaited Christ's future return in glory. For some years after his resurrection, Christ-followers still expected the completion of God's reign with the return of Christ to earth.

In the meantime, however, the early Christ-followers (including Paul) emphasized the importance of moral formation in the image of Jesus Christ for living in God's new age. They taught and demonstrated how people should walk the path to follow Jesus as Lord. In their Christ-patterned walks, they became active moral agents participating in the unfolding history of gospel-events. They became partners with God, who liberates the earth from the power of evil forces and reveals the presence of God's kingdom on earth. Paul states this connection clearly to the Thessalonians: "As you know, we dealt with each one of you like a father with his children, urging and encouraging you and bearing witness for you how to walk worthily of God, the one calling you into God's own kingdom and glory" (1 Thessalonians 2:11–12).

Paul's Mission Statement Grounds a New Moral Life in Christ (Philippians 3:10–11)

The death of Jesus is a prominent theme in Paul's gospel. Following his earthly death, God raised Jesus to new life. Death is defeated. Grounded in his apocalyptic perspective, Paul uses the language of death to highlight the discontinuity between new life in Christ and continuing life in the present evil age.[44] We have already heard Paul embrace this sequence of death to new life: "I died to the Torah, so that I might live to God; I have been crucified with Christ; and I am no longer living, but Christ is living in me" (Galatians 2:19–20). Paul closes the letter to the Galatians using a similar metaphor: "May I never boast of anything except the cross of our Lord Jesus Christ, by which *the world has been crucified to me, and I to the world*...I bear the marks of Jesus in my body" (6:14, 17).

The cross of Christ and his crucifixion ground Paul's metaphorical death to Torah. His death to Torah meant much more than simply dying to self, which is the way many contemporary Christians articulate Paul's perspective. Paul's death to Torah meant he no longer considered Torah as his *exclusive* pattern of life. His death to Torah ironically empowered him to "live to God" through his new life in Christ. In God's new age in Christ, all the dualities that oppose one another in the present evil age are dissolved. "There is no longer Jew or Greek, there is no longer slave or free, there is no longer male and female; for all of you are one in Christ Jesus" (Galatians 3:28, NRSV).

We have already seen how Paul's experience of the crucified and risen Christ turned his world upside-down. The only other time he writes about the consequences of that experience is in Philippians 3:2–11. There, he says that whatever successes he enjoyed as a rising star in Judaism pale in comparison with his experience of the risen Christ.

Latisha now rises in our circle of imaginary pilgrims. She's an elected member of the city council and is a lay leader in her local AME (African Methodist Episcopal) church. Latisha now reads these words of Paul:

> **Philippians 3:7** Whatever gains came to me, these I reckon as loss on account of Christ. **8** I regard everything as loss because of the surpassing value of knowing Christ Jesus my Lord. For his sake I have suffered the loss of all things, and I regard them as rubbish, in order that I may gain Christ **9** and be found in him, not having my own righteousness from the Torah, but, through the faithfulness of Christ, having the righteousness of God based upon that faithfulness. **10** I want *to know Christ* and the *power of his resurrection*, and the *partnership of his sufferings*, by *conforming myself to his death*, **11** if, somehow, I *might attain the resurrection from the dead*.

Paul's experience of the crucified and risen Christ led to this personal mission statement in Philippians 3:10–11. It embraces the gospel's fundamental sequence of death to new life. Paul pursued this multidimensional mission statement every day of his life in Christ. It was his lens for interpreting his lived experience. And it shaped every aspect of his ministry of formation, community building, and discernment among the Gentiles.

Paul's first step is to conform himself to the death of Christ by analogy in the contexts of his life. His death to Torah is analogous to the death of Christ. But his death to Torah was not just a onetime event. "I die daily," he tells the Christ-community in Corinth (1 Corinthians 15:31). Paul puts himself in harm's way every day because he continues to make the intentional choice to die to Torah, live to God in Christ, and endure the consequences of that decision.[45] Paul's choice to die to Torah exposes him to persecution by Jewish leaders and Jewish Christ-followers, on the one hand, and by Roman administrators, on the other. Because of this daily decision, Paul bears the marks of Jesus on his body (Galatians 6:17).

Paul's physical marks of persecution are also an aspect of his partnership (*koinōnia*) with Christ in his sufferings.[46] This partnership is not just an apostolic calling, but an aspect of life in Christ Jesus for every Christ-follower.[47] To know Christ includes the experience of suffering at the hands of those who live by the norms, values, and customs of the present evil age.

Paul's mission statement demands that he practice discernment. In the contexts of his own life and ministry, Paul seeks to align his actions by analogy to the pattern of the "faithfulness of the Son of God, who loved me, indeed, who gave himself for me." Paul comes to *know Christ* by embodying him in his own life: "It is my expectation and hope...[that] Christ will be magnified now as always in my body, whether by life or by death. For to me, living is Christ..." (Philippians 1:20–21).

This step of dying to Torah and embodying Christ reflects resurrection power at work in Paul's life. He tells the Corinthians, we are "always carrying in the body the death of Jesus, so that the life of Jesus may also be made visible in our bodies. For while we live, we are always being given up to death for Jesus's sake, so that the life of Jesus may be made visible in our mortal flesh. So, death is at work in us, and life in you" (2 Corinthians 4:10–12, NRSV). He also tells the Corinthians, Christ "was crucified in weakness, but lives by the power of God. For we are weak in him, but in dealing with you we will live with him by the power of God" (2 Corinthians 13:4, NRSV).

R. W. L. Moberly explains this death to new life sequence in Paul very clearly:

> For Jesus self-emptying has led to exaltation by God. This was through death. Paul is still part of life within this world, but that does not mean that exaltation is solely something to hope for in the future beyond the constraints of this present existence. For Jesus's death is a symbolic reality, a metaphor for that which happens already, here and now, to the Christian believer, and resurrection likewise becomes a presently operative reality.[48]

Paul's metaphor of death to new life became an important aspect of formation and the practice of discernment in Paul's communities. Just as Paul metaphorically died to the Torah as his exclusive pattern of life, he challenged Gentiles to die metaphorically to the norms, values, and customs of the Greco-Roman culture. Their metaphorical deaths empowered them to live to God by imagining actions that, by analogy, embodied the pattern of Christ's faithfulness in their own lives.[49] All Christ-followers, too, must choose this death *every day*.

To Know Christ Through Embodied Practice and Experience

The metaphor of death to new life also grounds formation and discernment in Paul's teaching of holiness in daily life to Gentiles. In their new life in Christ, Gentiles also come to know Christ by conforming themselves to the death of Christ. They turn away from their pagan idols and the norms, values, and customs of the Greco-Roman world to serve the living God in Christ.[50] Following their metaphorical deaths, they live to God, aligning their actions by analogy to the pattern of Christ's faithfulness in the contexts of their daily lives. Christ lives in them through their Christlike love embodied in acts of self-giving to others. In these actions they demonstrate God's resurrection power at work in their own bodies, energizing their new life in Christ.

Paul uses experiences in his own life and the lives of his congregants to bear witness to what the living God is doing in the world and to interpret God's will for the world.[51] These experiences are, as Luke Timothy Johnson comments, a "constant and dominant feature" of Paul's letters.[52] This "constant engagement with experience, past, present, and anticipated in the future" is what gives Paul's letters an "intensely dynamic energy."[53]

Many biblical scholars, theologians, and church leaders, however, grow anxious when people focus on religious experiences. They argue that human experience is largely subjective and, therefore, often untrustworthy. Moreover, human experience in the first-century world of the Christ-movement is also beyond the realm of scientific study and historical proof by scholars. The tendency to discount experience is exacerbated by the fact that many scholars and theologians prefer concepts and ideas to the "messy stuff" of embodied experience in ordinary life.[54] "[T]o miss the experiential in Paul's letters, and to read them only at the level of the conceptual, is to miss their significance altogether."[55]

This resistance to considering the role of embodied experience is one important reason why, for centuries, many interpreters in the church and academy have characterized Paul as the church's first theologian—meaning a *systematic* theologian. For these interpreters, Paul's letters articulate a body of conceptual, theological doctrines. For example, systematic theologians describe Paul's "Christology," which refers to what Paul thinks and says *about* Jesus as the Christ. Disciples must then "apply" these theological doctrines deductively to ordinary situations in daily life. This task proves to be more challenging than it needs to be, especially when there is a way to read and hear Paul differently.

Paul is a first-century *pastoral* theologian.[56] He builds moral communities grounded in the resurrection power of God at work through the life, death, and resurrection of Jesus Christ. Experiences of resurrection power for new life are the bedrock of formation, community building, and discernment in Paul's Christ-communities. The more traditional, systematic approach to interpreting Paul snubs the significance of human experience for powerfully shaping how most people see, interpret, and respond to the world around them.[57]

Paul doesn't give a systematic treatise about a theological topic and then tell Christ-followers to figure out how to apply it to their lives. He lays a foundation for how to live Jesus (see 1 Corinthians 3:10–15). He teaches a practice of discernment to all his congregations that expects the capacity of human experience to identify events of resurrection power and link them to Christlike actions.

The practice of discernment Paul teaches minimizes the potentially distorting power of individual subjectivity. Every prophetic statement that claims to identify an experience of resurrection power or an act of Christlike faithfulness must be evaluated by the congregation through a process of proof through testing in discernment.[58] These guardrails are the genius of *communal* discernment in Paul's congregations.

Luke Timothy Johnson continually emphasizes that embodied human experience is the site of God's continuing power and presence in the world.[59] This necessitates discernment "in the complex world of human bodily experience."[60] As we mentioned earlier and will continue to see on each of our stops on this pilgrimage, "Paul is the New Testament writer who most explicitly and extensively speaks of discernment, and most emphatically places it at the heart of Christian moral life."[61] For contemporary Christians, "[s]cripture forms the minds of the faithful to perceive the work of God in the world"; thus, attention must be "turned to actual human experience in the world."[62] From this, "discernment is essentially learned through practice."[63]

The practice of discernment over time leads Christ-followers to practical moral wisdom. Practical theologian Ulla Schmidt says this wisdom develops "through experienced perception and judgment of the concrete particulars of situations, objects, and relations."[64] The authors of *Christian Practical Wisdom* agree: this wisdom "denotes a kind of knowing that is morally attuned...It is not a package of preplanned rules but stays open and adaptive to new situations.... Most of all, this knowledge is practical, grounded in ordinary experiences, and learned over time in the company of others and for the sake of others."[65]

Paul incorporates the concept of practice as knowing into his teaching on formation and discernment. He focuses the Christ-community's discernment on knowing Christ through embodied, Christlike practices and knowing God through experiences of resurrection power. Paul captures this dynamic connection for the Colossians: "[w]e have not ceased praying for you and asking that you may be filled with the knowledge of God's will in all spiritual wisdom and comprehension, so that you may walk worthily of the Lord, fully pleasing to him, as you bear fruit in every good work and as you grow in the knowledge of God" (Colossians 1:9–10).

By walking worthily of the Lord in ways that are pleasing to God, human actions bear fruit in the community. Discerning these connections leads Christ-followers to knowledge of God's will in particular situations. We will see this connection very clearly when we get to Rome (Romans 12:1–2). Similarly, discerning these connections leads the community to know God through experiences of God's resurrection power for new life. Over time, discerning these connections leads to spiritual wisdom that informs future deliberations about anticipated actions that will continue to bear fruit and build up the congregation.

By reflecting on their actions and experiences, and making these connections in their practice of discernment, Christ-followers become mature disciples. And forming mature disciples in the image of Jesus Christ is the essence and goal of Paul's mission and ministry: "It is [Christ] whom we publicly proclaim, admonishing everyone and teaching everyone in all wisdom, so that we may present everyone mature in Christ" (Colossians 1:28).[66]

Ekklēsia Denotes a "Deliberative Assembly" in a Specific Place

In his letters, Paul usually addresses the local Christ-communities he founded using the Greek noun *ekklēsia*. He often adds the descriptive phrase "in Christ Jesus." The word *ekklēsia* is always translated into English as "church." But this can be very misleading for contemporary Christians, who often think of the "church" as a building or the collective group of people in a congregation.

In the Greco-Roman world, the word *ekklēsia* designated the assembly of a city council that gathered to deliberate on decisions affecting the welfare of the community (see Acts 19:32).[67] In the LXX the word referred to the assembly of God's people.[68] Paul likely chose *ekklēsia* because it was a secular political and religious term that both Gentiles and Jews would recognize. The word *ekklēsia* perfectly describes the *activities* of formation and discernment that take place in each of Paul's local Christ-communities. After they finished their shared meal, the assembled members of the congregation deliberated on moral issues affecting the welfare of the community and the formation of individuals in the image of Jesus Christ.

Thus, Paul's use of the term *ekklēsia* implies the community's task of moral formation.[69] The *ekklēsia* is not for Paul "an optional supplement to a private spirituality of dying and rising with Christ," but represents "what God is up to in the world: re-creating a people whose corporate life tells the world what the death and resurrection of the Messiah is all about."[70] Accordingly, throughout this book, I refer to each *ekklēsia* as the "deliberative assembly" of Christ-followers gathered in a particular location. They come together "in Christ Jesus" to be formed individually in the image of Jesus Christ and collectively as the Body of Christ in their local setting.

Summarizing Our Stop on the Road to Damascus

Paul's encounter with the risen Christ on the road to Damascus created a condition called "cognitive dissonance."[71] The experience created a tension for Paul that challenged two deeply held convictions. On the one hand, the Torah promised life to those who keep its commandments (Leviticus 18:5, quoted in Galatians 3:12). On the other hand, according to the norms of Torah, Jesus lived his life as a sinner and his death was cursed by God (Deuteronomy 21:23, quoted in Galatians 3:13). Jesus died accursed by God according to Torah.

Experiencing the risen Christ created an existential dilemma for Paul. Either Torah remains as his exclusive pattern of life and decrees Jesus to be a fraudulent Messiah. Or God was at work raising Jesus from the dead, which means Torah cannot continue as Paul's *exclusive* framework for interpreting and teaching holiness in daily life. If Paul trusts his experience—which he does—he has to reimagine Torah's role for his life and teaching.

Paul never writes about how or when he arrived at these conclusions. I've always imagined they might be the fruit of his time in Arabia (Galatians 1:16–17). His brief mention of Arabia mirrors the stories of Jesus being driven by the Spirit into the wilderness immediately after his baptism. There, in the wilderness, Satan tempted Jesus and helped him clarify the contours and boundaries of his divine calling. Maybe Paul's sojourn in Arabia presented a similar opportunity for him to explore and clarify the significance of his own calling by God.[72]

Through Paul's experience of God's resurrection power at work in the risen Christ, he discerned a prophetic call *within* Judaism.[73] He interpreted the resurrection of Jesus as the start of God's new age and fulfillment of Israel's expectation that God would one day unite all people—Jews and Gentiles—under their one God. Rather than prompting a "conversion" from one religion to another, this encounter with the risen Christ empowered Paul's lateral movement within Judaism. He left the leadership group of Pharisees to join the marginalized Jewish sect focused on proclaiming the crucified and risen Jesus as Messiah and Lord.[74] Paul took his appointment to proclaim the gospel of Christ among the Gentiles to be part of his Jewishness.[75]

In this new calling, God honored Paul's previous expertise as a Pharisee using Torah to teach holiness in daily living. Paul interpreted his experience as a divine call to become a teacher and model of holiness in daily living focused on the crucified and risen Christ. He embodied Christ in the contexts of his life and ministry among the Gentiles. And through his embodied life in Christ, he mediated persuasive experiences of resurrection power for others. His experience of the risen Christ inspired and energized his new vision for formation, community building, and discernment in his own life and in the lives of the Gentiles who would later populate his deliberative assemblies (*ekklēsiai;* the plural form of *ekklēsia*). Practicing discernment to connect Christlike acts of faithfulness with experiences of God's resurrection power became the heartbeat of formation and community building for new life in Christ.

Paul's life-changing encounter with the risen Christ on the road to Damascus launched his embodied, prophetic proclamation of Christ to the

Gentiles. The event grounds his vision of formation, community building, and discernment in his Gentile congregations.

Pilgrims Reflect on Their Experience

The first stop on our pilgrimage has come to an end. The pilgrims gather after dinner in the hotel meeting room in Damascus to reflect on their experience. They're pretty tired after a long, hot day and have not yet caught up with the dramatic time change. I'll share with you some of their conversation. Maybe their insights will help us clarify some of our own.

"That was not what I expected," says Sarah, a considerate, self-aware owner of a local business. She is also a leader in her local Episcopal church. "I didn't know there was any other story of Paul's conversion than the one we know from Acts."

"And it was not really a conversion, since Paul remained part of the Jewish people to the end of his life," adds Reynoldo, a deacon in his local Baptist church. Reynoldo manages a grocery store for a major grocery chain and also volunteers at the local food bank on weekends.

"I've never heard that the risen Christ was revealed *in* Paul," Diane says surprisingly. She's an experienced elementary school teacher who was raised in the Church of Christ tradition and knows the Bible backward and forward. "It's easy to understand a person being changed dramatically by a bright, blinding light and voice coming at you from heaven. I'm less comfortable with Paul saying that Christ now lives in him. That sounds a bit arrogant. It's as if he's become demonically possessed by him."

"But if human beings are made in the image of God, which is what we believe as Christians, is it so surprising that Christ might spark and energize that divine image in Paul, or you, or me?" asks Robert, a high school teacher who recently joined the United Methodist Church. During our travel to this first stop, Robert let the group know that he hopes this pilgrimage will lead him to greater understanding of his faith and discipleship.

"Jesus is divine, but I'm just human," cautions Philip, an idealistic Presbyterian who has already shared with the group his displeasure with the way older people are running the world. "I'd be uncomfortable saying that Christ lives in me."

"Philip, I once heard a church leader call what you just said heresy and false humility," says Esperanza, a wise and experienced Roman Catholic lay leader best known for her political activism in the local community. "Because Jesus was fully human, too. That's why Paul makes him the foundation and model for our faithfulness."

"I've never considered that, Esperanza," Philip responds. "Thank you."

An intrusive waiter interrupts the conversation to take orders from the group. Several pilgrims respond impatiently, reflecting the stressful impact of their altered body-clocks. After the waiter finally leaves, the conversation picks up again.

"I've always had faith in Jesus Christ," says Jean, the chair of a local nonprofit board and an active member of a large, nondenominational church. "I'm not sure if I ever thought of it as entrusting myself *exclusively* to his way of life. That's a much more active and serious commitment."

"That's why you're also entrusting yourself to the resurrection power of God," concludes Dante. "Don't forget that Christ's faithfulness led to his death."

"What really resonated with me was to hear that embodying Christ in my daily life was my way of announcing God's powerful reign on earth," says Gail, a practicing oncologist, well-known for her groundbreaking research and teaching, who is active in the local Mennonite church. "That's a level of responsibility I've never considered. But I find it very energizing and it dovetails perfectly with how I understand my medical practice!"

"Not only that," interjects Dante, "but I love the idea that I might come to know Christ at a more personal level, living in me through my own practice of discipleship. That's exciting and promising!"

"I've always been a rule-follower and never considered that there might not be any preformed rules in the life of faithfulness," ponders Ann, a reliable community volunteer who never says "no" to a worthy cause and has recently joined a local Episcopal church. "That offers some freedom as we try to help each other discern God's will in the nitty-gritty of daily life. But it does make me a little nervous. I hope Paul will say more about this later."

"Speaking of love, Dante, I heard something new today," says Jean. "Paul summarized the pattern of Christ's faithfulness as 'loving others through acts of self-giving for them.' That's a helpful refinement of the word 'love' for me. I always have concerns when someone says, 'God is love,' and then proceeds to define love in a thousand different directions. To understand 'love' as an act of self-giving for others is more manageable."

"Hmm..." responds Dante. "I'll have to give that more thought. Maybe it will come up again in another letter."

Latisha, who's been pensively listening, now opens up: "I've never considered the gospel to be an 'event'—something that happens over and over. I'll have to give that more thought."

"Yes! I love Paul's conviction that there will be a never-ending series of gospel-events," says Ann, enthusiastically.

"That's because God and God's life-giving power are eternal," concludes Jim, an administrative executive in the health-care industry who worships at a nearby Lutheran church.

"I want to ask the group a different question," says Esperanza. "I've always had the vague sense that there is evil in the world. But I've never thought of evil as an actual spiritual power. What do you think?"

"I find Paul's apocalyptic perspective helpful," offers Philip. "There are clearly spiritual forces that influence our daily decisions and actions—sometimes for good and sometimes not. Words from political leaders can influence how we act. The same is true for advertising. I'm starting to think that we need to ask the question, 'what spirit is at work?' in a particular situation."

"That's a great idea," adds Latisha. "I hope Paul says more about that at another stop on our pilgrimage."

"Do you think we live in the present evil age?" asks Jean. "That sounds pretty harsh. I can't say that I need to be set free from this age and I'm not sure I want to be."

"There's a lot about this world that seems to be influenced by spiritual forces of evil," responds Esperanza. "Maybe we have to have Christ living in us before we decide whether we are set free or need to be."

Jim speaks up, saying, "I like what you're suggesting Esperanza. I'm wondering how to go about imagining ways to embody Christ. That sounds like challenging work."

"I heard in our discussion that Paul teaches people a practice of discernment to help with that work," says Sarah. "I hope we hear more about that. It sounds important."

"Sarah, what do you think discernment is all about?" asks Diane. "I only think of that word when I have the occasional crisis or dilemma that requires a decision in my life. So, I look around for a book or other resource to read, in the hope that it will give me some direction."

"I've been pretty limited in my understanding of discernment, too," responds Sarah. "I thought it only had to do with deciding where to go to work or whether to become a pastor in a church."

"John gave a short definition of discernment during our preparations for this pilgrimage," Gail remembers. "And John's definition sounds a bit like our practice of discernment in the Mennonite church. But our practice is mostly about how we make decisions for the whole community. John's definition sounded much broader. Maybe we'll get more insight on this pilgrimage."

"Turning in a different direction, I'm so accustomed to using the word 'church' for everything," Gail confesses. "The building; what happens in it; and everything the congregation undertakes. I even hear my pastor occasionally talk about new ways to 'do church.' It may take me some time to adjust to Paul's terminology of 'deliberative assembly.'"

"Me, too," adds Robert. "I might have trouble thinking I'm part of a 'deliberative assembly.' That phrase suggests an activity I'm not familiar with. It sounds like the community regularly deliberates on people's faithfulness. In my church on Sunday, we listen to readings and hear a sermon. There's no conversation."

"What I'm realizing," says Reynoldo, "is that we have a lot more resources for our practice of discernment today. We have Scripture passages about Jesus that might stimulate our imaginations for how we might embody him in a given situation."

"I can't wait to see how all of this unfolds," says Sarah. "Where do we go next?"

"We're headed to Philippi," I say to the pilgrims. "I don't intend to tell you too much in advance of each stop. But I think you'll really enjoy this next congregation. Paul has a deep love for the Philippians,. They've been partners with him in the gospel from early in his ministry. This will be a very important and illuminating time for all of us!"

CHAPTER TWO

Christ-Patterned Moral Reasoning in Philippi

"Reason This Way Among You, Which You Have in Christ Jesus" (Philippians 2:5)

Our pilgrimage takes us next to the Roman province of Macedonia, part of northern Greece today. In this chapter we visit the assembly of Paul's Christ-community in Philippi. The city lies on the Via Egnatia, a major Roman trade route that was a key link connecting Rome with Byzantium (later called Constantinople, now modern Istanbul). In the next chapter, we will travel 100 miles west along the Via Egnatia to Thessalonica, where we enter Paul's congregation in that city. Although Philippi was a Roman colony and Thessalonica a free city, the churches both shared some common concerns and challenges, including suffering from persecution at the hands of their pagan neighbors.

Where Are We?

Our first stop in Macedonia is the Christ-community Paul founded in Philippi. The city lies near the northern coastline of the Aegean Sea. Paul probably arrived in Macedonia by ship at the nearby port city of Neapolis. He then walked the remaining twelve miles to Philippi on the cobblestone road called the Via Egnatia. Paul was surely aware of the city's historical importance and that probably influenced his decision to travel there. The history of the city is still important, even today, as Philippi has been designated as a UNESCO World Heritage Site.

Dating back to the fourth-century BCE, Philippi was named for Philip of Macedon, the father of Alexander the Great. By the time of Paul's arrival, the city probably had 10,000 inhabitants.[1] With its nearness to the port of Neapolis and location on the Via Egnatia, Philippi was a crossroads for travel and commerce in Paul's first-century world.

Philippi also played an important role in the birth of the Roman Empire. In 42 BCE, on the fertile farmlands just west of Philippi, the decisive battle of the Roman civil war took place. Armies led by Octavian and Mark Antony defeated the forces of Brutus and Cassius, who had assassinated Julius Caesar. Following their victory at Philippi, however, Octavian then defeated Antony at the Battle of Actium in 31 BCE and assumed leadership in Rome. After that victory, in 27 BCE, the Roman Senate conferred on Octavian the title of Augustus ("revered one"), effectively ending the Roman Republic. This act empowered the emergence of the Roman Empire and promoted the divine status of the emperor, with its accompanying cult of worship.

Octavian was welcomed as Rome's savior and the incarnation of divine good news [*euanggelion*] for the whole world.[2] The emergence of the Roman Empire under Octavian ended a period of civil strife and was thereafter associated with the vaunted *Pax Romana*—the "peace of Rome." This peace was forged through the construction of good, safe roads, effective governmental administration, and a powerful military. But the *Pax Romana* also had its dark side: the empire grew through conquest, subjugation of conquered people, intimidation, and the imposition of high taxes on conquered lands. The peace was maintained through violence, with crucifixion as the penalty for anyone who threatened the peace.[3]

In the same year Octavian defeated Antony, he also refounded the city of Philippi as a Roman colony and took the city under his personal patronage.[4] He settled Philippi with Italian farmers and Roman army veterans who had served under him in the civil war. Both groups were granted Roman citizenship and awarded various land rights and privileges. Octavian also conferred Italian legal status on the city and exempted the colonists from various Roman taxes. In return, he expected all residents of the city, whether they were Roman citizens and colonists or not, to obey Rome's imperial reign and participate in the new cult of the emperor.

Roman citizens and institutions, including various social, political, economic, and religious groups, exercised powerful influence over the city's residents during the early years of the Christ-community in Philippi.[5] The city in the first century CE is experiencing the thoroughgoing impacts of Roman citizenship and rule which tested the church's *exclusive* commitment to Jesus Christ as Lord and shaped Paul's letter responding to these challenges.

Why Are We Here?

For their work and witness on behalf of Christ and the gospel, Paul was suffering in a Roman prison and the Christ-followers in Philippi were suffering from local Roman persecution. This persecution probably resulted from the perception that Paul's gospel was "an un-Roman or anti-Roman Jewish message targeting Gentiles."[6] Paul's subversive gospel—his *euanggelion*—was not the good news of Caesar's reign but the good news of God's reign through Jesus Christ for life, peace, and salvation on earth. Paul and the members of his congregation were deemed to be unpatriotic by the city's residents. They were confessing and following Jesus Christ as their exclusive Lord, rather than worshiping the divine emperor and Rome's many other gods. This did not fit well with the fully Roman character of Philippi.

The experience of suffering for Christ tested the members of the congregation. The intimidating and coercive power exercised by their neighbors was pressuring them to compromise or abandon their exclusive devotion to Christ as Lord. This persecution and the challenges it created also seem to have put two women leaders—Euodia and Syntychē—at odds with each other about how to respond.

We are visiting this important Christ-community because its situation speaks to Western Christianity. Fewer and fewer members of contemporary Christ-communities today are exclusively committed to living the way of Jesus in the world. Those who do risk alienation from their neighbors. Their fellow citizens (some of whom are also Christians) often view them as unpatriotic and even antisocial. Often inspired by nationalistic fervor, their neighbors may use subtle tactics of intimidation to coerce faithful Christians to fall in line with their idolatrous worship of the nation and its culture, economy, and leaders.

As a result, many Christians today—myself included at times—are frequently tempted to compromise our baptismal commitment to follow Jesus as our exclusive Lord. We vacillate in a kind of double-mindedness. Whether intentional or not, we pick and choose when it's convenient to follow the costly way of Jesus and when to act in more comfortable ways that reflect the culture's norms and values and appease our neighbors and political leaders. We try to live with a kind of "dual citizenship"—living by two different sets of norms, values, and customs, depending on the context and situation. We stop in Philippi to hear Paul's response to this ancient and contemporary challenge.

What Words Matter?

There are a few Greek words in Philippians that are central to Paul's vision for formation, community building, and discernment. We will discuss different ways to understand these words: such as

- the noun *doulos* ("slave");
- the noun *hagios* ("holy one");
- the noun *eirēnē* ("peace");
- the verb *phroneō* ("to reason");
- the noun *koinōnia* ("partnership");
- the noun *agapē* ("love");
- the verb *dokimazō* ("to prove through testing");
- the noun *sōtērian* ("salvation"); and
- Paul's ubiquitous phrases "in Christ Jesus" (*en Christō Iēsou*) or "in Christ."

It's time to stop preparing and join the congregation!

Joining the Assembly in Philippi

Our pilgrims step off the Via Egnatia and walk steadily uphill through the streets of Philippi toward the house of the family hosting the gathering. The pilgrims pause to look back at the breathtaking view to the west. Just beyond the Via Egnatia, they see the city's *agora*, the central marketplace still bustling with late-afternoon commerce. Beyond the *agora*, pilgrims can see the lush, fertile valley spread out between the city and the distant mountains. It was in this same valley nearly a century earlier that armies led by Octavian and Mark Antony defeated the forces of Brutus and Cassius, thus setting the stage for the emergence of the Roman Empire. The pilgrims' view on this early evening is made all the more spectacular by the late afternoon's low clouds obscuring the tops of the mountains in the distance.

After a few comments on this memorable snapshot of natural beauty and the significance of this place in world history, the pilgrims continue to walk uphill to their destination. They enter the home of their hosts for this gathering. The community has assembled to share a meal and then to hear Paul's messenger read and explain his letter. At the conclusion of the reading, the Philippians will consider Paul's counsel and deliberate together in discernment focused on confronting the challenges of life in Christ in the midst of the Roman world of Philippi.

Paul Introduces Formation and Discernment Right Away! (1:1–11)

Everyone has now crowded together in this one large room. The dishes have been removed and the meal formally ended. There were no leftovers. The hungry group consumed all the bread and olive oil for dipping, beans, fresh fruit, and the few pieces of broiled fish that were placed on the table. The host leaves a half-full wine carafe on the table. Several congregants fill their glasses before the letter-reading commences. Of course, Paul is not here, but he's sent someone to deliver his letter.

A man enters the room and a great cry of joy goes up throughout the room. It's Epaphroditus![7] He is returning to Philippi after an extended stay with Paul. The congregation sent him to Paul earlier as their messenger, bearing a gift of support. During his absence, the community heard that Epaphroditus had almost died in his service to Paul. What a joyous homecoming—an event our pilgrims won't soon forget. This will probably be the pilgrims' only encounter with Epaphroditus. He is not mentioned anywhere else in Scripture or in later writings from the early church.

Epaphroditus carefully removes the letter from his carrying case and begins to read the opening paragraphs. Paul immediately emphasizes formation and discernment. He introduces major themes of the letter and highlights the key practice of discernment.

Paul introduces himself and Timothy, his coauthor, as "slaves" (*doulos*) of Jesus Christ (1:1). Paul immediately aligns himself by analogy with Jesus Christ who, later in the letter, Paul will characterize as the one who emptied himself of status and power to take the form of a human slave (*doulos*) in obedience to God (2:6–8).

In urban areas of the Greco-Roman world, a high percentage of inhabitants were slaves. To be a slave in Paul's world was to belong to another person and to do that person's bidding. Many slaves were the product of Roman conquest or piracy. Others became slaves after being abandoned at a young age. Still others were born into slavery—a slave's children also became the property of the slave owner. Slaves were bought and sold both privately and through public processes. Unlike our American understanding of slavery, however, slavery in the Greco-Roman world was not based on race.[8]

God Forms a Holy People Set Apart Exclusively to Serve God (1:1)

Paul greets all the "holy ones [*hagioi*] in Christ Jesus [*en Christō Iēsou*] in Philippi." Most of Paul's letters open with a greeting to the holy ones (*hagioi*) in that particular city.[9] The plural *hagioi* signifies a community of individuals set apart from the surrounding culture to serve the living God of Israel. Individually and collectively, "holy ones" publicly embody and bear witness to God's life-giving reign and healing presence in their lives.[10] Each local group of "holy ones" becomes the place and the means by which the character of God, revealed in Jesus Christ, becomes visible in and among the lives of its members.[11] *Holiness is all about formation in Paul's congregations!*

The word "holy" also expresses the early Christ-community's sense of being a countercultural society. They understood themselves to be a sacred people with a pattern of life that differs from that of the world.[12] Since Jesus Christ is the embodiment of divine holiness (*hagiasmos*) for Paul,[13] the commitment to Christ's distinctive pattern of life sets Paul's congregations apart from the culture.

What counts as being holy in Paul's churches is being *Christlike*.[14] And holiness regularly "entails observable behavior."[15] Formation in Christ's pattern of life happens for individuals and for the collective Body of Christ in each local setting. "[J]ust as Christ assumes the form of the 'image' of God in public...so a holy people *manifest* their consecration to God" through the formation of their Christlike character.[16] God's call to holiness for individuals and the community requires a cross-shaped life of "costly, self-giving, status-lowering practices toward others."[17]

Baptism into Christ sets these holy ones apart for their exclusive service to God. But baptism only begins a lifetime process of formation in a community setting. It is a lifelong process of sanctification, of being made holy, through the transformation of people's hearts, imaginations, and wills in a communal life.

For this reason, Paul tells the Philippians that he is confident that God, "who began a good work in/among you,[18] will bring it to completion" by the time Christ returns in glory (1:6). This process of formation—where practices of holiness lead to sanctification—occurs over a lifetime of active participation in the story of Jesus. By sharing a meal and deliberating together to discern Christlike acts of faithfulness, they are transformed over time into the image of Christ.

Formation and Discernment Take Place "in Christ Jesus" (1:1)

Paul links the Philippians' ongoing process of formation in holiness to their participation "in [*en*] Christ Jesus." Scholars have debated for centuries without consensus the meaning of the phrases "in Christ Jesus" and "in Christ." The Greek preposition *en* can be used to denote a physical location (being made holy *in* Christ Jesus) or instrumentality (being made holy *by* Christ Jesus).[19]

When Paul speaks of being "in Christ Jesus" he is also speaking in political terms.[20] Paul has in mind "a community whose character and common life are defined by the Lordship of Christ"[21] rather than the lordship of Caesar. By using the phrases "in Christ Jesus" and "in Philippi" in 1:1, Paul sets up two contrasting political realms "vying for the allegiance of the Philippian Christians."[22] He distinguishes the new age of God experienced "in Christ Jesus" from the old age "in Philippi," dominated by spiritual forces of evil working through Rome's power. Dualistic contrasts like this one are common for Paul and others who share the apocalyptic perspective in first-century Judaism.

Paul emphasizes this important apocalyptic distinction later in the letter. He tells the Philippians that their "citizenship is in heaven" (3:20). Heaven denotes the spiritual realm where God eternally reigns with resurrection power for new life. Heaven characterizes God's new age revealed in Christ Jesus that has now descended upon his followers.

Paul also creates an apocalyptic moral contrast between human life in this new heavenly age and ongoing life in the old age under the oppressive power of Rome. Paul will elaborate this moral contrast later in the letter. Some people walk in God's new age according to the pattern of the faithfulness of Jesus Christ, such as Paul, Timothy, and Epaphroditus (2:19–3:21). Others continue to walk in the old age as "enemies of the cross of Christ" by "setting their minds on earthly things" (3:17–19). They look to the norms, values, and customs of the Greco-Roman world that is already passing away to engage in destructive actions that oppose God's will.

There is yet another social and political dimension to Paul's use of the phrase "in Christ Jesus." It signifies a practical aspect of the community's formation as a holy people. The phrase signifies the actual physical gathering of a specific group of people in their local *ekklēsia*. The phrase "in Christ Jesus" points to "the present social body that is the assembly...a bodily expression of the risen Jesus who has become a life-giving spirit...this assembly—'together with all those who call on the name of the Lord in every place.'"[23] The people who gather "in Christ Jesus" come together so they can be formed as God's holy people. This group of assembled Christ-followers is the "political and ecclesial space designated as [being] 'in Christ.'"[24]

Grace and Peace from God Our Father and the Lord Jesus Christ (1:2)

Epaphroditus continues with his reading of Paul's letter. In 1:2 Paul invokes the agency of God and Christ. They will provide the Philippians with grace (*charis*) and peace (*eirēnē*). Given their present experiences of suffering from persecution, this greeting offers the Philippians hope for divine peace. True peace only comes from God through Jesus Christ. This is part of Paul's anti-imperial *euanggelion*. Roman propaganda emphasizes the importance of the *Pax Romana* secured through their use of violence against anyone disrupting that peace. The peace of God is something much stronger and more reliable.

Partners in the Gospel, God's Economy, Grace, Suffering, and the Spirit (1:3–8)

Another major theme of the letter is introduced—*koinōnia*. Many modern Bibles translate *koinōnia* as "fellowship." This translation implies something hardly more than today's coffee-hour conversations. Relationships among partners in antiquity were much more complex. Partners were expected to put the interests of other partners ahead of their own.

Paul appropriates this well-known cultural word *koinōnia* in 1:5 and 1:7 to describe different aspects of their communal life and their relationship with Paul. He redefines the word in line with God's new age in Christ Jesus. First, the Philippians have been in partnership (*koinōnia*) with Paul in his gospel from the first day of his ministry (1:5). Paul will mention some economic aspects of this partnership near the end of the letter.

Paul also affirms that the Philippians are partners with him [*synkoinōnos*] in grace (*charis*), God's gift of life-giving power. They partner with Paul in grace in his "imprisonment and in the defense and confirmation of the gospel" (1:7). As in Paul's own ministry, God gives the Philippians grace to embody in acts of Christlike self-giving for the benefit of others. God's confirmation of the gospel takes place when the Philippians' embodied witness of Christ leads to experiences of resurrection power for new life in the community.[25]

The Philippians are also partners with Paul in God's grace in their shared experiences of suffering for Christ. Recall from our stop on the road to Damascus that part of Paul's mission statement includes being a partner with Christ in his sufferings (Philippians 3:10). We will look closer at this dimension of partnership in 1:29–30. Finally, the Philippians are also partners (*koinōnia*) with the Spirit of Jesus in the deliberative assembly, a topic we will explore in 2:1.

Paul Highlights the Practice of Discernment for Embodied Life in Christ (1:9–11)

The crucial practice of discernment comes clearly into focus in 1:9–11.

Philippians 1:9 And this is my prayer, that your love [*agapē*] may overflow more and more with knowledge and full moral understanding **10** for you to prove through testing [*dokimazō*] the things that really matter, so that in the day of Christ you may be sincere and blameless, **11** having produced the fruit of righteousness that comes through Jesus Christ for the glory and praise of God.

When Paul speaks of love (*agapē*), he is referring to Christlike acts of self-giving for others. We first encountered his understanding of love at our stop on the road to Damascus: "[t]he life I am now living in the flesh, I am living by the faithfulness of the son of God, who loved me, indeed, who gave himself for me" (Galatians 2:20). Christlike love, embodied in acts of self-giving for others, is the foundation of moral formation, community building, and discernment in Paul's communities. Over time, with practice, love becomes an established disposition among members of his congregations.[26]

In his letter Paul prays that the Philippians' acts of love will abound and lead them to knowledge and full moral understanding.[27] This prayer presumes the Philippians are practicing discernment—the active practice of reflecting on their actions and the consequences of those actions.

Indeed, they are to "prove through testing" (*dokimazō*) the things that really matter (Philippians 1:10). The basic sense of *dokimazō* is to test or to try something, usually in a public sphere.[28] *Dokimazō* describes the process by which an assembly tests the extent to which a particular action has produced some lasting effect in the community.[29] Paul regularly uses *dokimazō* to describe the practice of discerning God's will in all his congregations.[30] "Proof through testing" is one of the essential elements in the after-dinner practice of discernment in Paul's congregations. Here's how it works:

Christ-followers always hope their Christlike love embodied in acts of self-giving for others will be pleasing to God and lead to experiences of resurrection power in the community. But there is never any certainty in advance that a particular action will be pleasing to God and bear fruit. In their after-dinner moral deliberations, community members weigh alternative possibilities for how a person might embody Christ in a specific situation. This includes reflection together on past actions and consequences.

For instance, one of the Philippians asks the assembly how she might respond in a Christlike manner to her aunt and uncle, who are pressuring her to worship with them at the imperial temple. One congregant responds by recounting his refusal to accompany friends to the temple of Artemis, telling the friends that he only worships one God. He was beaten for his refusal. Another member of the community tells about a conversation with her mother in which she explained the story of Jesus and drew her mother into an ongoing conversation. Several other members of the assembly offer similar, fruitful experiences. They interpret their actions as Christlike self-giving because they took the risk of explaining their commitment to Jesus and introducing their neighbors to his new way of life. The actions seemed pleasing to God and improved their relationships with their pagan neighbors.

At a later gathering, the woman reports her decision to discuss the issue with her aunt and uncle. She explained to them that her commitment to the risen Jesus as Lord is exclusive and prevents her from accompanying them to the imperial temple. While they are disappointed, they admire her courage and commitment. They promise not to make trouble for their niece. She affirms her conviction to the assembly that the action was pleasing to God, since the discussion strengthened their relationship. Her story will be recalled by the assembly later, when someone else seeks to discern how to respond in a Christlike way to a similar situation.

Through this process of proof through testing in discernment, the Philippians enrich their knowledge and moral understanding of what God desires (1:9). They are proving through testing what is the will of God, what is good and well-pleasing to God.[31] Over time, they develop a sharp practical moral wisdom that informs their decision-making.[32]

Paul's Own Suffering Is Part of the Larger Story of Christ (1:12–26)

Despite his own suffering in prison (1:12–26), Paul encourages those suffering from persecution in Philippi. Contrary to all expectations, his imprisonment has nevertheless helped to spread the gospel, even among Caesar's imperial guard. It has also emboldened other disciples to speak fearlessly of Christ (1:12–14). Later in the letter, Paul even sends greetings to the Philippians from all the holy ones with him, especially those in Caesar's household (4:22).

Paul situates his own suffering as part of a larger narrative—"the story of God's economy of salvation"[33] in Christ Jesus. Just as Christ's unexpected suffering and death led to the dawn of God's new age of resurrection life, Paul's suffering has spread the gospel and emboldened the public proclamation of Christ (1:12, 18).

Paul also expresses confidence in 1:19 that through the prayers of the Philippians and with the help of the Spirit of Jesus Christ his troubles will nevertheless lead to his salvation.[34] Whether in life or death, he hopes to magnify Christ in his own body (1:20). He hopes his body will become "Christ's text rather than the empire's" text.[35] Paul reminds the Philippians that their actions display their understanding of the character of Jesus.[36]

Paul's joy despite his suffering for Christ anticipates part of his personal mission statement we've already examined: "I want to know Christ...and the partnership of his sufferings" (3:10). Through his own experience of suffering for Christ, Paul comes to know Christ at a greater depth. Participating this way in the story of Christ gives him joy. It's an ironic joy perhaps, but it is an important theme throughout this letter.[37] Paul closes the discussion of suffering for Christ with further proof of how he participates in the story of Christ (and by implication how they can too). Although Paul would prefer to die so he could be "with Christ" (1:23), he thinks he will continue to live Christ in his earthly life, as it will be an advantage for the Philippians if he can serve them in their "progress and joy" of the faithfulness (1:25).[38] Paul looks forward to the time when he will meet with the Philippians again in Christ Jesus (1:26), a time when he can share a meal and participate in their after-dinner discernment.

There Is No Dual Citizenship for Those in Christ Jesus (1:27–30)

Paul shifts the focus to the suffering in Philippi. In his absence, Paul exhorts them to understand that discernment is the key to their ongoing participation in the larger story of God's economy of salvation in Jesus Christ:

> **Philippians 1:27**: Y'all live out your citizenship in a manner worthy of the gospel of Christ so that, whether I come and see you or am absent and hear about you, I will know that y'all are standing firm in the one spirit [of Jesus], struggling together as one soul for the faithfulness [*pistis*] of the gospel, **28** and are in no way intimidated by your opponents; for them this is a demonstration of their destruction, but of your salvation from God.

I'm sure that Epaphroditus did not use the colloquial "y'all" in his reading. I use it here to emphasize that Paul is using the plural second-person form of the verbs. He is addressing everyone listening to his letter. Paul offers this encouragement as a tool to empower their moral deliberations while they figure out ways to respond to their suffering from persecution.

First, there is no dual citizenship for holy ones in Christ Jesus! Their citizenship is in heaven (3:20). When Paul first met them, he probably characterized their life in God's new age in Christ as heavenly citizenship. This required a commitment to walk exclusively by the pattern of the faithfulness of Jesus Christ; and not by the norms, values, and customs of the culture. They must not be double-minded in their faithfulness. They cannot be fair-weather followers, who walk in the footsteps of Jesus only some of the time and at other times choose to walk with residents of Philippi and the Roman empire. Double-mindedness undermines their exclusive and holy devotion to God in Christ Jesus.

Paul also wants the Philippians to remember that their suffering is analogous to his own suffering. This should be a cause for joy as this, too, is a gift from God. "God has graced [*charizomai*] you on behalf of Christ not only to trust into Christ [in baptism],[39] but also to suffer on his behalf, since you are having the same struggle you saw I had, and now hear I still have" (1:29–30). The verb *charizomai* is rooted in *charis* ("grace"). The verb denotes God's active gift of grace—a gift of God's life-giving power. The call to trust into Christ in baptism is a gift of grace. So, too, it is a gift of grace to suffer for Christ. Both are actions and experiences by which they participate in the story of Jesus. In both ways, they come to know Christ intimately in their own lives (3:10).

Not *all* suffering is a gift of God's grace, he advises—only when Christ-followers endure suffering for their exclusive commitment to Jesus as Lord. It is with this end in mind that Paul tells the Philippians about his own suffering and how it has nevertheless led to the spread of the gospel. To be partners in the gospel (1:5; 4:15–16) and holy ones dedicated to serving God in the world requires metaphorically sharing the "profits" (salvation!) and the "losses" (suffering!) of their common calling "in Christ Jesus."

Paul encourages the Philippians to live out their citizenship in a manner worthy of the gospel of Christ (1:27). So, Paul shifts his focus to their practice of discernment. He candidly alludes to the deliberations that will soon follow the reading of his letter. The Philippians must stand firm in their commitment to be led in their discernment by only one Spirit—the Spirit of Jesus.[40] He also acknowledges that these after-dinner discussions, where they struggle together side by side in their moral deliberations about faithfulness, are part of their ongoing formation in Christ. It is one of the critical practices through which God builds up relationships in their community. "Paul's language of 'striving side by side'. . .suggests this is not a solitary journey. . . Paul's practice of moral formation in Philippians relies heavily on *fostering significant relationships* within the community."[41]

Paul insists that by walking resolutely on the path of Christ, struggling side by side in discerning the faithfulness of the gospel, they experience and demonstrate salvation from God (1:29). They exhibit relationships that, despite their suffering, also share the surpassing peace that only God can provide to those who walk exclusively in the ways of God's Son.[42] This surpassing peace of God will always exceed the promises and experiences of the *Pax Romana*.

Christlike Moral Reasoning Shapes Discernment (2:1–4:23)

In 2:1–11 Paul presents Christlike moral reasoning as the ground for contextual discernment in Christ Jesus. It's the framework for how they will live out their citizenship in a manner worthy of the gospel of Christ.

Moral Deliberations in Christ Jesus Build up a Community of Care (2:1–5)

Although there will be struggle, Paul is now emphasizing that the Philippians will also practice care for one another during these moral deliberations in discernment (2:1–4). Through these experiences, God builds them up into a community of care[43] as they become partners (*koinōnia*) with the Spirit of Jesus (2:1). Mutual encouragement, loving consolation, agonizing compassion,[44] and mercy (2:1) will create a shared purpose among them. And by shunning ambition or conceit and embracing humility, they will also put the interests of others ahead of their own interests (2:4).

During their moral deliberations in discernment, they should also "reason [*phroneō*] the same way," "reason [*phroneō*] the one way," (2:2), and "reason [*phroneō*] this way among you which is in Christ Jesus" (2:5). English translations usually turn this active verb *phroneō* into a passive noun—"mind"—alluding to the mind (*nous*) of Christ. Unfortunately, this distorts the active practice of Christlike moral reasoning that is crucial for their moral deliberations in discernment.

In this letter, Paul employs the Greek verb *phroneō* ten times.[45] According to Stephen Fowl, Paul uses *phroneō* to "manifest a common pattern of thinking and acting" that leads the community to see things the same way.[46] It is a framework for exercising moral judgment in all kinds of different situations and circumstances.[47] Paul assumes that if the Philippians employ this common, Christlike perspective in their practice of discernment, faithful and fruitful Christlike actions will follow.

Phroneō is part of a word-group closely associated with the noun *phronēsis*. This word-group was commonly used in the ancient world, particularly in discussions of the moral life.[48] *Phronēsis* is often translated as "practical reasoning" or "practical wisdom." It was an important aspect of Greco-Roman moral philosophy as far back as Aristotle.

Phronēsis is adaptive and engaged. It depends on ways of knowing that are embodied, relational, and situation-specific. Practical wisdom takes shape over time as moral communities reflect and deliberate together on their actions and experiences in daily life. With practical wisdom, communities learn over time how to do the "right thing, in the right way, and at the right time" within the constraints of changing circumstances and different contexts in life.[49] According to Aristotle, *phronēsis* is best learned by observing those who act in ways that lead to good experiences for people.

Paul used this framework for action and reflection in his prayer for the Philippians in 1:9–11. He prayed that their love, embodied in acts of self-giving for others, would produce fruit. And that, over time, the connections between their actions and the fruit would lead them to knowledge and full moral insight concerning God's will.

Paul incorporates the language and concerns of Greco-Roman philosophy but he transforms them by attributing them to the pattern of reasoning and acting reflected in the life of Jesus Christ (see 2:5). Accordingly, as Wayne Meeks notes, "this letter's most comprehensive purpose is the shaping of a *Christian phronēsis*, a practical moral reasoning that is 'conformed to [Christ's] death' in hope of his resurrection."[50]

The Story of Christ Provides the Shape of His Pattern of Moral Reasoning (2:6–11)

Paul reminds the Philippians of the one, unifying pattern of moral reasoning to use in discerning Christlike faithfulness. Fowl characterizes this pattern of moral reasoning as the story of Christ.[51] It shapes the moral deliberations of the community in their practice of discernment. It is the "concrete expression of a shared norm or rule from which Paul and the Philippians can make analogical judgments about how they should live."[52]

Paul sets out this story of Christ and his pattern of moral reasoning in what is commonly thought to be in the form of a hymn or confessional statement familiar to the Philippians:

> **Philippians 2:5** Reason this way among you, which you have in Christ Jesus,
> 6 who, though he was in the form of God, did not regard equality with God as something to clutch tightly,
> 7 but emptied himself, taking the form of a slave [*doulos*], being born in human likeness. And being found in human form,
> 8 he humbled himself and became obedient to the point of death— even death on a cross.
> 9 Therefore God also highly exalted him and graced [*charizomai*] him with the name that is above every name,
> 10 so that at the name of Jesus every knee should bend, in heaven and on earth and under the earth,
> 11 and every tongue should confess that the Lord is Jesus Christ, to the glory of God the Father.

Paul depicts Christ as the one who emptied himself of his heavenly status and power and took the human form of a slave to give himself for others (2:6–7). He humbled himself and became obedient to God, which led to his death on a cross (2:8). This narrative of "downward mobility"[53] provides the contours for practical moral reasoning in discernment. This practical moral reasoning is "a comprehensive pattern of judgment that involves thinking, feeling, and acting," a pattern "the Philippians are to embody in conformity to Christ."[54]

This story of Christ includes a crucial second dimension that also informs the practice of discernment. By raising Jesus from the dead, and gracing (*charizomai*) him with the name that is above every name, God put the divine stamp of approval on Christ's pattern of moral reasoning and action. This story of Christ offers the promise of new life from God to all those who embody self-giving actions discerned through this pattern of moral reasoning.

As we have seen from the moment Epaphroditus started reading this letter, discernment has been Paul's primary focus. Fowl suggests "Paul is trying to form in the Philippians the intellectual and moral abilities to be able to deploy, by means of analogy, their knowledge of the gospel in the concrete situations in which they find themselves."[55] Paul next urges the Philippians to employ this moral reasoning in their deliberations and discernment.

Y'all Work Out Your Own Salvation. . .for God Is Working Among You (2:12–16)

After setting out Christ's pattern of moral reasoning, Paul makes no suggestions for concrete actions. Instead, he urges the Philippians to take responsibility for discerning acts of self-giving that will build up their common life and lead them to experiences of salvation.

> **Philippians 2:12** Therefore, my beloved, just as you have always obeyed [God],[56] not only in my presence, but much more now in my absence, y'all work out your own salvation [*sōterian*] with fear and trembling; **13** for God is the one working among you, enabling y'all both to will and to work in ways that are well-pleasing to God. **14** Do all things without grumbling and arguing, **15** so that you may be blameless and innocent, children of God without blemish in the midst of a crooked and perverse generation, in which you shine like stars in the world. **16** It is by your holding fast to the logic [*logos*] of life that I can boast on the day of Christ that I did not run in vain or labor in vain.

Paul knows the Philippians will soon begin to deliberate in their practice of discernment. Christ's moral reasoning set out in 2:6–11 will guide their deliberations. In 2:16 Paul characterizes this pattern of moral reasoning as the "logic [*logos*] of life." I have translated *logos* as "logic," rather than its usual translation as "word," because Christ's pattern of moral reasoning is *not* just a spoken or written word *about* something. It "is an *enacted* pattern of behavior"[57] that leads to Christlike actions and experiences of resurrection power for new life. The goal of their moral deliberations is to employ the logic of life to discern Christlike actions through which members of the community will experience moments of the new life of salvation (2:12–13).

Paul understands salvation in social rather than individual terms.[58] It is something that occurs in this life.[59] The word *sōtērion*—salvation—describes present, earthly experiences in human relationships. The goal of their moral deliberations is to discern Christlike actions that lead to gospel-events of God's saving power in their communal relationships.[60] They do the work of discernment with fear and trembling because, in earthly life, there is never any certainty about whether an action will be pleasing to God and bear fruit. Thus every action must be undertaken with humility and openness to sometimes missing the mark.

This focus on humility leads to another often-overlooked dimension of Paul's exhortation to discernment in 2:13. God is the one working gospel-events—experiences of saving power—in the community. God is the one working through Christlike actions with resurrection power creating experiences of new life. The discerning community should recognize these experiences of new life and work back from them to identify the Christlike actions that precipitated them. In this way, God is enabling the community to will and to work for God's good pleasure.

While the Philippians may struggle together in these moral deliberations (1:27), Paul encourages them to reason together without complaint (2:14). They are, he says, citizens of heaven, residents of God's new age in Christ, a field of stars amidst a crooked and perverse age.

Most importantly, Paul urges the Philippians to hold fast to this logic of life (2:16) he laid out for them in the pattern of Christ's moral reasoning in 2:6–11. This is the pattern of reasoning that leads them to the discernment of Christlike actions and experiences of resurrection power for new *life* in the community.

Paul Gives Contextual Examples of Christlike Moral Reasoning in Action (2:19–4:3)

Paul prepares the Philippians for using the logic of life in their moral deliberations. He stimulates their moral imaginations by providing real-life contextual examples of Christlike attitudes and actions that, by analogy, reflect Christ's pattern of moral reasoning. By doing so, he also anticipates his guidance to Euodia and Syntychē in 4:2.

Paul presents the ministries of two coworkers, Timothy and Epaphroditus.[61] Timothy does not seek his own interest (see 2:4), he does not seek his own advancement. His actions are analogous to those of Christ, who emptied himself of status and power and humbled himself to become a human slave in service to others (2:6–8). Timothy is embodying Christlike actions and attitudes that, by analogy in his own life, reflect the fruit of Christlike moral reasoning. Timothy's care for the Philippians is genuine.

And Epaphroditus—who is now reading Paul's letter—does not hesitate one bit when he reaches the part of the letter that presents his own actions as examples of Christlike moral reasoning. He risked his life to serve Paul on behalf of the Philippians and almost died for this work of Christ (2:27, 30). Paul has now sent Epaphroditus back to Philippi, even though he had been ministering to the needs of the imprisoned Paul. Paul wants everyone to rejoice at being reunited with Epaphroditus and to celebrate his recovery from illness (2:28–30).

Both Timothy and Epaphroditus are Christlike models for emulation by the Philippians. They put the interests of others ahead of their own interests in their distinctive contexts. Epaphroditus, especially, serves as another example of someone who has partnered with Christ in his suffering by putting himself at risk for the sake of Christ, Paul, and the gospel (see 3:10).

By recounting more of his own story, Paul also presents himself as a model of Christlike moral reasoning in 3:2–9.[62] He emptied himself of his status and power by surrendering the gains from his rapid advancement in Judaism (3:4–8). This is part of the cost of the "surpassing value of knowing Christ Jesus my Lord" (3:8). In fact, Paul has suffered the loss of everything for the sake of Christ (3:8). This is part of the metaphorical "losses" associated with being partners in the gospel (1:5), partners in God's grace (1:7; 1:29), and partners with Christ in his suffering (3:10).

Further, in 3:15–4:3, Paul exhorts the Philippians to adopt this same pattern of Christlike moral reasoning in the contexts of their own lives. He points to himself and others as examples of being mature in Christ because they all reason (*phroneō*) the same way as Christ (3:15). Similarly, Paul encourages two leaders, Euodia and Syntychē, two women who have struggled side by side with him in the work of the gospel, "to reason [*phroneō*] this same way in the Lord" (4:2). While some of the Philippians may still be reasoning according to a different pattern (Euodia or Syntychē may fall into this category), Paul is confident that God will ultimately reveal to them the efficacy of Christ's exclusive pattern of moral reasoning (3:15). He urges them to walk in line with this same pattern of moral reasoning already being used in Philippi (3:16).

As we have already seen, according to Aristotle, *phronēsis*—practical moral wisdom—is best learned by observing those who act in ways that allow others to flourish. To wit, Paul invites them to continue in this learning process in their upcoming discernment. He also offers cautionary examples of those who walk as "enemies of the cross" because they reason (*phroneō*) according to earthly norms, values, and customs (3:18). He ends this part of the letter with a recognizable refrain: "Therefore...stand firm in the Lord in this way" (4:1).

Paul Offers Advice to Guide Their Moral Deliberations (4:4–23)

Finally, Paul starts to close the letter. The Philippians will soon begin their moral deliberations. Paul has more suggestions. He encourages them not to be anxious in their deliberations. He invites them to pray and to let their requests be known to God as they seek to embody Christ in acts of self-giving that will lead to gospel-events of salvation in the community. He assures them that "the peace of God, which surpasses all understanding," will guard their "hearts and thoughts in Christ Jesus" (4:7). Deliberating together in discernment is hard but godly work, so God promises to protect them in this process.

Paul offers himself yet again as an example of Christlike reasoning and action:

> **Philippians 4:8** Whatever is true, whatever is honorable, whatever is just, whatever is pure, whatever is lovely, whatever is commendable, if there is any excellence and if there is anything worthy of praise, take account of these things. **9** Keep on practicing the things that you have learned and received and heard and seen in me, and the God of peace will be with you.

Paul reminds the Philippians that discernment involves looking back on past actions and their consequences. He encourages them to recall particular actions he has taken that have proven through testing to bear fruit in their community. He wants them to connect specific Christlike actions with gospel-events of God's saving power. *He is giving them a shorthand rendition of the practice of discernment that has been in view since the letter's opening verses.* And he is assuring them that some of these past actions will lead them yet again to experiences of the peace of God that passes all understanding.

As he nears the end of the letter, Paul offers more words of encouragement. He thanks them for the latest gifts they sent with Epaphroditus to him in prison (4:10), gifts that are well-pleasing to God (4:18). These were probably gifts of food and clothing, since the Roman prison system provided very little in the way of material support for prisoners. "You did well partnering with [*synkoinōneō*] me in my affliction" (4:14). Not only were they partnering with Paul in his affliction, by sending their own resources they were also partnering with Christ in his suffering (3:10). He further reminds them that when he left Macedonia, they were the only congregation who partnered (*koinōneō*) with him in the practice of giving and receiving (4:15). Even when Paul was in nearby Thessalonica, the Philippians sent financial support to him more than once (4:16).

Paul weaves this into a theological framework. Their partnership in the gospel and generosity to Paul are increasing the fruit being deposited into their account with God (4:17). He assures them that God will satisfy every need they have in their community in Christ Jesus (4:19).

Epaphroditus finishes reading the letter. The Philippians will soon begin their moral deliberations in discernment. They will be seeking to discern actions based on the analogies they draw between the moral exemplars Paul has given them and the contexts in which they find themselves.[63]

Our pilgrims depart the gathering. They will reconvene later this evening to reflect on their experience.

Pilgrims Reflect on Their Experience

The pilgrims gather after dinner to reflect together on what they saw and heard in this assembly of Christ-followers in Philippi. They are sitting on the hotel's outdoor patio, surrounded by its beautiful garden, where colorful poppies and kalanchoes are flourishing. It's a pleasantly cool evening, so some of the pilgrims are wearing light sweaters. It's surprisingly quiet for a weekend night.

Latisha can hardly wait for everyone to be seated in our circle before saying, "The Christ-followers in Philippi really seemed to enjoy one another and they all treated one another respectfully."

"Yes, I really saw the kindness and patience of Jesus reflected in the different ways they responded to one another," adds Reynoldo. "They have been formed over time in those attitudes and practices by deliberating together in Christ Jesus."

"I heard Paul say twice that this congregation has been a partner with him in the gospel from the start of his ministry, even to the point of contributing to him financially several times," says Sarah. She then adds, "That means they've been meeting together for a meal followed by their practice of discernment for quite a while. Most of them seem to be mature in their formation in Christ."

Latisha joins in again, "I can understand why Paul is confident that God will continue to knit this group together. They have learned how to be a community of care, despite some apparent disagreements about how they should respond to the intimidation from their neighbors."

"I love how Paul realistically characterized their moral deliberations in discernment as 'struggling together for the faithfulness of the gospel,'" says Esperanza. "I bet that's hard work."

"Picking up on our discussion on discernment at the last stop," Gail responds, "what do you think it means to be struggling together for the faithfulness of the gospel?"

"I think they're wrestling with how that story of Christ—his pattern of moral reasoning—actually gets applied to situations in daily life," says Sarah.

"That's what I'm starting to think," says Gail. "Discernment is not just about decision-making for the whole group, which is what I'm familiar with, but about how the community reasons together using Christ's pattern of moral reasoning to help an individual imagine how to respond to a specific situation."

Jean speaks up and turns the conversation to another topic. "I've never really thought much about what it means to claim Jesus as Lord. I don't think I've ever heard it stated so clearly in my church that baptism into Christ means I've made an exclusive commitment to follow Jesus as Lord of my life. In fact, I got a little nervous when I heard that there is no dual citizenship involved in following Jesus. I've spent most of my life compartmentalizing my life of faith and my public life."

"I agree," says Robert, who adds pensively, "I've never considered that my commitments as a Christian included changing my entire way of life. I've always known that following Jesus means doing some things differently. But Paul is talking about doing things according to Christ's pattern of faithfulness in every aspect of our lives. He taught folks how to engage these questions every week after they finished their meal. That puts the primary emphasis on Christian formation in the church, rather than the ways we currently worship on Sunday."

"Yes, I heard that, too," offers Ann. "I also heard Paul emphasize that after their meal they should deliberate on these issues without grumbling and arguing. I can't tell you how often grumbling or arguing about something takes on a life of its own for me. They often cause me to get defensive. That distracts me from staying in the present moment and focusing on the issue we're discussing. One year I even tried giving up grumbling as a Lenten discipline! I didn't even make it a week before failing."

Robert sits up straight in his chair and says, "I understand a little bit about what the Philippians must have been experiencing from their neighbors. My wife and I gave up our membership in an exclusive, all-white private social club, because we didn't think it was aligned with our Christian values. Some of our friends then stopped including us in other social activities. They stopped inviting our kids to their children's birthday parties. It was hard to explain in response to our kids' disappointment at not being included."

"That's a high price to pay," says Jean. "I don't know if I'm ready for that."

"I know what you mean," says Diane, looking chagrined. "I've never heard so much talk about suffering with Christ. And to hear that I'm supposed to be joyful about being Christ's partner in suffering comes as a real surprise. I've always believed Jesus died for my sins to save me. I never knew there was a lot more to it."

"Yes," says Dante, diving into the conversation. "A lot of people in my church understand salvation as something they look forward to in heaven, after death. Paul has a very different understanding of salvation. But, you know, it makes our daily lives much more meaningful! Paul says I have a role to play in my own community's experience of salvation."

"I agree," says Ann. "It sounds like we're supposed to use our imaginations as we try to reason like Christ in ordinary life. I'm starting to think how good we have it—we have the Scriptures to help stimulate our moral imaginations. They only had Paul's letter and his earlier teaching and modeling of Christlike actions."

"Yes, I heard several times about the importance of drawing analogies between the contexts and actions that serve as our moral examples and the contexts of our own lives and situations," observes Robert. "John, can you explain anything more about this idea of analogy that Paul used in connection with Timothy and Epaphroditus?"

"Sure, see if this helps," I respond. "An analogy is a partial similarity or correspondence between two things that are different. In the case you're talking about, Timothy and Epaphroditus are two very different people from Jesus and from each other. But each of them embodies a certain aspect of the story of Christ and his moral reasoning. There is a partial similarity or correspondence between their actions and Christ's reasoning. Here's another way to look at it. Mark Twain is often quoted as saying that 'history never repeats itself, but it sure does rhyme!' What you're looking for here is a rhyme between some aspect of Christ's reasoning and some action by Timothy or Epaphroditus. Later, we will talk about finding the rhyme between a biblical passage and some event happening in your life or the life of another pilgrim. Catching the rhyme helps us to interpret and imagine possible responses to a current event in somebody's life.[64] Does that help?"

"Yes," says Robert, "but it's going to take us some time to get used to making those kinds of comparisons and connections."

"Yes, I agree," says Philip. Many other pilgrims nod in agreement.

"We'll continue working on this throughout our time together," I assure them.

"Imagine for a minute what it would look like if our civic or educational leaders were Christians who were formed in this kind of weekly practice of discernment," muses Sarah. "It might go a long way toward creating an atmosphere of cooperation and collaboration rather than the hostility and dysfunction that is tearing the fabric of our communities apart. Can you imagine our leaders struggling together side by side to solve some of the challenges we face today?"

"Not just our civic leaders," says Esperanza. "This kind of formation would change some people's opinions about Christianity. Right now, based on what they see and hear in the public square, many of our fellow citizens think Christians are hard-hearted and even hateful toward those who don't share their strict beliefs or, worse yet, just don't look like them."

"I didn't hear much of anything about beliefs in Paul's letter," adds Latisha. "He's clearly focused on forming his congregants so they can embody Jesus in their daily lives. He's given them this pattern of moral reasoning and practice of discernment to support that goal. He even reminds the Philippians—and us!—that their actions display their understanding of the character of Jesus."

Diane jumps in again, "And look at the culture this practice has built up in the church in Philippi. That's a church I'd like to join."

"How could we incorporate this discipline in our churches?" asks Robert.

"Do you think this kind of discernment might work for a church's leadership group?" asks Latisha.

Philip responds, "that's a good question, Latisha. It resonates with me. I've never seen anything in Scripture about deciding issues by voting. I think in one case they cast lots to decide who would replace Judas Iscariot and the lot fell on Matthias. There was nothing about a vote. My church leadership team always seems to have some conflict erupt after they vote on something. Discernment seems to be the heart of decision-making in the early church because the practice helps build healthy relationships. If only that was the case now."

"I want to go back to something we haven't discussed fully. What about this whole issue of patriotism?" Ann is now raising a sensitive question. "What does it really mean to be patriotic? My son serves in the Army and my father fought in Vietnam. Although he's drifted away from the church more recently, my son spent his early years going to Sunday School every week. Can he be a Christian and a soldier, too?"

Up to now, Jim has been unusually quiet. He finally opens up. "That's another great question, Ann. I've been wondering about something similar. I'm not sure how Christ's pattern of moral reasoning would help me in my workplace. It's a pretty competitive and, at times, even cutthroat place to work. I don't think it would be advantageous for me to put the interests of my coworkers ahead of my own interests. Nor would my employer appreciate me giving up my status and power when I'm negotiating with one of our suppliers. I'm conflicted about whether this is a good place for me to work."

"Well, that's just the business world, Jim," Jean says consolingly. "It's important for you to compartmentalize your work world from your church world if you want to continue to move up the ladder of success."

"Wait," says Esperanza. "Isn't that the point Paul is making when he tells the Philippians there is no dual citizenship for those of us in Christ? And what about Paul's apocalyptic perspective? If we're really committed to living in God's new age, don't you think we should be walking in Christ's footsteps no matter the outcome?"

"Oh, my," gasp Jim and Jean almost simultaneously. "What then should we do?" they ask.

"That's a great question," I say to the group. "But I think it's time we paused our helpful discussions—we'll continue them later. Let's pack our bags and get on the road to our next stop at the church in nearby Thessalonica."

CHAPTER THREE

Pastoral Care as Formation in Holiness at Thessalonica

"Therefore, Encourage One Another..." (1 Thessalonians 4:18; 5:11)

After leaving Philippi, our pilgrims follow in the footsteps of Paul on the Via Egnatia heading west. For the second time, our sandal-clad feet walk along the large stone slabs of the Via Egnatia. It's the Roman road constructed between 146 and 120 BCE that served as an important route for East-West trade and communication. The 700-mile road connected Dyrrhachium on the Adriatic coast (now in modern Albania) with Byzantium (later called Constantinople and, finally, modern Istanbul).

We trudge along the road for 100 miles to the walled city of Thessalonica, where we will enter the assembly of Christ-followers in Paul's congregation. They face issues of suffering from persecution, similar to the experiences of the Philippians.

There are two short letters from Paul to Thessalonica, designated "First Thessalonians" and "Second Thessalonians." First Thessalonians is Paul's earliest surviving letter and, thus, the earliest preserved Christian writing. We will hear First Thessalonians as it is read to the assembled Christ-followers.

Where Are We?

Thessalonica was the capital of the Roman province of Macedonia in northern Greece. It was founded in 316 BCE by Cassander, king of Macedon. He named the city for his wife, Thessaloniki, the half-sister of

Alexander the Great. The city was the largest in Macedonia, with an estimated population of 100,000, living both inside and outside the city's walls.[1]

Unlike neighboring Philippi, the city was not a Roman colony. It was a "free state" administered by an independent government. The city was originally populated with Greek immigrants from the south. During the Roman civil wars, Thessalonica experienced an influx of Latin-speaking people, particularly merchants and imperial administrators.[2]

By the time of Paul's visit and founding of the church in the late 40s CE, Thessalonica had become the largest port on the Via Egnatia, with economic and political importance throughout the Roman Empire.[3] Despite maintaining its Greek heritage, Thessalonica had become a center of the Roman imperial cult. The city also featured many temples to various pagan gods worshiped by the local population. With a clear view of Mount Olympus across the bay, home to many of the gods, residents were reminded daily of the influence of the gods in their lives. Most historians further conclude that by the first century CE the city had a significant Jewish population as part of the centuries-long Jewish Diaspora.[4]

According to Acts 17:1–10, following a harrowing experience in Philippi, Paul, Silvanus, and Timothy spent about three weeks proclaiming the gospel in Thessalonica. During that time, however, a mob of Jewish residents and ruffians complained to the city authorities that Paul and his colleagues were "turning the world upside down." According to the rioters, Paul and friends were acting contrary to Caesar's decrees and proclaiming another king named Jesus.

Members of the congregation then hustled Paul, Silvanus, and Timothy fifty miles further west to Beroea, where they had more success among that city's Jewish residents. But when the Thessalonians heard of their success in Beroea, they hurried there and stirred up another mob against Paul and his coworkers. Shortly thereafter, the Christ-followers once again collected Paul and escorted him to Athens (Acts 17:14–15).

Paul's first letter to the Thessalonians mirrors certain aspects of the narrative in Acts. Paul affirms in 1 Thessalonians 2:2 that he and his colleagues arrived in Thessalonica after being shamefully treated in Philippi. It's hard to imagine, however, that they only spent three weeks in Thessalonica.

The community to whom Paul writes seems well-informed about common convictions and practices Paul taught to all his churches. These include the crucial role of proof through testing in discernment we examined in Philippi. There also seems to be some functioning local leadership in place. Moreover, between the time of Paul's founding of the church and the writing of this letter from Corinth (probably 50 CE), the Thessalonians participated in the rapid spread of the gospel throughout Macedonia and Achaia (1 Thessalonians 1:7–8). The strength of this community's formation and practice suggests that Paul was probably in Thessalonica for much longer than just three weeks before departing.[5]

Why Are We Here?

Paul's first-century world was polytheistic. People were devoted to countless deities and local idols. The emperor's divine status, with his imperial cult, demonstrated that there was no such thing as the separation of religion and politics.

Ancient people worshiped the gods primarily by offering sacrifices at their local temples. These sacrifices were attempts to persuade a god to bestow favor and protection on the people of a town or region. In return, the deities required regular sacrifices to accommodate the people's expectations.

Divine-human relationships were contractual and focused on these ritual sacrifices. The gods made no ethical demands on their worshipers.[6] Most religions in the ancient world did not teach a complete way of life. Judaism and Christianity were prominent exceptions. They were more akin to the philosophical schools, like Stoicism, Cynicism, and Epicureanism, which each taught a distinctive way of life. Leaders of these philosophical schools gathered a group of followers and taught their way of life primarily by living and modeling it for their students.

Most of Paul's converts in Macedonia—including Thessalonica and Philippi—were probably poor members of the artisan class.[7] They likely included some skilled craftspeople like blacksmiths, carpenters, masons, potters, weavers, and jewelers, who produced goods using their hands and tools in workshops. In two other letters, Paul praises the Macedonians (including the Thessalonians) for their overwhelming generosity to other Christ-communities despite living in extreme poverty.[8]

Paul most likely taught the Thessalonians in a workshop, much like the philosophers who taught the moral life while working at a craft.[9] This letter's language implies that the group probably met in someone's home, which served two functions. The home provided a room for worship and created space for the manual laborers among them to practice their trade.[10]

To follow Jesus, these new Thessalonian converts had to renounce their former social and religious affiliations, including the imperial cult. From experience, Paul knew this would lead to local persecution. He warned them of this likelihood during his visit (3:4). True to Paul's warning, as we saw in Philippi, the Thessalonians were suffering from persecution by their local neighbors (2:1). This persecution may have involved "ostracism, mob activity, legal proceedings, and even killings."[11] In fact, some beloved members of the community died after Paul's visit, possibly through martyrdom. Paul is writing to ease the Thessalonians' concerns about those who have died (4:13–17).

Given their cultural background, Paul knew that the conversion of Gentiles required a resocialization process.[12] Formation, community building, and discernment were the keys to resocializing pagan Gentiles in Christ Jesus. Paul had to teach these converts Christ's new way of life as their exclusive pattern for walking in the world. He also knew that Christ's way of love, embodied in acts of self-giving for others, would seem foolish to the pagan culture. So, Paul built a network of friends in Christ for formation and pastoral care to sustain these small countercultural communities after he left town.[13]

Paul was also concerned about other issues for this young community in Thessalonica. First, he was anxious that these persecutions were tempting the Thessalonians to abandon their exclusive commitment to Jesus as Lord. This is the same concern we saw in nearby Philippi. So, Paul again raises the theme of holiness—their set-apartness to God in Christ. Paul was also worried that their inexperience in following Jesus would adversely impact their practice of discernment. He wondered whether their imaginations had been sufficiently transformed to give them the *"ability to discern* how their fidelity to God...should be embodied in the myriad of circumstances that they might face."[14] Third, in the early church, Christ's return in glory to claim the earth for God was anticipated with excitement and thought to be imminent. By the time Paul writes to the Thessalonians, however, nearly twenty years have passed since Christ's death and resurrection. His imminent return seems to be delayed. This has created an issue in this local church to which Paul responds.

The same persecutions experienced by the Thessalonians probably also caused Paul to make a hasty departure from Thessalonica under duress.[15] The chaos of his premature exit, possibly instigated by fellow Jews,[16] may have raised questions in the congregation about his trustworthiness as a Jewish teacher. Paul grew anxious about whether these persecutions had shaken their trust and confidence, not only in the gospel, but in Paul himself.

Given these concerns, Paul sent his trusted colleague Timothy to Thessalonica. Paul asked him to determine the state of their well-being, to assess their ongoing allegiance to Paul as their teacher and moral model, and to strengthen and encourage their practice of faithfulness (3:1–5). Immediately following Timothy's return and report, Paul, Timothy, and Silvanus write this first letter to the Thessalonians. For the sake of simplicity once again, I will refer to Paul as the author of this letter, always bearing in mind the inclusive meaning of his name.

As he writes, Paul knows that, after hearing this letter, the Thessalonians will reflect, discern, and deliberate together on their life in Christ Jesus. So, Paul directly addresses the assembly gathered to hear his letter. He intends for his reminders, insights, and suggestions to encourage them, give them hope for the future, and influence their deliberations.

What Words Matter?

The chapter introduces the following important words and phrases:

- the verb *parakaleō*;
  This is one of Paul's most important words focused on community building. It has a wide range of meanings that include Paul's attempts "to encourage" his congregants; to "comfort" and "console" them; and "to exhort" or "to urge" them to specific actions. Paul uses the verb

eight times in this short letter (2:12; 3:2, 7; 4:1, 10, 18; 5:11, 14). This reflects his desire to encourage a new community beset by persecution and to urge them to Christlike actions that will comfort, console, and build up the community in their new life in Christ.

- the noun *parousia*;
  The most common cultural translations point to a person's "presence," "coming," or "arrival." For centuries, however, this word has taken on an added layer of theological interpretation. The word is understood as a technical term for Christ's future "coming" or "arrival," often called his "second coming" by many modern Christians. Paul uses *parousia* four times in this short letter (2:19; 3:13; 4:15; 5:23).
- the phrase "Day of the Lord";
  Throughout the Old and New Testament Scriptures, this phrase denotes the day of God's final entry to reclaim and judge the world. It's the day when God fully reigns for life on earth in the new age of God's kingdom. We will explore Paul's distinctive, apocalyptic understanding of this event—a part of his "already but not yet" perspective.
- the verb *oikodomeō* ("to build up" or "to edify");
  This is part of a word-group that is crucial in his vocabulary of formation, community building, and discernment.

I continue to develop our understanding of other important Greek words in Paul's lexicon of formation, community building, and discernment introduced at earlier stops:

- the noun *pistis* ("faith," "trust," "faithfulness");
- the noun *prophēteias* ("prophecies");
- the noun *hagiasmos* ("holiness");
- the verb *dokimazō* ("prove through testing"); and
- the phrase *en Christō Iēsou* ("in Christ Jesus").

Enough talk about the letter's backstory! It's time for pilgrims to enter the assembly of the Thessalonians and to hear Paul's messenger read his letter.

Joining the Assembly in Thessalonica

The pilgrims step off the Via Egnatia and pause to take in their surroundings. It's a beautiful, clear, late-afternoon day on the coast of the Aegean Sea. Looking south from their vantage point, pilgrims are mesmerized by the vibrant, deep-blue sapphire color of the ocean just a few blocks from where they stand. Known for its crystal-clear waters, the Aegean Sea provides food for the local citizens and a safe harbor that boosts many trade opportunities. Looking southeast, pilgrims see Mount Olympus rising high into the late-afternoon sky. The setting sun creates a beautiful alpenglow effect on the west-facing side of the mountain. No wonder this was the home for so many Greek gods in the ancient world! Finally, looking to the southeast, pilgrims are treated to a rare view of Mount Athos. Now an important center for Eastern Orthodox monasticism, in Paul's day it held pagan religious significance.

It's now time to join the Thessalonians' congregation. The pilgrims make their way to the workshop-like setting of a congregant's home. They join the group that has gathered to share a meal and to hear Paul's letter read and explained.

Silvanus is introduced to the assembly. He is a coauthor of the letter[17] who will read it and answer questions. Following the reading, the members of the community will reflect on Paul's counsel and deliberate on ways to embody Christ in their challenging context.

Paul Offers Thanksgiving to God for the Thessalonians (1:1–10)

Silvanus carefully removes Paul's letter from his bag and begins to read. Paul greets "the deliberative assembly [*ekklēsia*] of the Thessalonians in God the Father and [in] the Lord Jesus Christ" (1:1). Members of this community have assembled "in the Lord Jesus Christ." This is a countercultural social and physical space where members share a common meal and then engage in face-to-face deliberations in discernment. It's the space where they learn from one another how to walk in the ways of Jesus Christ and be formed in his image. It's the physical space where formation, community building, and discernment take place.

Paul offers an extended thanksgiving (*eucharistia*) to God for the recipients. It begins in 1:2 and continues, off and on, through 3:10. Three different times (1:2; 2:13; 3:9) Paul gives thanks to God for some aspect of life in Christ among the Thessalonians.

Paul introduces major themes. He remembers in his prayers the Thessalonians' "work of faithfulness [*pistis*] and labor of love [*agapē*] and steadfastness of hope in our Lord Jesus Christ" (1:2–3). In this letter *pistis* consistently connotes the sense of faithfulness (1:3, 8; 3:2, 5, 6, 7, 10; 5:8).[18] At key moments Paul continues to link *pistis* and *agapē* throughout the letter (1:3; 3:6; 5:8). As we first saw on the road to Damascus and in this letter, too, *agapē* denotes Christlike love embodied in acts of self-giving for others (3:6, 12; 5:13).

Paul's emphasis on their "work" and "labor" implies low-status activities, suggesting that many of them are manual laborers.[19] He highlights the Christlike nature and importance of their efforts by setting up an analogy between their "labor" and "work" and the "labor" and "work" of Paul and his colleagues (2:9). Paul and his associates worked night and day so they would not be financial burdens on the Thessalonians. Their actions reflect, by analogy, Christ's own pattern of love embodied in acts of self-giving for others. Later in this letter, Paul encourages the Thessalonians to continue their own acts of manual labor so as not to become dependent for support on people outside the Christ-community (4:12). This is one of the ways the Thessalonians become imitators of Paul and the Lord Jesus (see 1:6).

Paul Introduces the Important Role of Experience (1:4–5)

Experiences of resurrection power transformed Paul's life and the lives of the Philippians. In this letter Paul emphasizes the revelatory and persuasive role of human experience in these gospel-events. At least fifteen times in this short letter—and ten times just in the letter's first two chapters—Paul emphasizes experience. He reminds the Thessalonians of their earlier experiences when he was first with them, using phrases such as "just as you know" (1:5; 2:11), "as you know" (2:2, 5; 3:4), and the emphatic "you yourselves know" (2:1; 3:3; 4:9; 5:2). These phrases refer directly to his readers' own experiences, a theme that predominates in this letter.[20] Paul also speaks of his own experiences. He uses phrases such as "we know" (1:4) and he talks of "bearing witness" to experiences, either by God (2:5, 10), the Thessalonians (2:10), or by him (2:12).

Paul introduces these crucial references to human experience in 1:4–5:

> **1 Thessalonians 1:4** *We know*, brothers and sisters, beloved by God that God has chosen you **5** because our gospel proved to be present [*ginomai*] in/among you [plural], not in word only, but also in power and in the Holy Spirit and with full conviction, *just as you know* what kind of persons we proved to be [*ginomai*] among you for your sake.

Paul is persuaded ("we know") that God has chosen the Thessalonians because he witnessed a gospel-event of God's powerful reign for new life among the Thessalonians. He reminds them that they experienced this power in the Holy Spirit.[21] From this experience, they turned their lives over to God and abandoned their idols (1:9). Paul offers these words as encouragement, reminding them that they turned in this new direction with full conviction. They did not waver in making their original commitment. So, now is not the time for them to vacillate. Paul is starting to rebuild their confidence in Christ's new way of life, a trust that may have been "shaken by these persecutions" (3:3).

Paul also reminds the Thessalonians that their own experience ("just as you know") of God's life-giving power took place through Paul's Christlike manner of life on their behalf (1:5). As we learned on the road to Damascus, Christ came alive in Paul when he experienced the resurrection power of God in the risen Christ. Paul thereafter patterned his earthly life on the faithfulness of Jesus Christ, "the one who loved me, indeed, who gave himself for me" (Galatians 2:20). Paul's Christlike actions among the Thessalonians led to their experiences of resurrection power. Both his oral speaking and his embodiment of Christ's pattern of faithfulness "became the channel…through which the Holy Spirit began" to transform their lives.[22]

There is a direct connection between Paul's embodiment of Christ and experiences of divine power among his congregants. As Sumney has noted: "Paul sees his life as a reflection of the gospel and believes that his manner of life has a role in communicating his gospel."²³ In 1 Thessalonians 1:4–6, Paul "connects the Thessalonians' conversion with how he lived among them...Paul thought his life played an important role in communicating the gospel to the Thessalonians...[He presents] himself as a model...the relationship between his message and his life follows the practice of the popular philosophers who presented their lives as models."²⁴

We will hear some of Paul's specific, Christlike actions in Thessalonica when Silvanus reads 2:1–13. Until then, though, we should recall that Paul embodies Christ by analogy in a variety of ways in different situations. His actions in Philippi led to their experiences of God's life-giving power.

Paul emphasizes the connection between actions, experiences, and understanding. He uses the verb *ginomai* twice in 1:4–5. The verb denotes a person, place, or event that "becomes" or "proves to be" something more than what it was originally seen or thought to be. He uses the verb eleven times from 1:5 through 3:4. While *ginomai* is a common verb, such an extensive use within such a short span of the letter seems intentional.

Paul uses *ginomai* to emphasize how human experience can be transformative and lead to new understanding. By observing the gospel-events taking place among the Thessalonians, Paul came to know that God had called them to this new life in Christ. Similarly, the Thessalonians have come to know for themselves that these gospel-events are linked to Paul's manner of life.

Paul wants the Thessalonians to know that the persecution they are enduring has much more meaning beyond just the suffering. He offers four different interpretations of their experiences to give them hope and confidence they are actively participating in the story of Jesus Christ.

> **1 Thessalonians 1:6** You proved to be [*ginomai*] imitators of us and of the Lord, for in spite of persecution you received the word with joy inspired by the Holy Spirit, **7** so that you proved to be [*ginomai*] an example to all the faithful ones in Macedonia and in Achaia. **8** For the word of the Lord has sounded forth from you not only in Macedonia and Achaia, but in every place your faithfulness toward God has gone out, so that we have no need to speak about it. **9** For the people of those regions report about us what kind of first

visit we had among you, and how you turned to God from idols, to enslave [*douleō*] yourselves to a living and true God, **10** and to wait for his Son from heaven, whom he raised from the dead—Jesus, who is delivering us from the wrath that is coming.

Through their experiences of persecution, with abiding joy, the Thessalonians proved to be imitators of Paul by analogy in their own context. As we saw in Philippi, Paul, too, has suffered from persecution for Christ (Philippians 1:12–26). Nevertheless, he always remains joyful despite the suffering (Philippians 1:18; 2:17, 18, 28; 3:1; 4:4, 10).

The Thessalonians also proved to be imitators of Paul and the Lord by enslaving themselves to the living God (1:9). As we saw in Philippi, Jesus Christ emptied himself of power and status and took the form of a slave (*doulos*).[25] He humbled himself and became obedient to God, even to the point of death on a cross.[26] Paul, too, is a slave of Jesus Christ (Philippians 1:1).

Despite the persecutions, the Thessalonians remained steadfast in their commitment to embodied faithfulness. So, they also proved to be an example of faithfulness throughout Macedonia and Achaia. Their exemplary acts of faithfulness grounded the report that spread throughout Greece about their powerful conversion and exclusive commitment to serve God in Christ.

Paul encourages the Thessalonians once again in 1:10. People have also heard of their commitment to wait for God's Son from heaven, whom God raised from the dead. Virtually all of Paul's interpreters see this as a reference to waiting for Christ's return to earth—his "second coming" as the catalyst for the Day of the Lord—when the spiritual forces of evil will be conquered and God will reign supreme over all the earth.

The verb "delivering" in 1:10, however, is in the present tense. Grounded in his apocalyptic perspective, the present tense of the verb suggests an active and *ongoing process* of divine deliverance that is *already* underway. Paul is speaking in 1:10 about a "dynamic sort of waiting"[27] for revelations from the risen Jesus that take place during their deliberations in the community's practice of discernment.[28] These revelations inform their ongoing practice of Christlike faithfulness. And it is through their acts of Christlike faithfulness that they are currently being delivered *out of* the old age that's passing away and being delivered *into* God's new age and kingdom "in Christ Jesus."[29]

The faithful are also being delivered from the future wrath that will take place when people experience the destructive consequences of their own actions. This wrath is not an attribute of God. It describes the consequences of human brokenness, idolatry, and actions that harm others, destroying human relationships and God's created order.[30] In fact this wrath is already being experienced in Paul's world (see 2:15–16). Paul interprets it as God's active judgment, allowing people to experience the consequences of their own actions.[31] We will revisit this dynamic understanding of discernment and divine judgment later, when we consider Paul's apocalyptic scenario in 1 Thessalonians 5:1–10.

Paul nurtures pastoral relationships and builds a culture of mutuality (2:1–10)

In the first-century world, teaching and mentoring a way of life was most effective in face-to-face encounters.[32] Embodied models were much more effective than oral instruction.[33] Recently converted Gentiles needed living models to stimulate their moral imaginations for how to embody Christ by analogy in their own lives.

Paul is mindful of the Thessalonians' relatively recent conversion to a new, Christlike way of life, value system, and practice of discernment. His concern lies with their ability to discern together how their faithfulness should be embodied in all the circumstances of their daily lives.[34] So, Paul reminds them of some of the ways he first embodied Christ by analogy in the contexts of his ministry among them. In that first visit he began a process of nurturing relationships through pastoral care that he now wants them to recall and reclaim. We saw a similar pattern in Philippians where Paul, in absentia, highlighted the ways he, Timothy, and Epaphroditus, embodied aspects of the story of Jesus by analogy in their own lives.

In 1 Thessalonians 2:1–10, Paul invites them to remember what they experienced through some of the ways he embodied Christ in serving them. "You yourselves know" that the time they spent with him did not prove to be (*ginomai*) in vain (2:1). Rather, their time together bore fruit in the lives of the

Thessalonians. "As you know," despite his suffering and shameful treatment in Philippi, Paul boldly proclaimed the gospel in Thessalonica in the face of great opposition (2:2). Paul subtly encourages the Thessalonians to continue their own influential faithfulness, despite similar opposition, and to trust that their acts of faithfulness will be pleasing to God and bear fruit.

"As you know and as God is our witness," Paul proclaimed the gospel with integrity and authenticity and not with deceit or trickery (2:3). In fact, he says, "we have been proven through testing [*dokimazō*] by God to be entrusted with the gospel" (2:4). Paul is inviting the Thessalonians to look back on his past actions that produced fruitful consequences among them. He uses the important verb *dokimazō* to describe the process of looking back on past actions and connecting them with their consequences. The *fruitful* consequences of his past actions establish that God was well-pleased with Paul's embodied proclamation of Christ. God demonstrates this approval by working powerfully among the Thessalonians through Paul's acts of Christlike ministry. This is how God bears witness to the divine approval of Paul's proclamation.

Moreover, says Paul, this is an ongoing process. God is continuously "proving our hearts through testing [*dokimazō*]." Life in ministry, serving God, is not static, but is dynamic and fluid. Discernment always includes looking back and paying attention to one's motives and actions to determine whether they were pleasing to God and bore fruit.

As we saw in Philippi, this practice of "proof through testing" is a crucial aspect of discernment in Paul's communities.[35] Paul uses the related adjective *dokimos* to describe persons whose trustworthiness in Christ has been proven through testing over time.[36] Conversely, he uses another adjective, *adokimos*, to characterize those whose thoughts and actions have proven through testing *not* to be trustworthy and faithful.[37]

"As you know" from your own experience (2:5), says Paul, I did not use words of flattery or act with a greedy motive. Similarly, though Paul might have burdened them with an apostolic demand for support, he proved to be (*ginomai*) gentle among them like a nurse caring for her own children (2:7). "You remember," he says, how I worked day and night not to be a financial burden on you (2:9).

Through these multifaceted, embodied portrayals of Christ by analogy in his own ministry, Paul bore witness to actions that were "pleasing to God" (2:4). Paul then summarizes these recollections:

1 Thessalonians 2:10 *You are witnesses, and God also*, how pure and just and blameless we proved to be [*ginomai*] among you, the faithful ones; **11** *just as you know*, how we dealt with each one of you as a father to his own children,[38] **12** encouraging [*parakaleō*] and reassuring and bearing witness for you how to walk worthily of God, who is calling you into God's kingdom and glory.

Through their experiences of mutuality, Paul and the Thessalonians have come to know that God works powerfully among them through Christlike actions. God bears witness to Paul's acts of Christlike faithfulness by providing the Thessalonians with experiences of resurrection power in the community. The Thessalonians continue to experience God's calling by walking worthily of God in Christ's way of life by analogy in the contexts of their lives. Recognizing the experiences of divine affirmation is an important aspect of the practice of discernment in Thessalonica.

Paul also gives thanks to God that the Thessalonians heard and heeded the word of God despite persecution from their neighbors (2:13). In this way, they proved to be imitators of the "deliberative assemblies [*ekklēsiai*] of God in Judea in Christ Jesus," who suffered at the hands of their fellow Jews (2:14).

Notice what might seem to be a redundancy in 2:14. Most readers assume that "the *ekklēsiai* of God in Judea" refers to *all* the Christ-communities in Judea. This reading renders the additional phrase "in Christ Jesus" repetitious. This is not the case. Instead, Paul may be distinguishing two different forms of Christ-communities in Judea. On the one hand, "the *ekklēsiai* of God in Judea" might be congregations of Jewish Christ-followers who are Torah-observant and require Gentiles to convert fully to Judaism to join the congregation. On the other hand, "the *ekklēsiai* of God in Judea *in Christ Jesus*" are Christ-communities that accept Gentiles without full conversion to Judaism. These assemblies ground formation and discernment in the person of Jesus Christ, not Torah. These Judean congregations "in Christ Jesus" are the *ekklēsiai* who once endured violent persecution from Paul before he experienced the risen Christ and began to proclaim the faithfulness he once tried to destroy among those congregations.[39]

The Thessalonians' Faithfulness Creates a Gospel-Event in Paul's Life (3:1–10)

It's no surprise that Paul has grown anxious about the state of their faithfulness (3:5). He fears that, in suffering from persecution, "the tempter" might have "tempted" them, causing his earlier, fruitful work to now be (*ginomai*) in vain (3:5). He's worried that their hope might be waning.

This language reflects Paul's Jewish apocalyptic perspective. He knows there are spiritual forces of evil actively opposing God's will for the Thessalonians. Paul previously told them how "Satan"—Paul's personified name for "the tempter"—had already interfered in the relationship between Paul and the Thessalonians (2:18). So, now, Paul justifiably fears that Satan might be taking advantage of their suffering on behalf of Christ. He may be tempting them to abandon their exclusive commitments to serve God by walking in the ways of Christlike faithfulness.

When he could bear it no longer, Paul sent Timothy, his coworker with God in the gospel of Christ, to evaluate the state of their faithfulness (3:2, 5). Timothy's assignment was also to strengthen and to encourage (*parakaleō*) them in their faithfulness (3:2). Timothy has now returned and reported to Paul: the Thessalonians are firm in their commitments to God and to Paul as their teacher and mentor (3:6).

Having received Timothy's report, Paul shares another way God is working through the Thessalonians to bring new life to the world. Paul tells them that Timothy has "gospeled [*euanggelizomai*] us concerning your faithfulness and love" (3:6). Paul uses *euanggelizomai*, one of his favorite verbs we first examined during our stop on the road to Damascus. There, God revealed the gospel and Christ in Paul, so that he might gospel [*euanggelizomai*] Christ among the Gentiles.[40] We saw how Paul uses *euanggelizomai* to characterize his own embodied, Christlike actions that lead to gospel-events in the lives of others.

In this case, however, Timothy's report created a gospel-event in Paul's life! The enduring commitments of the Thessalonians to serve God in Christ and to love Paul as their mentor became a channel of resurrection power for new life in Paul. "For this reason, brothers and sisters, despite all our distress and affliction, we have been encouraged [*parakaleō*]...through your faithfulness" (3:7). God *delivered* Paul (see 1:10) from his anxiety and concerns for their well-being. Paul has new life through this gospel-event. Just as Paul first served as the conduit for God's life-giving power that transformed their lives, the Thessalonians have now become a conduit for new life in Paul. "For we now live, if you continue to stand firm in the Lord" (3:8).

Acts of encouragement (*parakaleō*) are key pastoral practices that build up the community. Christ-followers commit to practice Christlike care, concern, and love for one another. Acts of encouragement like this one nurture relationships in a culture of pastoral care. Mutual encouragement is a never-ending circle of practice that builds up congregations through their experiences of resurrection power for new life.

Paul Prays for the Thessalonians to Be Formed in Holiness (3:11–13)

Paul concludes the extended thanksgiving section of the letter by praying for the Thessalonians. He introduces the theme of holiness (*hagiasmos*) that dominates the rest of the letter and foreshadows his advice on holy living in chapters four and five.

Paul beseeches God and Christ to facilitate another face-to-face visit with the Thessalonians. Then, he prays only to the Lord Jesus for two things. First, he asks the Lord to cause the Thessalonians' love (*agapē*)—their acts of self-giving for others—to increase and abound, not only for one another, but among outsiders, too. Second, he also prays that the Lord will strengthen their hearts, "blameless in holiness [*hagiasmos*], before our God and Father in the presence [*parousia*] of our Lord Jesus with all his saints" (3:13).

The fact that Paul prays only to the Lord Jesus in 3:12 is instructive. His petitions presume that the Lord Jesus actively guides the community's moral deliberations and discernment. He is asking the Lord to continue to confirm their Christlike acts of faithfulness as they grow stronger in holiness.

Recall from our stop in Philippi that holiness means being set apart from the culture and dedicated to serving the one God through Christ. Paul defines holiness exclusively in moral rather than ritual terms.[41] Jesus Christ is the incarnation of holiness in human life.[42] His earthly life is the source and model for holiness in the Christ-community.[43] Holiness is the goal of a congregation's *process* of formation over time in Christ's pattern of life. Holiness is the goal of their preparation for Christ's ultimate return in glory.[44] This ongoing process contributes to their formation in holiness—their formation in the image of Christ.

Paul's prayer in 3:11–13 mirrors his prayers for the Philippians (1:9–11) and Colossians (1:9–10). In these letters, Paul prayed that his congregants' practice of walking in love might multiply and lead to wisdom and moral insight, along with knowledge of God's will and God's life-giving power. All three of the prayers describe the process and goal of discernment in Paul's communities: over time, through their Christlike actions and reflection on the consequences of their actions, they are being formed in holiness and practical wisdom and, ultimately, will be found blameless in the future day of Christ's glorious return.

God's Will for the Thessalonians Is Holiness (4:1–8)

Still pursuing the themes of formation, community building, and discernment, Paul turns to the specific circumstances in Thessalonica. His focus now, however, shifts from building up the confidence of his beleaguered converts to encouraging them (*parakaleō*) to recall what they learned from him during his earlier visit: "how it is necessary for you to walk and to please God (just as you are walking)" (4:1).

This statement presents Paul's foundational understanding of moral life in Christ. Walking in Christlike ways that are pleasing to God leads over time to formation in holiness—formation in the image of Jesus Christ. Thus, says Paul, "continue to do so more and more" (4:1; see also Philippians 1:9).

Paul directly addresses the congregation[45] and reminds them again of his earlier teaching: "For you know" (from your own experience with me!) "the instructions we gave you through the Lord Jesus" (4:2). "This is the will of God: your holiness [*hagiasmos*]" (4:3). Paul uses the noun *hagiasmos* to refer to the goal of the process of formation in Christ's pattern of life.

As we learned in our stop in Philippi, what counts as being holy in Paul's communities is being Christlike.[46] God carries out this process of formation by means of their cross-shaped actions.[47] This formation of Christlike character happens for individuals and for the collective Body of Christ over time in the deliberative assembly in Christ Jesus.

Paul has more advice. This time on matters of sex! In 4:3b-8 he warns them to keep their distance from sexual immorality. Interpreters have debated for millennia without consensus on the precise nature of the issues of sexual immorality Paul is addressing. What is clear, however, is that his words are directed toward discerning holy actions—actions that set the Thessalonians apart from those who embody the sexual norms, values, customs, and practices of the Greco-Roman culture.

Discerning holiness in Paul's communities is not a static, passive state, but one of dynamism, activity, where the Holy Spirit shapes Christlike actions in a divine process of transformation (4:8).[48] After all, says Paul, "God did not call us in [acts of] impurity, but in [acts of] holiness [*hagiasmos*]" (4:7). Acts of holiness are Christlike acts of self-giving for others. Just as Christ-followers come to know Christ through their acts of Christlike faithfulness, they also experience God's call while carrying out these Christlike actions.[49]

The Thessalonians Have Been God-Taught to Love One Another (4:9–12)

In 4:9–12 Paul responds to a question concerning mutual love (*philadelphia*) among the members of this congregation. Interpreters are divided about why the Thessalonians would inquire about mutual love. In Paul's world, however, mutual love was almost exclusively reserved for blood sisters and brothers. So, their acts of mutual love in the congregation helped to create a new sense of identity and commitment among people who had no preexisting basis for such intimate, familial relationships. But some of the Thessalonians may be wondering whether their commitment to mutual love extends to those in the community who have stopped working and are looking to the congregation for support (these are the "idlers" mentioned in 5:14).

Paul deflects the question and once again offers encouragement. He tells the Thessalonians that he doesn't really need to write to them about this issue because "you yourselves have been God-taught [*theodidaktos*] to love one another, just as you are doing" (4:9–10). Once again he uses the emphatic "you yourselves" to highlight what they have already learned about this practice from their own experiences in the Body of Christ.

Paul coins the new word *theodidaktos* for this mode of experiential learning. God alone empowered them in their new life in Christ to practice love for one another beyond what the outside culture requires. They have experienced God's power for new life in the community through their love embodied in acts of self-giving for one another. In fact, their embodied acts of love even extend beyond their community to all the Christ-followers throughout Macedonia, and Paul encourages them to do so more and more (4:10).

Paul also may be making another point with this response. He has already praised their labor of love (1:3) and prayed that the Lord would increase their love for one another (3:12). Now, he encourages them to live quietly and work with their hands, so that they might "walk properly toward outsiders and have no need of anything from them" (4:11–12). In this instruction, Paul is illustrating an important aspect of Christlike love embodied in an act of self-giving for others. Just as Paul worked day and night not to be a burden on the Thessalonians (2:9), he now encourages them to work so that they are not a burden on outsiders. Their work is a labor of Christlike love—an imitation of Jesus Christ. It is love embodied in an act of self-giving that benefits others by relieving them of the burden of support.

Paul Encourages Those Who Are Grieving the Deaths of Friends and Family (4:13–17)

The Thessalonians are grieving the loss of loved ones, possibly through martyrdom. They are anxious about whether those who have died will miss out on the general resurrection of the dead when Christ returns in glory. In the letter's opening paragraph, Paul praised the Thessalonians for their "hope in our Lord Jesus Christ" (1:3). He now helps them to maintain that laudable level of hope, despite the circumstances.

Paul assures the Thessalonians that, at Christ's return, God will bring "with him those who have died" (4:14). In fact, says Paul, the dead in Christ will rise first (4:16), even before those who "are living and remaining in the presence [*parousia*] of the Lord" (4:15; see also 3:13). Then, only after the dead are raised, will those who "are living and remaining" be raised, too (4:17). As for this last group—those still living and remaining on earth when Christ descends from heaven—they "will *always* be with the Lord" (4:17). They are the ones still living their earthly life with the risen Lord in Christ Jesus. They continue to live with the Lord (see 5:10) who is guiding the gathered community until they, too, are raised from the dead on the day of Christ's return.

Therefore, says Paul, "encourage [*parakaleō*] one another with these words" (4:18). As he has done throughout this letter, Paul uses the polysemous word *parakaleō* to support the Thessalonians in a variety of different circumstances. Here, he prescribes words and actions that comfort, console, and encourage those who are grieving their loss and anxious about those who have died. Prior to Christ's return, they are to continue offering encouragement, comfort, and consolation to one another (4:18). Encouragement is an action proven through testing to build up the community in Christ.

Apocalyptic Language Encourages the Practice of Discernment (5:1–11)

Having comforted and consoled the living in their grief, Paul now turns to address another question,[50] maybe brought from them by Timothy. Paul's response reflects his "already but not yet" apocalyptic perspective. By raising Jesus from the dead, God has defeated evil and death; but God's reign is not yet complete. Paul reminds them how they ought to continue walking in the light that shines on them in their deliberative assembly during their practice of discernment.

We don't know the exact question they put to Paul, though his response gives us clues. The situation involves a concern for the timing and nature of the divine reckoning associated with "the Day of the Lord" (see 5:1–2).

In the Jewish Scriptures/Christian Old Testament, "*the* Day of the Lord" is the future day when YHWH intervenes to judge the world and to set things right in human affairs. Throughout the early writings of the Christ-movement, the future return of Christ in glory will be the catalyst for this event. It will include the resurrection of the dead into eternal salvation and the raising of those who are still living with the Lord (4:15–17). "[T]he imagery underscores the unpredictable timing of the Day of the Lord and colors it as a threat that comes suddenly and unexpectedly—at least for some."[51]

Paul's response follows a familiar pattern. The Thessalonians have no need for Paul to write to them about this issue (5:1; see also 1:8; 4:9). This is because "you yourselves know *very well* that *a* day of the Lord *comes* like a thief in the night" (5:2). He wants them once again to recall and reflect on their own relational experiences. In this case, however, Paul stacks one emphatic phrase on top of another. The first emphatic phrase—"you yourselves know"—follows a similar pattern in this letter.[52] But then Paul adds the *even more emphatic* phrase "very well" to what he wants them to recall from their experience. This tells us that their earlier experience is crucial for answering their question.

Most interpreters conclude that what the Thessalonians "know very well" is simply Paul's teaching about "the Day of the Lord"; his teaching about this final day of divine judgment that will come at an unexpected time "like a thief in the night" (5:2).[53] These interpreters translate the Greek verbs *erchomai* (5:2) and *ephistēmi* (5:3) as "will come"—future tense—even though both verbs are written in the present tense and can be translated as "comes." Applying the future tense of these verbs supports their interpretation that Paul is referring to "*the* Day of the Lord" that will arrive at some future time.

Paul's terminology begs for a closer look. There is no Greek article "the" preceding the phrase "Day of the Lord" in 5:2. Paul does include the Greek article "the" in 5:4, referring to "the Day." This *may* signal a distinction Paul is making between *the* final Day of the Lord that will come unexpectedly in the future and *a* Day of the Lord, where a divine judgment is being rendered in the *present* time.

For Paul, as with the Hebrew prophets, "the Day of the Lord" has a moral dimension.[54] Further, this "[j]udgment does not remain a future certainty; it is in some way a present reality that comes upon people."[55] Thus, I suggest that, in 5:1–11, Paul is referring to an event of divine judgment the Thessalonians *know very well* from their own past, relational experience in the community. In some way they experienced "*a* day of the Lord." One or more of them have experienced a moment of judgment revealed by the risen Lord Jesus in their moral deliberations in discernment. It is a divine judgment they all "know very well" because they experienced it in their common life together.

The Thessalonians learned from their experience of judgment. This is exactly what Paul expects from a community that practices discernment together. The risen Lord delivered them (see 1:10) from their metaphorical darkness by the judgment that led them to amend their actions. They are now "children of light" and "children of the Day" (5:5). Light shined on them in "*a* day of the Lord" and brought them out of darkness into light. They are now better prepared for "*the* Day" that will come unexpectedly in the future (1 Thessalonians 5:4).

Nevertheless, Paul recognizes the dynamic and challenging life of earthly faithfulness. So, he exhorts them: "let us not fall asleep as others do; let us keep awake and be self-controlled" (5:6). *This is the language of communal discernment!* The community's practice of discernment keeps them awake to all that is happening in their lives and relationships. It is where they maintain mutual accountability to one another.

"Since we belong to the day," Paul says, "let us be self-controlled, clothing ourselves [*enduō*] with the breastplate of faithfulness and love and, as a helmet, the hope of salvation" (5:8; see also 1:3). Paul frequently uses the metaphorical image of being clothed (*enduō*) with Christ in baptism.[56] He uses the imagery of putting on armor to defend oneself in the struggles of life,[57] something particularly important for a community enduring ongoing persecution. It is not surprising that Paul occasionally uses military imagery, since the human body is the site of apocalyptic resistance to the influential spiritual forces that actively oppose God's will for the world.[58]

This metaphor of clothing oneself with Christ is a major focus of the practice of discernment in Paul's congregations. Discerning Christlike actions, using Christ's pattern of moral reasoning, leads to experiences of

God's saving power (Philippians 2:6–13). "For God has not appointed us for wrath but for acquiring salvation through the Lord Jesus Christ, who died for us, so that whether we are awake or sleeping, we might live with him" (1 Thessalonians 5:9–10). As we saw in Philippi, salvation is worked out through deliberations in discernment. It takes place among those who are awake and living with the risen Christ in the deliberative assembly.

Paul ends his apocalyptic interpretation of living with Christ with yet another community-building exhortation: "[t]herefore, encourage [*parakaleō*] one another and build up [*oikodomeō*] each other, one to one, as indeed you are doing" (5:11).[59] Paul encourages honesty with care, especially in their one-to-one engagements. They will soon deliberate in discernment as a community of mutual accountability when Silvanus finishes reading this letter. They will speak as prophets to one another—to encourage, console, and build up one another.[60] Paul knows the importance of these practices for establishing trust in this process.

In 5:11 Paul introduces us to the verb *oikodomeō*—"to build up" or "to edify."[61] This verb is part of the *oikodom-* word-group that is so important in Paul's vocabulary of formation, community building, and discernment. The verb points metaphorically to human actions that are building blocks in the construction of the Christ-community. Christ-followers are responsible for taking actions that build up and edify the whole community;[62] edification "encompasses all of a person's behavior" directed to individual members.[63] At our next stop in Corinth, we will see the consequences when some Christ-followers don't take this responsibility to heart.

Paul Suggests Concrete Actions to Encourage
and Build up Everyone (5:12–15)

Throughout the remainder of chapter five, Paul offers advice on how the Thessalonians should speak to one another, one to one, and how they should act to build up individuals and the entire community. This advice starts in 5:12–15:

> **1 Thessalonians 5:12** Respect those who labor among you and who exercise leadership in the Lord and those who are admonishing you;

> **13** regard them highly in love [*agapē*] because of their work. Be at peace among yourselves. **14** And we encourage [*parakaleō*] you, brothers and sisters, admonish the idle ones; console the discouraged; help the weak; be long-suffering toward everyone. **15** See that none of you repays evil for evil, but always pursue the good for one another and for everyone.

Paul recognizes the challenges associated with building up a community of mutual accountability. Those who exercise leadership are often viewed with a mixture of envy toward their authority and resentment to the exercise of that authority. Similarly, admonishment from a peer is often hard to hear and at times provokes a defensive response.[64] Thus, at the end of this letter, he urges them to be at peace with one another (5:13). This will prove to be especially important when it comes to admonishing the idle ones. They may be members of the community who stopped working in the expectation of Christ's imminent return.

Paul also encourages members of the community to take the humble step of commending those who exercise leadership in the Lord, especially those who admonish the rest of the community for their own good (5:12–13).[65] Mutual accountability is built on the premise that there is a shared responsibility to examine and, if necessary, critique one another's faithfulness, accompanied by a corresponding humility to receive the critique graciously.

A merciful community also understands how to be long-suffering in bearing with irritations caused by others, including outsiders. The Greek verb *makrothumeō* in 5:14 is usually translated as "patient," but "long-suffering" is a more literal translation, as well as a more challenging, Christlike characteristic. Consider whether Jesus was just "patient" with his disciples or was "long-suffering" with the way they constantly misunderstood his teaching!

Human nature often prompts one's desire to respond to what is perceived as an attack with a corresponding counterattack. But Paul, like Jesus, teaches against retaliation and prohibits the repayment of evil with evil (5:15).[66] Pursuing the "good" of others (5:15) is paramount to building up the deliberative assembly (see Philippians 2:4) and, for that matter, establishing healthy and fruitful relationships outside the *ekklēsia*.

Paul Becomes More Directive Regarding Their Upcoming Deliberations (5:16–18)

Probably mindful that the Thessalonians will soon begin to deliberate on their issues and consider what he has written,[67] he persists in suggesting specific actions, confident that through these actions God will continue to build up and strengthen their communal life and enhance the formation of individual members in holiness.[68] Andy Johnson emphasizes that Paul here is shaping their communal life "in ways that contribute to *improving their ability to discern* how their faithfulness (*pistis*) should be embodied in the various circumstances that might confront them in their ancient Mediterranean society."[69]

"Rejoice always" (1 Thessalonians 5:16); "pray unceasingly" (5:17); and "give thanks in everything, for this is the will of God in Christ Jesus for all of you!" (5:18) Paul inserts the phrase "in Christ Jesus" to emphasize that these actions are God's will for how they should conduct their deliberations when they are together. By repeating the phrase "this is the will of God" from 4:3 in 5:18, Paul connects the acts of rejoicing, praying, and giving thanks with their ongoing formation in holiness.

Paul regularly encourages his congregations to rejoice together despite their suffering. We saw this clearly in our visit to Philippi. Paul encourages the assemblies to rejoice because suffering on behalf of Christ is an essential element of participating in the story of Jesus. Their steadfast faithfulness in partnership with Christ in his suffering[70] is reason to rejoice! In 5:16, Paul urges the congregants to rejoice together and to give thanks in everything—not *for* everything[71]—when they have gathered "in the Lord" for their meal and discernment.

Prophecies Inspire Moral Imaginations for Discerning Christlike Actions (5:19–22)

As Paul nears the climax of the letter, he takes a prophetic turn that will edify the community. "Do not quench the Spirit" and "do not reject prophecies [*prophēteias*]" (5:19–20). Instead, they must "prove everything through testing [*dokimazō*]" (5:21).

Prophets (*prophētēs*) and their prophecies (*prophēteias*) are essential for the practice of discerning faithfulness in the moral life in Christ. As we will see when we get to Corinth, Paul democratizes the role of prophets in the practice of discernment in his local congregations. In fact, he tells the Corinthians, "you can *all* prophesy [*prophēteuō*] one by one, so that all may learn and be encouraged."[72] Those who prophesy speak to others for upbuilding (*oikodomē*), encouragement (*paraklēsis*), and consolation.[73]

Paul tells the Thessalonians not to quench the Spirit by rejecting prophecies. It is likely that the community's experience of judgment that underlies 5:1–11 was in some way related to one or more prophecies offered in the congregation. Paul is concerned that this experience might cause the Thessalonians to reject *all* prophecies.[74] Paul wants to be clear that he is not criticizing prophets and prophecy, *per se*. Rather, he is simply insisting that all prophecies be subjected to the process of proof through testing to determine their fruitfulness in the community. Paul knows that prophecies stimulate Christ-patterned moral imaginations. Prophecies help the community to imagine and discern ways to embody the faithfulness of Jesus Christ, the one who loves others by embodying acts of self-giving in various situations.

While they must continue to hear and evaluate prophecies, Paul exhorts the Thessalonians to "prove everything through testing" (*dokimazō*). As we saw in Philippi and earlier in this letter (2:4), Paul uses the verb *dokimazō* for discerning whether a particular action is pleasing to God because it bears fruit in the community.[75] Not every prophecy leads to actions that please God and bear fruit. So, the community must practice discernment—they must examine the connections between past actions and their consequences. When a particular Christlike action pleases God and leads to an experience of God's resurrection power for new life, the congregation must "hold fast" to this action in similar, future situations (5:21b). Conversely, if an action appears to cause harm, or if someone experiences harm through actions from others (like persecution), they must abstain from that action or keep their distance from those who act in such harmful ways (5:22).

This practice of proof through testing in discernment is a crucial dimension of what it means to keep awake for those still living together in the presence of the risen Jesus. As Paul winds down this letter, he climactically emphasizes this practice of proof through testing in communal discernment. He has given them instructions for how they can continue to experience resurrection power for new life together.

Paul closes the letter with a prayer that recaps his emphasis on the community's process of formation in holiness:

> **1 Thessalonians 5:23** May the God of peace…make you [plural] entirely holy [*hagiazō*]; and may your spirit and soul and body be kept whole and blameless in the presence [*parousia*] of our Lord Jesus Christ. **24** The one who is calling you is faithful [*pistis*] and will do this.

Paul prays to God to continue the process of making the Thessalonians holy—both individually and as a community. This formation in holiness takes place through the power of God at work in the deliberative assembly. It happens over time, in the community's moral conversations in discernment and their community-building actions—their Christlike love embodied in acts of self-giving for others. "God carries out the process of sanctification" in holiness by means of the Christlike actions of the Thessalonians.[76] God transforms their character, dispositions, and allegiances, but this requires a network of communal relations in the deliberative assembly.[77]

This transformation depends on God, who, Paul assures the Thessalonians, is faithful (*pistos*) and will do this. Paul states this confidently. It's the persuasion that comes from his own experiences of God's faithfulness and life-giving power, proven through testing over time.

The traditional interpretation of this prayer focuses on the future coming (*parousia*) of Christ in glory. In this scenario, the prayer asks God to keep the Thessalonians whole and blameless until the time of Christ's return. I suggest, however, that given the congregation's fluid and dynamic process of formation in holiness through discernment, Paul is praying for continuing divine guidance of the community that eats and deliberates together in the presence of God and the risen Lord. For the discerning community that stays awake, God and the risen Lord faithfully keep the community whole and blameless, week to week, year to year. This is a dynamic and fluid process of formation in holiness that only comes to *completion* at the return of Christ in glory.

To ensure his persuasive influence on the whole community's practice of deliberation and discernment, Paul demands that his letter be read to everyone (5:27).

Silvanus has now finished reading the letter.

The room is silent.

Paul's final words have landed. They bring to mind the seriousness of the issues they face and the challenges for how they will respond. The Thessalonians take a short break before reconvening to deliberate. The pilgrims silently depart the scene, too. It's been an intense evening for everyone.

Pilgrims Reflect on Their Experience

Our pilgrimage group reconvenes to consider what they saw and heard in the assembly in Thessalonica. Tonight, we're gathered in a seating area in the lobby of our hotel. There are people coming and going all around us; some are checking into the hotel and others are leaving for a late dinner. Most of the pilgrims have now adjusted to the time change and are upright and alert in their seats, eager to debrief Paul's letter. There are no more drooping eyelids and big yawns that we saw the first two nights.

Robert begins the conversation. "I was surprised to learn that Judaism and Christianity were exceptions in the religious world of antiquity because they taught their followers a way of life."

Jean responds, "I see a lot of churches today that seem to have lost sight of their responsibility to teach and help disciples learn how to live Christ's way of life in the nitty-gritty details of daily life. I see a lot of churches spending too much time teaching people 'right belief' rather than 'right action.' Or, worse yet, trying to tell them how to vote."

"I loved the way Paul reminded the Thessalonians of their experiences of 'gospel-events' and how they were related to the various ways Paul embodied Christ when he was with them," says Sarah. "That helps me understand the connection between Christlike actions and experiences of new life. Then he showed them the mutuality of this practice in their own community."

"Paul even had the humility to share with them his own experience of a 'gospel-event,'" adds Reynoldo. "He experienced God's resurrection power for new life when his anxiety and concern for the Thessalonians was relieved. And all that from Timothy's report that they were standing firm in their practice of faithfulness despite the persecution and were still looking to Paul as their teacher and model."

Ann jumps in, saying, "I had an experience similar to Paul's recently. It started when I got a call from a receptionist at an airport lounge in Chicago. She said someone had turned in my husband's cell phone. It was still seven hours before his flight was scheduled to depart. Hours passed and I didn't hear from him. That made me very anxious, because his cell phone is more like a body part for him—it's never far from his consciousness." Concern shows on the faces of the pilgrims and they move forward to the edge of their seats, waiting for the next part of Ann's story.

"Finally," Ann continues, "just before his flight was scheduled to leave, he called. The lounge's receptionist had walked all the way from the lounge, down two floors to his gate. She called out his name, and when he stood up, she returned his phone. I was so relieved. It was a 'gospel-event' for me, just like it was for Paul. The receptionist's extraordinary Christlike act of self-giving led to my experience of resurrection power for new life when my high anxiety was finally relieved."

"That's a powerful story, Ann," says Sarah. "It has become very clear to me from our time in Thessalonica that Paul is almost exclusively focused on teaching and showing people how to live a Christlike life that, hopefully, leads to experiences of gospel-events of resurrection power. It's getting clear, too, that the practice of discernment is the key to their growing awareness of how and when these gospel-events take place. Paul prepared them for how to live faithfully without needing him to be present."

Philip now jumps into the discussion: "I can understand why Paul was so focused on moral formation. I never thought about discipleship as involving a process of resocialization, or that Christ's way of life was exclusive. That's pretty radical! I love it!"

"I think it's part of Paul's apocalyptic perspective," offers Diane. "He sees God's new age and kingdom in Christ as being *alternatives* to the way of life most people live in the world. It makes me think of the Amish or the Quakers in today's religious landscape."

"Is that what we're supposed to be and to look like?" asks Jim.

"Not necessarily," concludes Esperanza. "I think that's where analogy and context come into the conversation. Or, maybe I should start using Mark Twain's words and talk about catching the rhyme between the gospel stories and some aspect of my own life. It seems like, for Paul, every situation, every context is different. The group has to consider different ways to embody Jesus in response to changed circumstances."

Reynoldo enters the discussion adding, "the Thessalonians turned away from their many idols to serve the one true and living God we worship. I wonder what idols we still worship in today's world—the idols that distract us from serving the one God we have committed to serve in and through Christ."

"You mean idols like celebrities, sport stars, entertainers, and political leaders?" asks Anne.

"Maybe," responds Reynoldo. "But I was thinking more like the idolatries of chasing after 'success' or 'power.'"

"Yes, those are some worldly values that can lead us astray," says Dante. "I wonder if there is a spiritual practice that can help us 'keep awake' to these temptations. I know we're supposed to be thinking about reclaiming Paul's vision for formation. It's starting to look like the practice in a community of discernment is a major way to 'keep awake.'"

"Paul addressed one of my temptations," Sarah admits. "I'm not very gracious in receiving critique, or as Paul calls it, 'admonishment.' I can quickly become resentful and defensive."

"Yes, I've been on both ends of that," adds Reynoldo. "As a manager of a supermarket for my employer, I sometimes have to give job reviews, and I get mixed responses. I am also regularly reviewed by someone from the corporate office, and that tempts me to respond in ways I know I will later regret. I can understand the importance of creating a community of accountability where people learn how to give and receive that input."

Ann wonders aloud, "do you think the small group practice at St. Benedict's Workshop is structured to help disciples 'keep awake' to what's happening in their lives? That would include helping people process giving and receiving admonishment."

"That's why I've come on this pilgrimage," says Latisha. "I want to hear more about St. Benedict's Workshop and how its practice of discernment aligns with Paul's practice."

"Yes," I say in response. "The folks practicing discernment at St. Benedict's Workshop are 'awake' to some of the temptations we face. They also learn how to give gentle admonishment to others if it's warranted. But most of the time, they all can relate to someone else's stumble and they offer consolation and encouragement more than critique."

"That's good to hear," says Reynoldo. "What resonated for me was the way Paul addressed the Thessalonians' understanding of suffering for Christ. He turned suffering into something much more meaningful. He took the experience of suffering—which sounds negative—and gave us a reason to be joyful as active participants in the story of Christ."

"I can sense how Paul's approach might help me reinterpret my exhausting, and sometimes frustrating, late-night sessions with a struggling friend who is also one of my cancer patients," says Gail. "I might be participating in the story of Christ and not even know it."

"I had a similar insight," Philip says, "when I heard Paul speaking about waiting for Christ from heaven to deliver us from the coming wrath. It brought to mind my job setting where my boss verbally abuses me and my other coworkers almost every day. I keep praying and asking for help. I wonder if a discernment group in Christ Jesus might help me sort out how to respond."

"Something different resonated for me," says Esperanza. "I remember a time when a life-threatening health condition also jeopardized my job and marriage. I began to wonder whether God had abandoned me in my greatest time of trial. A community of pastoral care and support like the one in Thessalonica would have really helped. Do you think that's what these groups at St. Benedict's Workshop do?"

"I don't know," responds Latisha. "But I'm going to keep my eyes and ears open as we visit other sites. I'm starting to imagine a small group that meets like Paul's deliberative assemblies. I'll be watching for practices and actions to consider."

Now Dante, animated by these pilgrims' serious engagements with the letter, speaks up. "I was really impacted by the discussion of the experience of a present-day judgment on some of the Thessalonians. It reminded me of my experience in my old law firm. We got very focused on our own individual financial advancement at the expense of others in the firm. A conflict erupted that eventually destroyed the relationships among many of us who had been friends for decades. The firm split into parts. I now understand that those of us who were dedicated Christians in the firm experienced God's judgment because we were not focused on Jesus but on our own success."

"That's very interesting," says Sarah. "We had a similar kind of experience in my church. We got into an irresolvable dispute that involved politics. Some members of the church thought the preaching and teaching was too political and finally left the church. At first, I wondered if the church community had experienced God's judgment. Their departure saddened us, because many of us had been longtime friends. It also adversely impacted us financially. On the other hand, it strengthened us spiritually because we realized that the texts of Scripture should be the lens for evaluating every action we take. From the time we spent in Philippi and now this time in Thessalonica, I'm starting to reinterpret the event of our church split as an experience of being a partner with Christ in his suffering. That gives the experience a world of meaning!"

"I was intrigued by the word 'God-taught' Paul created in connection with loving one another in the church," said Philip. "I realized that we could be God-taught, too, if we were regularly connecting experiences of God's resurrection power to acts of Christlike faithfulness. I'm really intrigued by this practice."

"That would also require that we know what 'Christlike faithfulness' looks like," responds Jean. "I wonder how Paul's congregants went about that process."

"I think that's why Paul keeps talking about moral models and imitating how other Christ-followers walk in the world," says Dante. "But I'm also starting to get the impression that the people who met every week in one of his deliberative assemblies looked to one another as models, too. I am also seeing now that every one of Paul's letters offers some concrete suggestions for actions that Paul thinks might be Christlike in the particular situations faced by that congregation."

"Yes, I think that's right," agrees Ann. "I also think Paul's suggestions stimulate the moral imaginations of the participants. Some of his suggestions even stimulate my imagination in some of my current situations. He gets them to do their own work together. That's probably something we could do, too, if we set up our own deliberative assembly."

Latisha added, "Some of us from my church just recently did some hard work with our hands as we packed and moved heavy boxes of food for hungry people in our city. I think that's what Paul means when he talks about doing the good and walking properly toward those outside the church. We showed them Christ at work for the community, whether they knew that or not! I can see how we could use his letters and suggestions and translate them by analogy into our own modern contexts."

"I do the same thing two weekends a month," Reynoldo chimes in. "That's a helpful analogy—I mean, a helpful rhyme with my circumstances," he says with a big smile and a wink.

"That sounds exciting, Latisha," says Dante. "Let's give that some more thought."

"John, is it time to move to our next stop in Corinth?" asks Diane.

"Yes, it time to start moving again," I respond.

Diane continues, "I've read that letter before and there are a lot of issues. Paul is at his best trying to teach the Corinthians how to reason with what he called the 'logic of life' to the Philippians. I'm really looking forward to how Paul brings formation, community building, and discernment together with these conflicted groups."

"Let's go see!" says Ann as she gets up out of her chair and heads to her room to pack."

CHAPTER FOUR

Formation and Discernment Gone Awry in Corinth

"What Should Happen...When You Come Together?" (1 Corinthians 14:26)

Our pilgrimage now takes us to Paul's Christ-community in the thriving city of Corinth. We will join the Christ-followers who have assembled to share a meal and hear Paul's beloved coworker, Sosthenes, read and explain his first letter to them.

There are two long letters from Paul to Corinth in the canon of the New Testament. We only have time and space to examine closely what is designated as First Corinthians.[1]

Where Are We?

In First Corinthians, Paul is writing to a group of Gentile Christ-followers in the strategically important city of Corinth. Once an important and powerful Greek city-state, Corinth was destroyed by the Romans in 146 BCE. The city lay dormant for more than a century until it was refounded as a Roman colony by Julius Caesar in 44 BCE. He populated the city with freed slaves and poor immigrants. The city was made the capital of the province of Achaia by Augustus in 27 BCE.

Under successive Roman emperors in the first century CE, the city continued to build and be rebuilt. Its importance grew, to the extent that within the empire Corinth was ranked just behind Rome and Alexandria.[2] A visitor traveling through Corinth would notice that most of its public inscriptions were in Latin rather than Greek, even though Greek was probably the language still spoken by most of Corinth's residents. They would also find that Roman influence was most evident in the city's agora, its public marketplace, which was one of the largest in the Mediterranean world.[3]

A highly competitive social environment fueled Corinth's thriving economy. The pursuit of honor and the avoidance of shame motivated every level of this hierarchical society. In the absence of an indigenous aristocracy, those who colonized the city competed aggressively to acquire the marks of higher social status.[4]

By the time of Paul's arrival in Corinth in the 50s CE, the city had around 80,000 inhabitants. It was located on the narrow isthmus that connected mainland Greece to its southernmost Peloponnesian peninsula. This location, and its two busy ports, ensured that Corinth was an important center for trade, travel, religion, and governmental administration. Thanks to its ports, Corinth controlled the Asia Minor to Italy trade traffic.[5]

More than two dozen temples, statues, and monuments dedicated to major Greek gods and the Roman emperor were spread throughout the city. It would become a perfect strategic position for the spread of the gospel.[6]

Life in ancient Corinth had its challenges. Like many port cities throughout the ages, Corinth boasted a robust sex trade. This thriving industry was probably rooted in the city's longstanding relationship with its protector goddess, Aphrodite. Her primary temple sat atop the Acrocorinth, the acropolis towering 1,800 feet above the city. This sex trade, along with its highly competitive commercial environment, contributed to the city's troublesome reputation among travelers visiting the city. Those who knew this reputation even coined a verb—"to become Corinthianized"—which meant "to become thoroughly immoral and materialistic."[7]

These social and religious factors substantially contributed to the challenges Paul faced in formation, community building, and discernment in the Christ-community at Corinth.

The Two-Stage Dinner Party Structure of Worship in Paul's Congregations

Paul structured his deliberative assemblies according to the formal two-stage dinner party that was common in antiquity. It provided a conventional way for people to meet and celebrate shared values, commitments, and practice.[8] The first stage was an actual meal.[9] Paul calls it the "Lord's Supper" in 1 Corinthians 11:20. When Christ-followers came together to eat this meal, they were engaging in a practice common to many different religious, social, charitable, or other sectarian groups.[10] This communal meal had not yet developed into the separate "sacramental meal" that later became a liturgical ritual recognizable to modern Christians as a Eucharistic worship service.[11]

The meal was always followed by a drinking party frequently called the *symposium*.[12] It was a time dedicated to entertainment of the guests. In addition to drinking, this second stage usually involved music, dancing, and sometimes even more raucous and bawdy activities.

The two-stage dinner party served a crucial, formative social function.[13] It was the central social activity that exemplified the group's identity and solidarity.[14]

Another social function of the dinner party was to create partnership (*koinōnia*) among the diners. This was crucial in Paul's Christ-communities. His congregants came from culturally diverse groups and crossed rigid and hierarchical social, religious, economic, and ethnic boundaries to gather, eat, and discern together as the Body of Christ.[15] By taking part in this communal meal Gentiles, unconverted to Judaism, found true belonging in this nascent Jewish messianic sect.[16]

By the first century CE, the post-dinner *symposium* had been adapted by synagogues and philosophical schools to become a time for community conversation and moral deliberations.[17] Plutarch, the first-century poet, philosopher and historian, wrote that building friendship was one of the principal goals of this post-dinner conversation.[18] This was accomplished by selecting appropriate topics that were simple enough that everyone could take part in the discussion, even the less intellectually gifted guests, and by conducting the discussions in an orderly manner.[19]

A philosophical banquet featured stimulating discussion where all could contribute. Likewise, participants in Jewish synagogues used the *symposium* for discussions of the Jewish law (Torah).[20] Deliberations on the Torah and the faithfulness of participants were also crucial aspects of the common meals for the Jewish sect of Essenes at Qumran.

While only two texts from Paul's letters expressly refer to events that took place during the community's common meal (Galatians 2:11–14; 1 Corinthians 11:17–34), his letters contain numerous references to moral deliberations and discernment in the post-meal *symposium*. At each of our stops on this pilgrimage so far, we have seen how Paul's letters address each community's post-dinner conversations. He expected these post-meal deliberations and activities to include hymns, lessons, revelations, tongues, interpretations, and prophecy.[21]

In the early years of the Christ-movement, there is no evidence that they read what we call Scripture today. The principal document read after the community's common meal was the letter. The letters from Paul and other early leaders like Peter, John, and Ignatius of Antioch were explicitly written to be read after the community's common meal during the time set aside for moral conversation.[22] While readings from Torah probably took place in Jewish synagogues from earliest times, there is no direct evidence in Paul's letters that there were readings from Jewish Scripture. Paul's letters do reflect his biblical literacy, but the most likely sources of his knowledge were memorization and occasional access to local copies of specific texts during his travels.[23]

Similarly, there is no evidence in the early years of the Christ-movement that there was anything resembling what we know today as a sermon. In the post-meal conversations, no one person dominated the discussion. Paul anticipated a "whole procession of prophets, not one sole teacher...or oracle."[24] We get a picture from Paul of what Andrew McGowan calls "a collective set of inspired discourses, with neither 'sermon' nor reading of Scripture."[25] At this early point, there were plenty of opportunities for shared discourse, conversation, and "dialogical inspiration," which included "oral contributions of different length, content, and form from various participants."[26]

The oldest, clearest description of a Christian assembly with scriptural readings and a sermon comes from Justin Martyr in 160 CE.[27] In all likelihood, this format reflects a shift from the prophetic discourses at communal banquets in Paul's mid-first-century congregations to a "more textual and scholastic emphasis" that involved the reading and interpretation of Scripture in the early decades of the second century CE.[28]

The structure of Paul's communities also displays the first-century reality that the two-stage dinner party was a primary setting for education. The setting offered "enormous creative potential" for learning by providing a framework for improvisation and lively repartee among the participants.[29] These meals and their after-dinner deliberations created significant formative events and learning experiences.

In this stop at Corinth, we will see clearly how the two-stage dinner party is implemented in Paul's congregations. This structure represents one of Paul's "ways in Christ Jesus" that he teaches "everywhere in every *ekklēsia*" (1 Corinthians 4:17). We will also see how, despite Paul's lofty goals for this structure, things can go sideways. Depending on the attitudes and actions of congregants, the shared meal and the post-dinner moral deliberations in discernment can lead either to chaos or community building.

Why Are We Here?

What's distinctive about First Corinthians? It is Paul's most practical letter. From start to finish, he focuses on formation, community building, and discernment.

Paul is responding to a variety of relational issues. Paul first had sent his trusted colleague, Timothy, to remind the Corinthians of the ways in Christ Jesus that Paul teaches in all his congregations (1 Corinthians 4:17). He later received a now long-lost letter from some of the Corinthians, inquiring about troublesome issues. Paul then heard an oral report from some of "Chloe's people," who had just returned from Corinth (1:11).

Clearly, the Corinthians had become Paul's "problem child."[30] Michael Gorman summarizes the situation succinctly: they "managed to misunderstand just about everything Paul said and did, to their own detriment and Paul's utter astonishment."[31] They failed to grasp the communal implications of Paul's apocalyptic gospel and its consequences for formation and conduct.[32]

There were painful struggles between supposedly enlightened, affluent, elite members of the Christ-community and the so-called unenlightened, poor, non-elite members.[33] The actions of these privileged congregants, who enjoyed higher social status and wealth, continued to reflect the social norms, values, and customs of the Greco-Roman world, particularly a city of many vices like Corinth. They privileged their own interests above the needs of the poor, less educated, and beleaguered members of the assembly.[34] Because of their privilege, they failed to comprehend Paul's gospel, which was directly focused on an egalitarian social practice and living a Christ-patterned way of life.[35]

Reflecting the highly competitive culture in Corinth, some congregants were claiming an elite spiritual status grounded in their remarkable ability to speak in tongues. They thought of themselves as better than other members of the community. They were part of a larger group who, for a variety of reasons, had become "puffed up" (we might call them "arrogant") according to Paul's assessment of the situation.[36] To make matters worse, this group probably exercised a disproportionate influence on decision-making in the community.

According to the oral report to Paul from Chloe's people, there were serious quarrels and divisions in the community. Different leaders were baptizing (1:11–16) and teaching divergent ways about how to walk in the footsteps of Jesus Christ (3:1–5, 10–15). Congregants were acting in other ways that did not reflect a Christlike way of life. For example, they were suing one another in Roman courts (6:1–11), engaging in a variety of unacceptable sexual practices (5:1–21; 6:12–20), and eating meat sacrificed at temples of various gods and idols, which was leading other Christians astray (8:1–13; 10:1–33). They were also perverting the practice of the Lord's Supper (11:17–34) and competing for spiritual superiority by speaking in unintelligible tongues when they came together (14:1–23). Some influential members were failing to participate in the important after-dinner practice of moral deliberations in discernment or, at least, were refusing to consider the views of every member of the congregation in those discussions.[37] They were even denying the reality of resurrection from the dead (15:12).

From Paul's apocalyptic point of view, many of the Corinthians were forgetting that Jesus was the crucified and resurrected Messiah, appointed by God as the exclusive Lord of their lives. Jesus Christ was the one in whom God revealed resurrection power and divine wisdom that conflicted with what Paul calls the "wisdom of the world" (see 1:17–2:16) that was still influencing too many of the Corinthians.

Paul interprets the conflict and chaos tearing this community apart as clear evidence of a breakdown in the community's formation and practice of discernment. At least *eight* times in First Corinthians Paul refers to events occurring "when you come together" (11:17, 18, 20, 33, 34; 14:23, 26) and when they "assemble in the name of the Lord Jesus" (5:4). It was clear that when the members gathered for their meal and moral deliberations, some misunderstood their fundamental commitments to the crucified Christ as their exclusive Lord. Clearly, individuals had not been sufficiently formed in the image of Jesus Christ. Neither was there a functioning community of accountability, where every voice is heard and treated with respect and deference.

Paul vigorously responds with this letter that is "rich in 'discernment' language," according to Luke Timothy Johnson.[38] He expects the Corinthians to reason together in the ways he first taught them—the ways that accord with the spirit and mind of Jesus Christ.[39] He is confident that if they reason with the mind of Christ, they will distinguish between actions that are bearing good fruit and leading to new life and those that are producing chaos and destruction. Using the exclusive "logic of the cross" (1:18)—Christ's pattern of moral reasoning—he anticipates their collective ability to choose and embody Christlike actions that will build up the entire community rather than just individuals.

In the first four chapters, Paul concentrates on formation. He describes the shape of community life, and the relational pattern of morality required for effective moral discourse.[40] For the rest of the letter, Paul focuses on discernment and community building. He repeatedly uses ordinary situations to illustrate how to reason with the logic of the cross and discern Christlike actions through which God builds up the congregation.

Paul knows Sosthenes will read his letter after the community's shared meal and before the time set aside for moral deliberations and discernment. So, Paul crafts this letter offering his own prophetic voice and, at times, the voices of others, to contribute to their after-dinner moral deliberations on the contested issues.[41] Paul's goal is to inform their moral deliberations and decision-making. He wants to convince them to end their destructive ways, consistent with his prophetic counsel, and replace them with actions that enhance the community.[42] With only one exception, he never exercises his apostolic authority by ordering the Corinthians to take a specified action.[43] At least twice in the letter, he invites the Corinthians to "judge for yourselves" the wisdom of his prophetic insights.[44]

By the time Paul describes an ordered process for their communal discernment (14:26–33), he has provided them with numerous examples for how to reason with the logic of the cross in connection with their issues in daily life. By explaining these examples, Paul has shown the Corinthians how this prophetic, deliberative, revelatory process of discernment should unfold.

We are here in Corinth to rediscover Paul's vision for formation, community building, and discernment so prevalent in this letter. When implemented, Paul's deliberative process of discernment cultivates capable moral agents. The practice fosters moral communities through Christlike actions and shared experiences of God's resurrection power. For Paul discernment is the heartbeat of moral formation and community building in all his early Christ-communities. Wayne Meeks concludes that, over time, the "moral confidence" of congregants should advance "from a shallow self-confidence that purchases its security by excluding inconvenient considerations and inconvenient people, toward a confidence resting on the grace that makes dialogue possible."[45]

This hadn't happened in Corinth; hence Paul's letter.

What Words Matter?

At this stop in Corinth, some important new words and phrases include:

- the verb *hagiazō* ("to make holy");[46]
- the phrase *logos tou stauros* ("logic of the cross");[47]
- the noun *doxa* ("glory");[48]
- the verb *krinō* ("judge"/"examine closely"/"distinguish one from another");[49] and
- the verb *sumpherō* ("to bind together" or "to benefit").

We will continue to develop some other words previously introduced:

- the noun *charis* ("grace" or "gift");[50]
- the verb *dokimazō* ("prove through testing");[51]
- the verb *sōzō* ("to save");[52]
- the noun *koinōnia* ("partnership");[53]
- the verb *oikodomeō* ("to build up");[54]
- the noun *prophētēs* ("prophet");
- the noun *agapē* ("love");[55] and
- the noun *apokalypsis* ("revelation").[56]

We continue to build our own vocabularies and are beginning to imagine how to reclaim these words and phrases for use in the church today!

Pilgrims Enter the Assembly at Corinth

Pilgrims join the assembly that has gathered in the home of Gaius. He hosts gatherings of the whole assembly of Christ-followers in Corinth, which includes smaller house-gatherings from around the city.[57] His home is spacious, with beautiful tile mosaics on the floors and painted frescoes on the walls. We can hear water gurgling from the fountain in the central courtyard. And there are wonderful, complex smells wafting from the kitchen somewhere at the back of the house. We notice people continuing to drift into the gathering at various times.

Most of the Corinthians share their community meal spread across several rooms of the house. Some stragglers arrive late, however, after the tables have been cleared. They're too late for food. But they find places to recline at the back of the room where the reading will take place.

A local leader introduces Paul's emissary, Sosthenes. We learn that he cowrote this letter with Paul. He will deliver the letter to the assembled group and respond to questions.

Formation and the Shape of Community Life (1:1–4:21)

Paul Introduces Himself and Identifies the Letter's Recipients (1:1–2)

Sosthenes carefully removes the letter from his satchel, unseals it, and then unrolls the papyrus material on which Paul's letter is written. Knowing that the letter might be handled and read more than once to the various house-groups in Corinth, and might then be passed on to others, Sosthenes carefully holds the letter and prepares to read.

Papyrus was an ancient writing material created by drying, gluing, and pounding together at right angles strips removed from the stem of the papyrus plant. Producing a written letter like this long one to Corinth was an expensive and arduous project. Not only did Paul have to purchase the papyrus material, but he usually hired a scribe like Tertius (see Romans 16:22) to do the actual writing dictated by Paul and his colleagues. Occasionally, Paul would write a few sentences in his own hand at the end of the letter, like in this one (see 1 Corinthians 16:21; Galatians 6:11; Colossians 4:18).

In antiquity many letters followed a similar pattern. They had a standard, basic format. In Paul's day most letters began with a brief identification of the sender and addressee.[58] As Sosthenes begins to read, we hear Paul identify himself as an "apostle of Christ Jesus through the will of God" (1:1). He immediately affirms his status as an apostle. This is usually a red flag for readers. It indicates that he is writing to a community in which some people dispute his status as an apostle. That certainly turns out to be true in this case.

Paul greets the letter's recipients, identified as "the deliberative assembly [*ekklēsia*] of God in Corinth" (1:1). By using this phrase, Paul assumes that his letter will be read at a regular gathering of the *ekklēsia*, but not necessarily to all the different Christ-groups in the city at the same time.[59]

Paul characterizes those who have gathered as having been "made holy [*hagiazō*] in Christ Jesus, called to be holy ones [*hagioi*]." We have already seen that the plural *hagioi* signifies a community of individuals set apart from the surrounding culture to serve the living God of Israel and bear witness to God's life-giving reign and healing presence in their lives.[60] The word "holy" also expresses the early Christ-community's sense of being a countercultural society, with a Christlike pattern of life that differs from that of the world.[61]

The related verb *hagiazō* in 1:2 denotes the action of forming people in Christ's distinctive pattern of life. They have been "made holy in Christ Jesus." These holy ones who are set apart to serve God are "ideally *holy in life*, as a habituated pattern" that reflects the formation of their Christlike character.[62]

Because Paul refers to every Christ-follower as "holy," however, the term can be misleading. This proves especially true when *hagioi* is translated as "saints." The word "saints" conveys to many people today the sense of someone set apart to God through moral perfection. Nothing could be farther from the truth! We will see this reality up close in Corinth, where quarreling and bickering are destroying the Christ-community.

Baptism into Christ sets these holy ones apart for exclusive service to God. But baptism only begins a lifetime process of formation in a community setting. The perfect passive form of the verb *hagiazō* in 1:2 reflects a past event (baptism) with continuing effects resulting from divine activity. This is a lifelong process of being made holy through the transformation of people's hearts, imaginations, and wills in a communal life "shot through and through with self-giving actions."[63]

This process of being made holy is taking place "in Christ Jesus" (1:2). The preposition "in" can denote instrumentality, which leads some interpreters to say that the Corinthians have been made holy *by* what God has accomplished through Christ.[64] The preposition can also indicate location. So, other interpreters emphasize a kind of union with Christ or being-*in*-Christ as a theological concept. The idea denotes a person's inclusion in a larger community or body of people that share the status of being "in Christ."[65]

There is a practical dimension associated with Paul's phrase "in Christ Jesus" that we have discussed several times. The phrase describes the actual meeting of the local Christ-community that physically embodies the theological concept of being "in Christ Jesus." They gather as members of the *ekklēsia*—the "deliberative assembly" that comes together to form the Body of Christ in Corinth. They are "in Christ Jesus" because they are guided by the presence of the Spirit of the risen Lord in their deliberations and practice of discernment. Through their moral deliberations in discernment and their Christlike actions, God shapes and forms them as holy in the image of Jesus Christ.

Paul adds a phrase in 1:2 that is unique in his letters. The Corinthians are called to be holy ones "with all the ones calling on the name of our Lord Jesus Christ in every location, theirs and ours." Paul places the Corinthians within a much wider network of Christ-communities stretching around the Mediterranean world. Later, he will chide some of the Corinthians, who seem to think they enjoy an elite spiritual status that frees them from accountability to others.[66] Paul reminds them here that this is not the case.

God Enriched the Corinthians Through Their Confirmed "Witness of Christ" (1:4–9)

Paul offers a customary "thanksgiving" for the Corinthians that introduces some of the letter's major themes. He gives thanks to God for some of their positive attributes, accomplishments, and experiences. "I give thanks [*eucharisteō*] to my God always concerning you for the grace of God [*charis*] given to you in Christ Jesus" (1:4).

Many readers will immediately recognize this Greek verb *eucharisteō*. From the related noun *eucharistia*, a variety of churches today derive the name of the Christian sacrament of Eucharist. This is the practice of sharing bread and wine that represent the body and blood of Jesus Christ. In the worship of some Christian denominations, portions of this liturgy of Holy Eucharist are even called The Great Thanksgiving.

It is important to remember, however, that in the earliest days of the Christ-movement, members shared an actual meal rather than the sacramental meal later called Eucharist. The actual meal was the first stage of the two-stage dinner party that structured each gathering. It took nearly a hundred years for the sacramental meal called Eucharist to replace the actual meal that was part of these earliest gatherings.

Sosthenes continues reading from Paul's letter:

> **1 Corinthians 1:4** I give thanks to my God always concerning you for the grace [*charis*] of God given to you in Christ Jesus,

5 because in all kinds of ways you have been enriched in him, in speech and knowledge of every kind—**6** when the witness of Christ was confirmed among you—**7** so that you are not lacking in any embodiment of grace [*charisma*] as you eagerly await the revelation [*apokalypsis*] of our Lord Jesus Christ, **8** who will indeed confirm you blameless to the end, in the day of our Lord Jesus Christ. **9** God is faithful [*pistos*]; by whom you were called into the partnership [*koinōnia*] of his Son, Jesus Christ our Lord.

Before Sosthenes can continue reading, a man reclining at the end of the table near the back wall stands up and starts to speak.

"Sir, I don't understand what Paul is talking about. Can you help me?"

Sosthenes pauses, puts down the letter, and patiently responds, "Of course. I'm here to answer your questions. Paul is reflecting on some good things he's heard about recent experiences in the community here. And he's using language from his earlier teaching when he was here in Corinth for those many months."

"But I'm a fairly new member of this community," the man says, "and I haven't heard anything about Paul's earlier teaching. Can you enlighten me and a few of the other new folks?"

Sosthenes, who is clearly not in a hurry and makes no attempt to brush off his question, replies, "Yes, I'll be glad to help. Paul and I expected there would be people who needed some background."

Sosthenes then continues: "In this thanksgiving Paul is reflecting on experiences here in the Christ-community. His principal focus is the crucial role of discernment that takes place 'in Christ Jesus' in the presence of the Spirit of the risen Christ. Paul taught that practice when he was here.

"In this paragraph Paul draws on his fundamental understanding of discernment and the role of grace (*charis*). Grace is God's gift of life-giving power that abounds for new life in the world through the person of Jesus Christ.[67] Christ dispenses this grace to you and me and every other member of his body in stewardship for the life of this community and the world.

"Each Christ-follower exercises this gift of grace—this gift of God's life-giving power—by embodying it in a Christlike act of self-giving for others. If the act pleases God, those on the receiving end of the action will experience God's resurrection power for new life.

"That's the background," says Sosthenes. "So, Paul is now reminding all of you of these connections. He is giving thanks to God for the gifts of grace given to the Christ-followers in Christ Jesus. Some of you, in your practice of discernment, have determined ways to embody your gifts of grace in Christlike acts of self-giving to the community. Paul calls these embodiments of grace *charismata* (the plural form of *charisma*).

"He is also pointing out that Christ has confirmed the Christlike nature of these acts of self-giving—your 'witness of Christ.' Christ did this by revealing the connections between Christlike actions and the experiences of God's resurrection power that enriched this community with all kinds of new speech and knowledge (1:5–6).[68] Paul taught the community to practice discernment in which revelations by the Spirit of the risen Christ connect Christlike actions with experiences of resurrection power. By discerning these connections, the community learns to anticipate future Christlike actions that will, hopefully, lead to more experiences of resurrection power among you.

"Paul is also expressing confidence that you will not lack any future embodiments of grace—the *charismata* (1:7). This is because revelations from the risen Christ will continue to confirm your witness of Christ by connecting them to experiences of resurrection power from now until the time of his final return (1:7–8). As long as this community continues to practice discernment, Christ will show you the connections between Christlike actions and experiences of God's resurrection power. In this way, the revelations of the Spirit of the risen Christ keep you blameless until his final return.

"Finally, and equally important," says Sosthenes, "Paul also promises that God is faithful (*pistos*) to this process and relationship (1:9). God has called all of you into a partnership (*koinōnia*) with Jesus Christ the Lord. God will continue to enrich this community with experiences of resurrection power for new life through your future 'witness of Christ' in Christlike acts of self-giving to others."

"Thank you, sir," the questioner responds. "That helps me understand why some things here have gone awry and why some of our relationships have soured."

Paul's thanksgiving emphasizes three crucial foundations for the practice of discernment. First, human actions are always subject to divine evaluation. They are either confirmed or judged as inadequate. Second, in discernment the community should always be connecting actions with their consequences. Third, revelation (*apokalypsis*) happens during the community's moral deliberations in discernment.[69]

In 1:4–8 Paul praises their "witness of Christ" that was divinely confirmed by their experiences of resurrection power. For most of the letter, however, Paul will point out where their embodied actions are being divinely judged as deficient. Paul will show that their practice of discernment is failing to recognize these experiences of chaos and destruction resulting from actions that do not meet the test of being Christlike.

Finally, Paul emphasizes the importance for Christ-followers of being called by God into the partnership (*koinōnia*) of the Lord Jesus Christ. One of the primary goals of the two-stage dinner party is developing a partnership (*koinōnia*) among those who dine and deliberate together. In 1:9 Paul adds a theological and moral dimension to this partnership: the faithful God and the risen Lord Jesus Christ are their principal partners in this relationship.

Reasoning with the Logic of the Cross Leads to Experiences of God's Power (1:10–2:5)

Sosthenes returns to Paul's letter. Paul states his aim for the letter in 1:10: "I urge you, brothers and sisters, through the name of the Lord Jesus Christ, that all of you speak the same way and that there not be any divisions among you, but that you be restored in the same mind [*nous*], that is, the same way of judging" (1:10).

Paul de-emphasizes the role of human leaders, who he considers part of the problem (1:11–16). He places the power of moral deliberations on contested issues back into the hands of the entire discerning community ("all of you"). He urges all the members to speak the same way. He may be emphasizing their common confession: "Jesus is Lord" (12:3). But he may also be anticipating the problem that some of them speak in unintelligible tongues, which is unproductive and shows a lack of rationality (14:14). He wants them to be restored in the same mind (*nous*)—the "mind [*nous*] of Christ" (2:16)—that is, restored in the same way of judging in discernment. As Paul is about to show, everyone should be reasoning and discerning with the one mind of Christ and his logic of the cross.

By describing his own call, Paul seeks to reduce the influence of the various leaders baptizing in Corinth:

> **1 Corinthians 1:17** For Christ did not send me to baptize but to gospel [*euanggelizomai*], and not with eloquent words of human wisdom, so that the cross of Christ might not be emptied of its power. **18** For the logic of the cross [*logos tou stauros*] is foolishness to those who are perishing, but to us who are being saved [*sōzō*] it is the power of God.

We first encountered the verb *euanggelizomai* when Paul was describing his call in chapter one. The verb characterizes his embodied witness of Christ that sparks gospel-events of resurrection power among the Gentiles. Paul is responding in part to some of the Corinthians who have become overenamored with eloquent and entertaining preaching by other leaders (probably including Apollos). He insists the gospel's persuasive force lies in the tangible experience of the cross and resurrection, not in eloquent words alone.

Paul's embodied witness of Christ in word and deed is grounded in "the logic of the cross" (*logos tou stauros*). This phrase defines Christ's moral reasoning, which should guide the Corinthians in discerning Christlike actions. This is *not* a spoken, oral "message about the cross" (NRSV 1:18). That translation misses the active, moral function of "the logic of the cross." Jane Patterson stresses this logic as the key to Paul's embodied gospel: "Rather than speech *about* something," the *logos tou stauros* "is an *enacted* pattern of behavior."[70] We saw Paul use a very similar phrase in Philippians 2:16—the "logic [*logos*] of life"—to characterize Christ's same pattern of moral reasoning set out in Philippians 2:6–11.

Paul knows from his own embodied experience of gospeling Christ that, as Patterson suggests, "[t]he saving power of the cross is released when one lives into a pattern of action consistent with its 'logic,' namely, giving up what one might be entitled to, for the advantage of the (weaker) neighbor."[71] The embodied "witness of Christ" (1 Corinthians 1:6), discerned using the logic of the cross, leads not only to experiences of resurrection power for new life in the community, but also to "[o]ne's own process of healing, or salvation...in this pattern of self-giving...."[72]

Christ's love, Paul concludes, embodied in acts of self-giving for others, is utter "foolishness to those who are perishing" (1:18); contrary to the "wisdom of the world"; and "foolishness to Gentiles" (1:23). It makes no sense in a world dedicated to pursuing and achieving honor and status.

On the other hand, the "logic of the cross" is the "power of God to the ones being saved [*sōzō*]" (1:18). Those who embody Christ's love in acts of self-giving for others unleash a transformative resurrection power, which fosters a new life that deeply enriches their relationships in the community (recall 1:4–8). In the "wisdom of God," through Paul's own embodied proclamation of Christ crucified, God is well-pleased to save (*sōzō*) the ones who entrust themselves to Christ's pattern of life (1:21, 23).

From Paul's apocalyptic point of view, God has intervened in the world in the death and resurrection of Jesus Christ to render the earthly "wisdom of the world" futile. By raising Jesus from the dead, God has revealed two aspects of earthly reality. First, God demonstrated that "the foolishness of God" (Christ's pattern of self-giving for others) is wiser than human wisdom (1:25). Second, the "weakness of God" (Christ's pattern of self-giving that led to his death on the cross) is "stronger than human strength" (1:25). Through the apocalyptic intervention of God's resurrection power, Paul and the Corinthians are now "in Christ Jesus," who became for them God's wisdom, holiness (*hagiasmos*), righteousness, and redemption (1:30).

In keeping with Paul's divine call to gospel (*euanggelizomai*) rather than baptize (1:17), he reminds the Corinthians of what happened during his first visit. Through his embodied proclamation of Christ crucified, they first experienced the resurrection power of God for new life:

> **1 Corinthians 2:1** When I came to you, brothers and sisters, I did not come to you proclaiming the mystery of God in superior speech or wisdom. **2** For I judged [*krinō*] to know nothing among you except Jesus Christ, and him crucified. **3** And I came to you in

weakness and in fear and in much trembling. **4** My logic [*logos*] and embodied proclamation were not in persuasive words of wisdom, but in a demonstration of Spirit and power, **5** so that you put your trust [*pistis*] in the power of God rather than human wisdom.

Paul understands from his own experiences that Gentiles are persuaded to entrust their lives to the logic of the cross when they *experience* God's resurrection power. These experiences do not happen through eloquent or entertaining words of human wisdom. When he got to Corinth, Paul embodied the logic of the cross—"Jesus Christ crucified"—in his own life. This led to a public demonstration of Spirit and resurrection power that brought new life to some people in Corinth.

Paul introduces the Greek verb *krinō* in 2:2. The word denotes a considered judgment or decision rendered by someone—a clear allusion to Paul's own practice of discernment. He uses *krinō*, and other compound words rooted in *krinō*, twenty-nine times in this letter! He will employ an impressive cascade of these words (four times) in the next verses at 2:6–16, building on the theme of discernment that undergirded his thanksgiving in 1:4–9.

Spirit-Led Discernment Compares Spiritual Things with Spiritual Things (2:6–16)

Paul knows he's writing to some Corinthians obsessed with spiritual elitism and to others enamored by worldly wisdom. He responds by describing God's wisdom, understood only by those who are mature (2:6–7). God decreed this wisdom for human glory (*doxa*) and recognized Jesus as the "Lord of glory [*doxa*]" (2:8).

Paul's use of *doxa* reflects the Jewish concept of God's manifest glory in both past and future divine encounters.[73] It denotes the radiance of God and God's power in earthly existence.[74] As the "Lord of glory," Jesus Christ embodies and shapes human actions that lead to the manifestations of God's glory—experiences of God's resurrection power—in human lives.

God's wisdom also involves the apocalyptic process of Spirit-led discernment. Paul distinguishes the "spirit of the world" and the "Spirit from God" that is received by the mature. This Spirit from God reveals to mature, discerning Christ-followers the things graced (*charizomai*) to them by God (2:12).

The verb *charizomai* is rooted in *charis*—grace—God's gift of life-giving power. These gifts of grace occur at two levels—to individuals and to the community. The Spirit from God graces each of them individually. Each gift of grace must then be embodied in what Paul calls a *charisma* and put into service through a Christlike act of self-giving for others (see 12:4–7). The hope is that each embodiment of grace put to use in a Christlike action will please God and lead to an experience of resurrection power in the community.

Paul described this process in 1:4–8. Divine confirmation of the witness of Christ led to the enrichment of the community. In other words, the various embodiments of the gifts of grace to individuals, offered to others in acts of self-giving, led to their experiences of new life.

The verb *charizomai* also refers to the ways God graces the community with experiences of resurrection power for new life. The Spirit illuminates the Corinthians' discernment, enabling them to recognize these experiences and link them to embodiments of grace that are confirmed in acts of Christlike self-giving. This, too, was Paul's focus in 1:4–8. God enriched the community—i.e., God graced the community—with all kinds knowledge and speech when the witness of Christ was divinely confirmed among them.

As an added dimension of this Spirit-led discernment, mature Christ-followers also distinguish between the influences of the spirit of the world and the influences of the Spirit from God (2:12).[75] Such spiritual discernment involves a process of "comparing [*synkrinō*] spiritual things [*pneumatikos*] with spiritual things [*pneumatikos*]" (2:13). In this comparative process, the discerning community must know and apply an important distinction. On the one hand, the spirit of the world leads an individual to actions that only build up the self. The Spirit from God, on the other hand, leads an individual to acts of self-giving that build up others—strengthening relationships in the community. Paul will later contrast spiritual things (*pneumatikos*) that only build up the individual, of which the Corinthians are fond, with the *greater charismata* (12:31), which are the embodiments of the gifts of grace in acts of self-giving that benefit others.

Paul builds on this distinction in 2:14–16. The earthly human is one who has not yet accepted or received the Spirit from God (which Paul later identifies in 15:45–49 as the Spirit of the risen Christ, the man from heaven). As a result, the earthly person does not know or understand the distinction between the spirit of the world and the Spirit from God. Paul's description of the earthly person perfectly fits some of the Corinthians and some contemporary people who identify themselves as "spiritual" but not "religious." These are people who do not know the distinction between the Spirit from God that brings life to the world and the spiritual forces of the world that bring destruction and chaos.

The earthly person does not receive or understand the Spirit's gifts of life-giving grace and the embodiment of that grace in *charismata*. This is all foolishness according to the wisdom of the world (2:14). Only mature Christ-followers, who understand the distinction between the Spirit from God and the spirit of the world, can carry out this comparative process. They are able to recognize their divine gifts because they "closely examine [*anakrinō*]" these things spiritually (2:14–15) and distinguish which spirit is at work in any given situation. Those who have the Spirit from God "closely examine" (*anakrinō*) and understand all things (2:15). This process of spiritual discernment takes place, says Paul, because "we have the mind [*nous*] of Christ" (2:16). It is only by reasoning with the one mind of Christ and the Spirit from God that the mature perceive the "teachings of the Spirit" (2:13).

Jesus Christ Is the Foundation in Paul's Vision for Formation (3:1–4:21)

The evidence is clear. The Corinthians are still walking according to human norms, because there is jealousy and quarreling among them (3:3). They are still pledging allegiance to human leaders (3:4), such as Paul, Apollos, or Peter (1:12).

Paul responds by placing the role of leaders within God's larger economy of grace. Paul and Apollos are merely servants (*diakonos*) of God through whom the Corinthians entrusted themselves to the power of God at work in Christ (3:5; see also 2:4–5). Like all leaders, Paul and Apollos each have separate functions given them by the Lord (3:5). They each embody different gifts of grace (the *charismata*) that they activate in different Christlike acts of service to the community. Paul planted, Apollos watered, but God gave the growth (3:6; see 12:4–6)!

Addressing the spiritual elites and arrogant ones in the community, Paul says that neither he nor Apollos matter at all. Only God, who gives life to the community (3:7). As servants working cooperatively, Paul and Apollos are simply fellow workers with God (*synergos*) in service to the Christ-community that is God's field or God's building (*oikodomē*) (3:9).

Paul's approach to the moral life in Christ is set out in a nutshell in 3:6–9. God gives grace to each servant to embody (*charisma*) in an act of self-giving for others. God's resurrection power for new life works through each act of self-giving to "give growth" to a person, group, or the entire community. God gives the growth and enriches the interpersonal relationships among members of the congregation (see 1:4–8; 12:4–7).

The Greek noun *oikodomē* ("building") in 3:9 is part of the important word-group introduced when we were in Thessalonica. Paul uses this noun and its related verb forms fourteen times in this letter—more than in any other letter.[76] The metaphor portrays the Christ-community as God's building (3:9) and it becomes a dominant theme for the remainder of the letter.

In 1 Corinthians 3:6–9, Paul uses the metaphor of a field to describe the Christ-community he planted and Apollos watered. He then shifts to the metaphor of God's building in 3:10–15. The congregation's leaders and members continue to construct this building, but Paul started the project. "According to the grace [*charis*] of God given to me as a wise architect," says Paul, "I laid a foundation" (3:10), "which is Jesus Christ" (3:11). Paul laid this foundation by teaching and demonstrating in his own life how the Corinthians should reason with the logic of the cross to embody Jesus Christ in ordinary life.

But now, other leaders and members of the congregation are building upon (*epoikodomeō*) the foundation laid by Paul (3:10). This verb, another member of the *oikodom-* word-group, metaphorically points to human actions that are building blocks in the construction of the Christ-community. These leaders and other Christ-followers are responsible for actions that *should* build up and edify the community.[77] So, Paul issues a warning: "let each one see [*blepō*] how they are building on [*epoikodomeō*]" the foundation laid by Paul (3:10).

Paul's visual imagery is essential to his purpose. *He is speaking the language of discernment.* Each person must "see" the consequences of their actions holistically—the impact they are having on the community. The community evaluates the faithfulness of each member's contribution in this way. Paul is suggesting that the ongoing jealousy and quarreling (3:3) is *discernible evidence* that some of the Corinthians are not faithfully building on the foundation of Jesus Christ he first laid.

Some Corinthians—metaphorically speaking—are faithfully building by using enduring metals and minerals like gold, silver, and precious stones, while others are using ephemeral materials like wood, hay, and straw (3:12). In the "Day" of the Lord's judgment,[78] says Paul, a fire will prove through testing (*dokimazō*) the quality of the materials used in construction of the building (3:13). This does not bode well for a building metaphorically constructed with wood, hay, and straw. That testing fire is now raging, Paul implies, and it is manifestly discernible in the jealousies and quarrels taking place.

As we have already seen, the Greek verb *dokimazō* in 3:13 is significant for Paul's framework of formation, community building, and discernment. It describes the crucial process of "proof through testing" in the community's practice of discernment. By reflecting together on each other's actions and their consequences, the community "proves through testing" whether an action is pleasing to God, which becomes evident in experiences of new life in the community. This process requires respectful deliberation among all participants. Clearly, in Corinth, their process of "proof through testing" is failing. Some do not "see" (3:10) that their actions are destroying the community.

Paul raises the stakes by reminding them that they are God's holy temple and that the Spirit of God dwells among them (3:16–17). The Spirit opens the eyes of the discerning community to the things graced to them by God (2:12). The Spirit helps them "see" how they are building on the foundation of Jesus Christ (3:10).

He warns them, though, that anyone destroying God's temple will be destroyed (3:17). Those who are still enraptured by the wisdom of the world are fools in the eyes of God (3:18–19). To build God's temple on the foundation of Jesus Christ—a building that will survive the testing fires that always come—they must embody the logic of the cross, which is the power of God for those who are being saved (1:18).

Thus, the Corinthians' allegiance to human leaders is misplaced. These leaders are merely servants of the community that belongs to Christ, who belongs to God (3:22–23). So, says Paul, think of us as leaders this way: we are "subordinates of Christ and stewards of the mysteries of God" (4:1) who must be found faithful to that responsibility (4:2). Paul, it seems, is mindful of his critics who have been closely scrutinizing (*anakrinō*) him and his ministry (4:3). Only the Lord holds the authority to scrutinize (*anakrinō*) his actions (4:3–4), and therefore his critics should refrain from judging (*krinō*) him until Christ appears (4:5). When that happens, the Lord will reveal hidden secrets and expose the true motives of people's hearts (4:5). Until then, the Corinthians should look to Paul and Apollos as models for how to build faithfully on the foundation of Christ (4:6). They are not competitors, but cooperative collaborators working for Christ in service to the community.

* * *

As Sosthenes pauses to take a sip of water, another member of the assembly rises to ask a question. Visibly concerned by what he's just read, she asks, "Does this mean we have to wait until Christ's final return in glory to know whether Paul's actions or ours have been found to be faithful by the Lord? I'm not sure we can survive that long as a community."

Sosthenes smiles and responds in a gentle voice, "Be patient, my sister. Paul will address that very soon. But until then, I'll remind you of what he's already said. The Spirit sent from God guides your community's deliberations in discernment. The Spirit opens your eyes to see the ways God has graced each of you to serve the community and the ways God is enriching your community through Christlike acts of self-giving. The Spirit also opens your eyes in discernment to see the consequences of actions that are destroying the community because they do not reflect the foundation of Jesus Christ. Do you understand what I am saying?"

As the import of his words sink in, the woman replies, "Are you saying that in our discernment together the Spirit might also help us see the Lord's judgment on some of our actions?"

"Be patient, my sister," he responds. "Let's revisit this question soon."

Satisfied with his answer for now, the woman reclines again at the table. Sosthenes picks up the letter and starts reading again.

* * *

Paul launches into a rebuke of some Corinthians, employing biting sarcasm in 4:8–13. He contrasts their arrogance at being strong, wise, and honored in the world with his humility in being weak, foolish, and dishonored according to the standards of the world. Though he is sarcastic, he admonishes them as his beloved children (4:14). Although they may have ten thousand moral tutors[79] in Christ (referring to their so-called leaders), Paul reminds them that in Christ Jesus he became their father through the gospel (4:15). He planted the seeds of their new life in Christ and God gave them the growth (3:6).

By living a life considered foolish by the wisdom of this age, Paul exemplified the transformative logic of the cross and its central role in the foundation of Jesus Christ he laid. Among them, he embodied only Christ crucified (2:2). He exemplified what it means to be a witness of Christ. "Therefore, I urge you to become imitators of me" (4:16). Which explains why Paul earlier sent his "faithful child in the Lord," Timothy, to remind them of "my ways in Christ Jesus, just as I teach them everywhere in every *ekklēsia*" (4:17).

In Paul's absence, however, some of them have grown haughty ("puffed up," 4:18). God willing, he threatens to come to Corinth to find out how much power they really have, beyond their arrogant bluster (4:19). "For the kingdom of God does not emerge by talk, but by power" (4:20). The emergence of God's kingdom in resurrection power for new life comes through Jesus Christ and those who embody the logic of the cross in their own lives.

The Logic of the Cross and Discernment in Daily Life (5:1–11:1)

How should the logic of the cross and discernment be applied to situations in ordinary life? Paul sets out to demonstrate the application of the logic of the cross to a number of situations unfolding in their community. He begins by addressing the Corinthians who have "assembled in the name of the Lord Jesus" and with the presence of the "power of the Lord Jesus" (5:4). Paul pictures them together in their post-dinner time for moral deliberations and discernment that will follow the reading of this letter. He offers a wide range of advice and moral counsel, showing them how to reason with the mind of Christ and the logic of the cross. At every turn, his concern is with the life and health of their Christ-community more than individuals.

First, he insists that they expel a man from the community for a practice of sexual immorality that even pagans find unacceptable (he's sleeping with his stepmom!) (5:1). The problem, explains Paul, is that some members of the community have become arrogant rather than mourning the situation (5:2, 6). They are (wrongfully) taking pride in their countercultural approval of this relationship. They have also failed to recognize that this man's action is having a deleterious impact on the community (5:6–8). An important part of their responsibility to one another in discernment is to judge (*krinō*) the actions of those who are inside the community (5:12–13).

Next, Paul is incredulous that two members of their community have taken their dispute to a Roman court for resolution. The case will be decided by the norms and values of the Roman world rather than by the community of holy ones (*hagios*) (6:1). To be in litigation is already a defeat for the entire community, says Paul (6:7). It appears that no one in the assembly has been wise enough to distinguish (*diakrinō*) between the claims of these two contestants (6:5). Neither of the two legal combatants have embodied the logic of the cross in the situation (6:7–8); these failures risk their inheritance in the kingdom of God (6:9–11).

Paul tackles a situation where a Christ-follower has engaged in sexual relations with a prostitute in 6:12–20. As in 5:1–13, he is more concerned about the well-being of the community than the individual actor (though he disapproves of the action). What is at stake, once again, is the common life of those gathered in the name of Jesus Christ.

Paul addresses the conviction of some Corinthians that "all things are permissible for me" (6:12).[80] He doesn't deny the assertion, but he turns it on its head. All actions may be permissible for an individual, but not all things are helpful for the community. Gordon Fee summarizes Paul's point this way: "[t]ruly Christian conduct is not predicated on whether I have the right to do something, but whether my conduct is helpful to those about me."[81] In Christ Jesus, for the discerning community, all actions must be evaluated for their anticipated impact on the community. According to 6:12, to be Christlike and pleasing to God, the action must "bind people together" (*symphero*). That's the kind of action that serves the common good[82] and benefits[83] the entire congregation.

Paul is concerned with individuals who act without regard to the impact of their action on the community. Through baptism into Christ, their bodies become members of the one Body of Christ (6:15). They are, speaking metaphorically, limbs in Christ's body. Baptism also unites them in one spirit with the risen Christ (6:17). When an individual conjoins their body to that of a prostitute, they tear people apart from the Body of Christ. This individual action jeopardizes the future of the community as a whole (6:14).

Consequently, Paul tells them they must glorify God in their one, collective body, through moral deliberation and discernment of individual actions that bind people together. The logic of the cross puts the interests of others and the interests of the whole community ahead of an individual's personal interests and choices.

In 1 Corinthians 7:1–40 Paul responds to questions on marital and sexual relations put to him in an earlier letter from the Corinthians. He engages in dialogical persuasion with them, offering his opinions on actions that he thinks will please God in the various contexts involved. Paul emphasizes the importance of discernment in each situation. He acknowledges that each person has their own *charisma*—their own distinctive embodiment of God's gift of grace–and their own individual acts of self-giving to others. Paul will return to this important point later.

As Paul answers a question from the Corinthians (8:1–13), the logic of the cross—its embodiment and challenge—becomes sharply defined. Some community members are convinced that there is only one God. From that, they conclude that all the other gods, idols, and the emperor worshiped in the culture have no power over them. As a result, these Christ-followers freely attend events at local temples to eat the meat sacrificed to those gods and idols. It's the only meat to which most people ever have access. The issue arises when other Christ-followers, wary of the influence of these other gods and idols, eat the meat because they follow the example of more experienced or respected members of the congregation. In the act of eating the meat, they defile their own consciences.

Paul's response is bold. He tells them that "knowledge puffs up, but love [*agapē*] builds up [*oikodomeō*]" (8:1). He pairs together two of his key words crucial for formation and community building. We were introduced to the verb *agapaō* ("to love") on the road to Damascus. Paul characterized Christ as the one "who loved me, indeed, who gave himself for me." In 8:1 we encounter the related noun *agapē* ("love"). Here, love—embodied in acts of self-giving for others—build up (*oikodomeō*) the community. We were introduced to the verb *oikodomeō* on our last stop in Thessalonica. The verb denotes the consequences of actions that build relationships, binding people together. By embodying love in acts of self-giving for others, the community is built up and strengthened. These loving acts enrich the interpersonal relationships among members of the community.

Once again, however, Paul challenges the actions that are the subject of the inquiry. He tells them bluntly: anyone who thinks they know something with certainty, still has a lot to learn (8:2). In this earthly life, before God's new age is brought to completion, humans can only ever know in part, not in full.[84]

Paul agrees with the enlightened Christ-followers. There is only one God (8:6). But not everyone in the Christ-community is fully convinced of that reality (8:7). So, he warns them again, as he did in 3:10, to see (*blepō*)—to watch out—lest their actions become a stumbling block for others in the community (8:9). He emphasizes the crucial role of moral discernment in their collective decisions. To ensure that all voices are heard,[85] the deliberative assembly provides a crucial space for the injured Christ-followers to make their defiled consciences known and for the perpetrators to understand the harmful effects of their actions. In this case, as with many others, discernment has failed.

Paul concludes that the knowledge of the supposedly enlightened members who eat meat sacrificed to idols has, in effect, encouraged other Christ-followers to eat this meat and thus defile their consciences. The consequences of these actions are destroying those for whom Christ died (8:11). The enlightened members are sinning against Christ (8:12). Therefore, Paul states, if food causes another Christ-follower to stumble, "I will never eat meat" (8:13).

Christlike love in this case—embodied in an act of self-giving for others—is to *refrain* from taking an action otherwise appropriate for that person to take. Paul agrees with the supposedly enlightened community members—there is only one God. So, in the abstract, eating this meat sacrificed to idols has no consequences for the actor. But, in this case, the interests of *other* people must also be considered. This was an essential aspect of Christ's moral reasoning we examined in Philippians 2:4–11: putting the interests of the other person ahead of one's own interests. To protect other people's consciences, the supposedly enlightened congregants must refrain from eating this meat.

So far, this letter is Paul's clearest statement yet about the embodiment of the logic of the cross: putting the interests of others ahead of his own interests. Paul develops this theme further in 1 Corinthians 9:1–27 as part of the defense of his authority to those who are scrutinizing (*anakrinō*) his actions (9:3). He refuses to exercise his right to compensation for his gospeling activity. He wants to proclaim the gospel free of charge (9:18), rather than putting an obstacle in the path of the dissemination of the gospel (9:12, 15). By analogy to Christ's pattern of faithfulness, Paul embodies Christlike love. He renounces an unquestionable right for the sake of the others and for the gospel—an act of Christlike self-giving that benefits the Corinthians.[86]

Paul shows how agile and contextual his gospeling activity is in 9:19–23. He shapes his practice to best fit each group of people he is serving (9:19). "To the Jews, I became as a Jew to gain some of them" (9:20). Even though Paul is no longer under the Torah—having died to the Torah to live to God—he submitted to the Torah when he was gospeling those under the Torah (9:20). Even though he is "in the law of Christ," he became lawless to gain the lawless for Christ (9:21). He has become all things to all people in order that he might save some of them (9:22). "I do all things through the gospel, so that I might become a partner with [*synkoinōnos*] the gospel" (9:23). He is partnering with the power of God, facilitating gospel-events among different groups of people.

Each setting for Paul's ministry requires careful consideration about how to embody Christ in that distinctive context. There is a message here for the Corinthians, too: every context requires moral deliberation and discernment. Embodying Christ in acts of self-giving that, hopefully, will please God and bear fruit in the community, requires the deliberation and discernment of everyone in the community.

Paul addresses the ongoing debate concerning food sacrificed to idols in 10:1–33. Acknowledging their skills of discernment (*phronimos*), he tells the Corinthians to judge (*krinō*) for themselves what he says: flee idolatry (10:14–15), with its potentially destructive temptations (10:1–13). He reminds the Corinthians:

> **1 Corinthians 10:16** The cup of blessing that we bless, is it not a partnership [*koinōnia*] in the blood of Christ? The bread that we break, is it not a partnership [*koinōnia*] in the body of Christ? **17** Because there is one bread, we who are many are one body, for we all partake of the one bread. . . . **20** The things that they sacrifice, they sacrifice to demons, and not to God. I do not want you to become partners [*koinōnos*] with demons. **21** You cannot drink the cup of the Lord and the cup of demons. You cannot partake of the table of the Lord and the table of demons.

As we saw in our preparation for arrival in Corinth, meal practices in the ancient world were formative. More specifically, the practices of the Christ-community's shared meal of the Lord's Supper and their after-dinner deliberations are similarly formative. Recall, from the opening thanksgiving, that God called the Corinthians into the "partnership [*koinōnia*] of Jesus Christ" (1:9). The table of the Lord, and this partnership in Christ Jesus, are *exclusive* for the community set apart to serve God in Christ Jesus. These practices at the table and the after-dinner conversations in discernment form Christ-followers as friends and partners with one another and with Christ.

Christ-followers should not participate in a meal and gathering at the table of a demon. A demon is Paul's metaphorical characterization for someone or some group with influence and power in the old age that is now passing away. Paul does not want Christ-followers to be exposed again to the values, norms, and customs of the old age. Thus, they should "flee from idolatry" (10:14).

Paul explains the embodiment of the logic of the cross in this context using forceful language:

> **1 Corinthians 10:23** "All things are permissible," but not all things bind people together [*symphero*]. "All things are permissible," but not all things build up [*oikodomeo*]. **24** Do not seek your own advantage, but that of the other. **25** Eat everything sold in the meat market without closely examining [*anakrino*] it on the ground of conscience... **27** If an unbeliever invites you and you wish to go, eat whatever is set before you without closely examining [*anakrino*] the food on account of conscience. **28** But if someone says to you, "This has been offered in sacrifice," then do not eat it, to protect the conscience of the one who revealed that to you... **31** Therefore, whether you eat or drink—whatever you do—do all things for the glory [*doxa*] of God. **32** Be without offense to Jews and Greeks and to the deliberative assembly [*ekklesia*] of God, **33** just as I try to please all people in everything I do, not seeking my own benefit [*symphoros*], but that of the many, so that they might be saved [*sozo*]. **11:1** Become imitators of me, as I am of Christ.

Community building requires Christlike acts of self-giving to benefit others (10:24). Through these actions God builds up the community and binds Christ-followers together in meaningful relationships (10:23). Regard for the needs, concerns, and even the weaknesses of others are part of one's own discernment about how to embody Christ in daily life (10:25–28). "Do everything for the glory of God," says Paul in 10:31. Christ-followers should act in ways they believe will reveal God's glory—experiences of resurrection power for new life that become visible within the community. Paul links these experiences of God's glory to actions that embody the logic of the cross, which is why he ends with an exhortation to imitate him as he imitates Christ (11:1).

Faithful Discernment Is the Key to New Life in Christ (11:2–14:40)

In 11:2–14:40 Paul addresses the contentious issues arising when the Corinthians come together for their two-stage dinner party. He uses the verb *synerchomai* ("come together") *seven* times to unite his presentation in this section of the letter.[87] Both Aristotle and Paul use this verb to refer to the process by which humans are joined together to form a community.[88] Aristotle, Plutarch, and Paul all share a similar commitment to the importance of partnership and dialogue in the moral formation of an assembled community.[89]

Paul only uses *synerchomai* in this letter. This highlights his focus and concern on what is happening when they come together. These four chapters contain Paul's longest and most thoroughgoing discussion of his vision for the two-stage dinner party that structures worship in his congregations.

In 11:2–16 he enters a debate with some of the Corinthians about the proper way women should wear their hair as they prophesy to the gathered community. Because the issue is so tied culturally to first-century dress and decorum, I will only highlight two brief points. First, men and women are not independent of one another "in the Lord" (which I take as a reference to the assembled Christ-community). They speak to the assembled community with equal respect and authority, rather than conforming to the cultural hierarchy of men over women. Second, stepping back from the specific issue in 11:16, Paul chastises those who are contentious or argumentative—those who are fond of victory in a debate. Paul's *ekklēsiai*—his deliberative assemblies—have no such custom. Paul is indirectly pointing a finger at those who attempt to bully others in their moral deliberations.

"You Come Together in Ekklēsia" to Proclaim the Death of the Lord (11:17–34)

Paul critiques their divisive and destructive practices at the Lord's Supper. He tells them, "when you come together [*synerchomai*] it is not for strengthening but for weakening" (11:17). For one thing, says Paul, "when you come together [*synerchomai*] in *ekklēsia*, I hear there are divisions among you" (11:18). The phrase "in *ekklēsia*" confirms that Paul is addressing what takes place when the community *physically* assembles for their meal and moral deliberations. Hence, the accuracy of our translation of *ekklēsia* as the "deliberative assembly." The usual translation of *ekklēsia* as "church" substantially misleads most modern Christians because there is no deliberative element in the worship of most churches today.

In response to hearing about their divisions, Paul also tells the Corinthians in 11:19 that there must be such choices (*hairesis*—from which we get "heresies") so that it becomes clear who among them have proven through testing to be trustworthy (*dokimos*). The NRSV translation of *dokimos*—"genuine"—misses the word's connection to the verb *dokimazō*. Introduced in this letter in 3:13, I noted that *dokimazō* holds a special place in Paul's framework of formation, community building, and discernment. Paul describes individuals or groups as *dokimos*, signifying they have undergone rigorous testing (*dokimazō*) and emerged as trustworthy. Through reflection on past actions and experiences in discernment, they have proven to be trustworthy.[90]

Paul addresses the problem in 11:20: "when you come together [*synerchomai*] in the same place it is not to eat the Lord's Supper."[91] The social goals of sharing a meal are being subverted by the actions of the socially elite, privileged members of the congregation. The actions of this minority group[92] at the table of the Lord are perpetuating the cultural norms of social segregation. They are reinforcing the hierarchical class structure, with its divisions and power differentials. They are eating better food than other members of the community at a time of their own choosing, before some poorer members even arrive. This causes some to go hungry (11:21). By continuing these culturally divisive practices, they are undermining the transformative power of the community's shared meal.

Paul makes five crucial points in connection with this destabilizing behavior. First, in 11:23–25, he offers his interpretation of this meal practice: "as often as you eat this bread and drink the cup, you announce [*katanggelō*] the Lord's death until he comes" (11:26). The foundational assumption of his interpretation is that *embodied actions*—eating and drinking—are the means by which congregants "announce the Lord's death."

The Greek verb *katanggelō*, usually translated as "proclaim," carries overtones of public action. By eating this bread and drinking the cup, "the whole assembled congregation stands in a witness box" to proclaim their part in the death and resurrection of Jesus Christ.[93] Through their embodied actions of eating and drinking separately, however, this powerful minority group is unworthily proclaiming the Lord's death (11:27). They are failing to "die" metaphorically to their culture's divisive class structure, norms, and disparities of power. To worthily proclaim the Lord's death, they must share their higher-quality food with every member of the community after everyone has arrived. As we have seen regularly in Paul's letters, it is through this "death to new life" sequence that Paul and the members of his congregations faithfully proclaim in word and deed the good news of the death and resurrection of Jesus Christ.

Second, Paul reminds the Corinthians that there are destructive consequences to these actions. Some members of the Christ-community have become "weak and ill, and some have fallen asleep/died" (11:30). Paul may be speaking literally about the actual death of church members from malnutrition or starvation. Paul may also be referring to the physical condition of some of the poorer members of the congregation who seldom get enough to eat. Or, he may be speaking metaphorically about congregants who have "fallen asleep," meaning they are oblivious to the harm they are causing. They are failing to "see" the harmful impact of their actions on the community (3:10). Paul may also be alluding to the physical and spiritual harm to the group's elite members from their practices of gluttony from eating and drinking excessively without sharing.

Third, Paul points to these unhealthy physical and spiritual consequences as *discernible evidence* of the Lord's divine judgment on the actions of the privileged (11:32). They are being judged because they have perverted the proclamation of the death of the Lord by the ways they are eating and drinking the Lord's Supper. Instead of metaphorically dying to the cultural norms and values that allow them to eat better food without sharing, they are reinforcing these same cultural divisions and segregation by their practices. They are subverting God's will to reconcile all humanity in Christ by continuing their segregated and divisive practices at the Lord's Supper. Their perversion of the meaning of Christ's death has led to a community-wide experience of judgment and discipline (11:29).

This is similar to Paul's reasoning in 6:12–20. When one member of the community has sexual relations with a prostitute, there are harmful ramifications for the entire congregation. While this may seem unfair to modern sensibilities, it reinforces the importance and mutuality of interpersonal relations in the kingdom of God in Christ Jesus.

Paul also makes it crystal clear that this judgment of the Lord and the tragedy that has befallen the community have resulted from their failure to practice discernment, both individually and collectively. "Let each person prove themselves through testing [*dokimazō*]" before they eat or drink (11:28). Self-reflection on the visible consequences of their actions is an essential element for determining their worthiness to eat the Lord's Supper. Moreover, it is equally important that the shared meal not begin until everyone has arrived, "[f]or the one eating and drinking without distinguishing [*diakrinō*] who might be absent, eats and drinks judgment on themselves" (11:30).

With these warnings, Paul reinforces the formational importance of everyone sharing the meal together and the failure of their communal discernment. Community members *should* have *discussed, recognized, and acknowledged* the absence of some community members and the destructive effects of these actions during their moral deliberations in discernment. Had they reflected together—with equal respect given to every voice—they could have easily connected these harmful consequences with particular actions. The offenders would have been challenged to change their behavior to limit the injury to other members of the congregation.

Fourth, the logic of Paul's counsel makes it clear that the purpose of divine judgment and discipline is not retribution or punishment. It is the Lord's invitation for the community to amend its practices. If they do, they "will not be condemned" with the rest of the world (11:32) when the risen Lord returns in glory at the end of time.

Even though they have failed in their discernment to recognize the need for corrective action, all is not lost. Paul hopes they can change course. He has suggestions: "When you come together [*synerchomai*] to eat, wait for one another" (11:33). "If anyone is hungry, let them eat at home, so that you don't come together [*synerchomai*] for judgment [*krima*]" (11:34). Otherwise, those who are elite, privileged members of the community will continue to be disdainful of the *ekklēsia* of God, where the playing field *should* be leveled for everyone. They will continue to put to shame those who have nothing (11:22).

Finally, if we hope to understand Paul's vision of formation, community building, and discernment, we must recognize the active role of the risen Lord when the Christ-community "comes together in *ekklēsia*." The risen Lord—who Paul will soon characterize as the "life-giving Spirit" (15:45)—comes among them when they are assembled.[94] He guides their discernment of Christlike actions and confirms their witness of Christ (1:4–8). He judges actions that are proving to be destructive to individuals and tearing the fabric of the congregation. Through his judgment, the risen Lord leads the discerning community back to the place of life and peace, which is where the community wants to be in the final Day of the Lord that will come at the end of the age.

At this point, Sosthenes pauses in his reading. He looks straight at the woman who asked him whether the Spirit also guides the community to see the Lord's judgment on the community. She looks him squarely in the eye, says nothing, but gives Sosthenes a knowing nod of the head. The pilgrims on the balcony look at each other, knowing there will be fireworks when the deliberations begin after the letter is read.

The Divine-Human Relationship Guides Spirit-Led Discernment (12:1–11)

In our preparations for arrival in Corinth, I mentioned that one of the issues in this community was the assertion by some Corinthians of their elite spiritual status. Some are speaking in unintelligible tongues in the assembly and claiming an exalted spiritual status for themselves in the community.

In 12:1–11 Paul responds to questions from the Corinthians about various "spiritual things" (*pneumatika*). He begins to distinguish what the Corinthians call *pneumatika* that come from any source—including pagan idols that lead people astray (12:2)—from what Paul characterizes as the greater *charismata*. These are Spirit-inspired embodiments of God's gift of grace in acts of self-giving that serve and benefit the community.

Only the Holy Spirit empowers Christ-followers to confess "the Lord is Jesus" (12:3). Grounded in this confession, Paul summarizes in the next verses what might be characterized today as his moral theology:

> **1 Corinthians 12:4** Now there are distinctive distributions of embodiments of grace [*charismata*], but the same Spirit; **5** and there are distinctive distributions of acts of services/ministries[95] [*diakonia*], but the same Lord; **6** and there are distinctive distributions of effects [*energēmata*], but it is the same God effectuating [*energeō*] all these things in everyone. **7** To each is given the public manifestation of the Spirit for binding people together [*sympherō*].

When the community comes together, they are guided by this easily accessible vision of the divine-human partnership. It is simple enough that everyone involved in the deliberations can understand and participate.[96]

First, remember that grace (*charis*) is God's gift of life-giving power to each Christ-follower. The Spirit received from God (2:12) illuminates distinctive ways for Christ-followers to embody these gifts of grace in *charismata* (12:4). There are no gradations of grace—no sliding scale of the amount of life-giving power conveyed in the gift of grace. God's grace is the power to create new life in some way. Full stop. But the Spirit makes distinctive distributions of the *embodiments* of each gift of grace (*charismata*), based on each person's capabilities, context, and past experiences.

Second, each Christ-follower activates this gift of life-giving power through a distinctive act of service/ministry (*diakonia*) to others grounded in the service/ministry of the one Lord Jesus Christ (12:5). Just as Jesus taught and modeled for his disciples how they are to walk in his ways, so, too, Paul carries out that same Christlike service/ministry in the contexts of his own life (3:10).

Third, there are distinctive distributions of effects—i.e., experiences of resurrection power for new life. But it is the one God who powerfully effectuates all these experiences. For example, look back to 1:4–8. The risen Lord confirmed the Corinthians' witness of Christ, but God enriched the community in all kinds of speech and knowledge through the embodiments of grace (*charismata*) put into acts of service.

Finally, to each person is given the public manifestation of the Spirit that binds people together in the community (12:7). The noun *symphoros* (7:35; 10:33) and the verb *symphero* (6:12; 10:23; 12:7) are usually translated as "beneficial," or actions taken for the "common good." These are, of course, helpful and legitimate translations. But both Greek words share the prefix *syn-* ("with") and thereby carry the richer meaning of joining, binding, or bringing people together with one another. This is Paul's real purpose. Actions that foster unity and reconciliation among conflicting parties contribute to the common good of the community.

Nobody Matters Unless Everybody Matters in the Body of Christ (12:12–13:13)

In his popular novels involving the shrewd Los Angeles police detective and Vietnam veteran Harry Bosch, author Michael Connelly quotes Bosch often as saying "nobody matters unless everybody matters." Bosch uses the phrase when he is being pressured by the brass to spend his investigative time focused on crimes against high-profile people rather than those at the lower ends of the social hierarchy.

Likewise, Paul levels the playing field in the Christ-community using similar images. Having challenged the privileged members of the congregation, who perverted the Lord's Supper at the expense of the poor, Paul subverts the cultural hierarchies in his description of the Body of Christ. In the Body of Christ, the value of each person is linked to the well-being of everyone. Unless each person is valued and respected, the entire group suffers. Unless each part of the body functions properly, the body suffers.

Each person is baptized into the one body, and each receives the same Spirit of the risen Christ, whether Jews or Gentiles, or slaves or freed persons (12:13). This body has many members (12:14). Paul analogizes each member of the Body of Christ to a particular part of the human body. He makes the point that each of them has need for all the others (12:15–21).[97] There are many members, but one body (12:20).

Paul levels the social playing field in the Body of Christ. "The members of the body that seem to be weaker are essential; and the ones we think are without honor we surround with abundant honor; and we confer elegance on our shameful ones" (12:22–23). The elegant members have no need for this. But God has mixed together the body, giving greater honor to the one lagging behind (12:24).

God has done all of this for a purpose: "that there may be no division in the body, but the members have the same concern for one another" (12:25). "If one member suffers, all the members suffer together with that one; and if one member is glorified [*doxazō*], all the members rejoice with that one" (12:26). "You yourselves are a body of Christ, and each one of you a part of it" (12:27). God has placed in the *ekklēsia* a wide variety of Christ-followers to serve the entire community (12:28–30).

The Corinthians inquired of Paul in 12:1 about spiritual things (*pneumatika*). Instead, he urges them to "seek the greater *charismata*"—the embodiments of the gifts of grace put into the service of the community through Christlike acts of self-giving for others (12:5, 31). This is the way of walking in God's new age in Christ that is "beyond comparison" (12:31).

Paul's way of walking beyond comparison is the way of love, *agapē* (13:1–13). This is the love (*agapē*) we first encountered when Paul said that in his earthly life, he "lives by the faithfulness of the Son of God, who loved [*agapaō*] me, indeed, who gave himself for me" (Galatians 2:20). This is the way of love that "builds up [*oikodomeō*]" the community (1 Corinthians 8:1). Christlike love embodied in acts of self-giving for others builds up the Body of Christ. No action matters, and every action is useless, unless the actor embodies love with the "moral disposition that seeks the benefit of the other more than the self"[98] (13:1–3). Love embodied in acts of self-giving for others becomes the antidote to the competitive, arrogant, and self-referential actions destroying the community in Corinth.

Paul delineates the specific ways love behaves, and the actions it avoids. He depicts love as a moral actor. Love is the subject of the sentences in 13:4–7. Paul provides embodied examples of acts of self-giving for others to stimulate the moral imaginations of the Corinthians in preparation for their upcoming deliberations in discernment.

Love embodies long-suffering with others. Love is embodied in acts of kindness, not actions rooted in jealously. Love does not brag or promote self-importance. Love does not act shamefully, nor does it seek its own advantage! Love does not respond when provoked by others. Love does not keep a record of the times it has been subjected to evil. Love does not rejoice in acts of unrighteousness, but only rejoices in the truth. Love endures all things, trusts all things, hopes all things, abides all things.

Love is the greatest of all things, abiding eternally, even beyond faithfulness and hope (13:13). Everything else, says Paul, is only partial—prophecies, tongues, knowledge—they will one day end (13:8). In earthly life, a Christ-follower can only know in part and prophesy in part (13:9). But when the end comes, the partial will end (12:10). "Now, I know only in part," but when the end comes, we will see face to face, and be fully known (13:12). For now, though, we still "see life only by means of a mirror in an enigma [*ainigma*]" (12:12).

Paul's insight that humans can only know something in part in earthly life echoes what he said in 8:1–2: "knowledge puffs up, but love [*agapē*] builds up [*oikodomeō*]; anyone who thinks they know something with certainty, does not know as they ought to know." This profound insight challenges some of the Corinthians, whose actions are grounded in their moral, theological, and spiritual certainty. The awareness that we all still have a lot to learn is also the bedrock foundation for the essential role of discernment in the deliberative assembly.

Paul's insight that life is an enigma–a riddle–is equally important. The communal practice of discernment establishes a process for Christ-followers to use as they seek to engage and respond to the riddles of daily life. In their trial-and-error practice of discernment, they seek actions that will be pleasing to God and build up the community through experiences of resurrection power. Paul now turns to this critical, after-dinner practice of discernment, including an illustration for how it works and a structure for its orderly practice.

"What Should Happen... When You Come Together?" Discernment! (14:1–15:3)

Paul moves smoothly to the second stage of the dinner party in 14:1–40. At this point we do well to recall once again Plutarch's first-century view on the goal of building friendships in the post-dinner conversation. To achieve that goal, said Plutarch, the conversation must be conducted in an orderly manner and the topics should be simple enough for everyone to participate in the discussion.

Paul appears to share Plutarch's views on the goal and proper conduct of the post-dinner deliberations. While there are a variety of community-building practices that take place after the Lord's Supper, such as singing hymns, hearing lessons, and interpreting tongues (14:26), Paul focuses primarily on the critical role of prophecy (*propheteia*).

He starts his assessment of the post-dinner practices with a clear statement of their goal: "[p]ursue love [*agapē*] and seek the spiritual things [*pneumatika*], but so that you might prophesy [*prophēteuō*]" (14:1). For Paul, a prophet (*prophētēs*) is someone who has a gift of grace and activates that grace in acts of self-giving to evaluate whether human actions reflect or fail to reflect, by analogy, the faithfulness of Jesus Christ, the model for all Christ-followers.[99] Prophecy is a form of speech that engages the mind—the *nous* (see 14:14–15). Prophecy addresses whether a particular action or attitude reflects, by analogy, the mind of Christ or an action that embodies the faithfulness of Jesus Christ, "the one who loved me, indeed, who gave himself for me" (Galatians 2:20). It is intelligible speech by which everyone in the assembly can be built up, learn, and be encouraged (1 Corinthians 14:31). Contrary to popular belief, a prophet for Paul is not someone who predicts the future. Prophecy is an act of love embodied in self-giving for others.

In contrast to prophecy, speaking in tongues is only talk between the individual and God, since no one else understands what is being said (14:2). Unless interpreted, it is not an act of self-giving for others. This practice, so highly valued by some Corinthians as a sign of elite spiritual status, was probably the verbal expression of a powerful emotional state of the speaker. It is not a real language intelligible to others, but a kind of structured babbling.[100] As a result, uninterpreted tongues do *not* build up the assembly (14:4). Speaking in tongues may engage a person's spirit, but their mind is unfruitful (14:14). Even if one is offering a blessing or thanksgiving in tongues, someone who is uninitiated in the Christ-community will not be able to say "amen" or be built up (*oikodomeō*) by the tongues because they won't understand what is being said (14:16–17).

Those who prophesy, however, speak to others for their *edification* (*oikodomē*), encouragement, and consolation (14:3). Those who speak in tongues only build up (*oikodomeō*) themselves, while the one who prophesies builds up (*oikodomeō*) the *ekklēsia*, the deliberative assembly (14:4). Paul prefers for Christ-followers to prophesy; the one who prophesies is greater than one speaks in tongues, so that the *ekklēsia* might be built up (*oikodomē*) (14:5).

In his evaluation of the after-dinner discussions, Paul returns to the metaphor he introduced in 3:9. The community is God's building (*oikodomeō*) that is built up (*oikodomeō*) through Christlike actions (3:10–15). Tongues do not build up the entire assembly. Prophecy does. In the deliberative assembly (*ekklēsia*) it is more important to speak five words with the mind (*nous*) to instruct others than 10,000 words in tongues (14:19).

Paul provides a clear example for how prophecy should work in the assembly. He addresses a hypothetical situation where the "whole *ekklēsia* comes together" (14:23). He is probably depicting a meeting of all the various house-groups in Corinth. He also imagines that some outsiders and those who are uninitiated in the Christ-community will join this larger assembly. If everyone speaks in tongues, says Paul, the outsiders and the uninitiated will conclude that the Christ-followers are out of their minds (14:23). But if everyone is prophesying during the time for discernment, and some outsider or uninitiated enters in, that person will be closely examined (*anakrinō*) by everyone and put to shame ("convicted" in the NRSV)(14:24). The "hidden things" (*krupta*) of that person's heart will become manifest and that person will then fall on their face and prostrate themselves before God ("worship" God in the NRSV) and declare that "God is really among you" (14:25).

Paul's hypothetical recalls his earlier warning to the Corinthians in 4:5. He cautioned them not to judge him until the Lord comes, "who will bring to light the hidden things [*krupta*] of the darkness and will manifest the motives of the hearts, and then there will be praise to each one from God." Paul's hypothetical in 14:20–25 presumes just such a judgment of the Lord taking place in the assembly. In this case, the actions and hidden things in the heart of the outsider are revealed and judged as deficient. But the Lord's goal with this judgment is accomplished. The outsider recognizes his failure and is convicted by their close examination of his actions and motives. The outsider acknowledges God at work among the members of the assembly.

Just in case the Corinthians failed to appreciate what Paul said in 11:27–34, that the Lord had come and judged some of their meal practices as destructive, this hypothetical sets them straight. This is probably why Paul also, at the close of this letter, implores the risen Christ, "Lord, come! [*marana tha*]" (16:22). He is inviting the risen Lord to come into the assembly to persuade the Corinthians through revelation that Paul's other prophetic words in the letter reflect the Lord's judgment on some of their actions.

In 14:26–40 Paul finally addresses the chaos and disorder in the deliberations of the assembly, probably being caused by the proliferation of unintelligible and emotional tongues being spoken. He sets out an orderly process for how the post-dinner moral deliberations in the assembly should unfold.

"What should happen, brothers and sisters? When you come together, each one has a hymn, a lesson, a revelation, a tongue, or an interpretation. Let all things be done for upbuilding [*oikodomē*]" (14:26). Paul's goal is always the same: to promote love embodied in acts of self-giving for others that build up the community. Paul limits those speaking in tongues to two or three, speaking in turn, and they can only speak if there is someone to interpret what is said (14:27–28).

"Let two or three prophets speak, and the rest of the assembly must distinguish [*diakrinō*] what they are saying" (14:29). Paul uses the word *diakrinō* again to describe a process for distinguishing between the various insights of these prophets. Other members of the community must evaluate for themselves which prophecies best interpret a particular situation and suggest the Christlike responses most likely to result in experiences of resurrection power that build up the congregation.

Paul anticipates that during these moral deliberations, revelation from the risen Lord will happen. In that case, the speaker pauses to let the revelation be presented to the assembly (14:30). This is the way the Spirit of the risen Lord guides their moral discernment. Finally, Paul tells them, "you are all able to prophesy one by one, so that everyone may learn and be encouraged" (14:31).

The goal of prophecy in the deliberative assembly is to help everyone learn how to embody Christ faithfully in ordinary life (recall the imitation of Christ motif in 11:1) and to encourage them in the process. Prophecies also console the person whose action is deemed to be an insufficient "witness of Christ" (recall how that might help in 5:1–13; 6:1–11; 8:1–13; 11:17–34). Paul is satisfied that his counsel will bring order to the assembly, for God is a God of peace, not of anarchy and confusion (14:33). He closes by telling the Corinthians, "let all things be done fittingly and according to order" (14:40).

Paul thereby closes his lengthy discussion and evaluation of the Corinthians' two-stage dinner party. He then transitions to address the doubts of some Corinthians concerning resurrection from the dead. Since our pilgrimage is focused on Paul's vision for formation, community building, and discernment, I will highlight only a few important points from Paul's argument in 1 Corinthians 15.

In 15:1–2 Paul reminds the Corinthians of the gospel (*euanggelion*) he gospeled (*euanggelizomai*) to them. This is the gospel they received, in which they now stand, and through which they are being saved. This process of being saved will continue, suggests Paul, if they hold fast to the *logic* (*logos*) which he gospeled *(euanggelizomai)* to them (15:2). We have now seen Paul emphasize this logic twice in Philippi (Philippians 2:1–11, 16) and twice in Corinth (1 Corinthians 1:18; 15:2). The Corinthians must hold fast to this logic of the cross–the logic of life–if they expect to continue experiencing the resurrection power of God for new life and salvation. Their salvation that is underway (1:18; 15:2) depends upon using the one mind of Christ (1:10; 2:16) to reason with the logic of the cross and discern Christlike actions that build up the deliberative assembly. Their practice of discernment is the heartbeat of the flow of life-giving grace that keeps the people and their process of salvation on track.

The crucified Lord has become a life-giving Spirit in resurrection (15:45). He will continue to guide their moral deliberations in discernment (2:6–16), so they know the things graced to them by God—both individually and as a community.

Paul sums up his apocalyptic understanding of the moral life in God's new age in Christ Jesus in this closing exhortation to the Corinthians:

> **1 Corinthians 15:47** The first person [Adam] was from the earth's dust; the second person [Jesus Christ] is from heaven. **48** The person of dust is a model for the people of dust; and the one from heaven is a model for those of heaven. **49** Just as we have worn the image of the person of dust, let us also wear the image of the person of heaven.... **51** Behold, I speak to you a mystery: we will not all fall asleep in death, but we all will be changed... **52** the dead will be raised...and we will be changed... **58** Therefore, my beloved, stand firm, immovable, always abounding in the work of the Lord, knowing that in the Lord your labor is not in vain![101]

Discernment in the deliberative assembly is the place and the practice where the Corinthians debate and decide how to wear the image of the person of heaven. And, through Christlike love, embodied in acts of self-giving for others, they anticipate future experiences of resurrection power for new life in Christ Jesus. Paul closes his moral exhortation by telling the Corinthians, "let all things be done in love [*agapē*]" (16:14). Let every action be one of Christlike love, embodied in an act of self-giving for others. "Come, Lord [*marana tha*]!" (16:22). Persuade this assembly of the need for Christlike action!

Paul Highlights the Transformative Practice of Discernment (2 Corinthians 3:12–18)

In Second Corinthians Paul describes how the practice of discernment becomes transformative for those who come together to share a meal and moral deliberations in discernment. He writes:

> **2 Corinthians 3:14** [I]n Christ... **16**...one turns to the Lord... **17** Now the Lord is the Spirit, and where the Spirit of the Lord is, there is freedom. **18** And all of us...seeing the glory [*doxa*] of the Lord reflected as in a mirror, are being transformed [*metamorphoō*] into the same image from glory [*doxa*] into glory [*doxa*]; for this comes from the Lord, the Spirit.

The verb *metamorphoō* only appears four times in the entire New Testament. The verb describes the transfiguration of Jesus Christ on the mountaintop (Mark 9:2; Matthew 17:2). Paul also uses the verb twice—here and in Romans 12:2, another passage focused on communal discernment. In both cases, Paul describes the process of transformation that is underway for Christ-followers who participate in the moral deliberations and discernment that are the heartbeat of worship in God's new age in Christ.

In the natural world, the verb *metamorphoō* describes the physical changes of a caterpillar as it is transformed in its cocoon and finally emerges as a beautiful butterfly. This natural process aptly captures Paul's vision for the transformation of humans into the image of Jesus Christ. Over time, Christ-followers are transformed into the image of Christ in the practice of discernment in their metaphorical cocoon—the *ekklēsia* in Christ Jesus! In death, they leave their earthly cocoon, transformed for eternal life in Christ Jesus.

Paul is also speaking very practically in this passage. As Luke Timothy Johnson notes, in antiquity "following a leader or teacher meant, in fact, learning through imitation the character of the teacher in order to translate that character into the circumstances of their own lives."[102] We still learn the moral life in Christ today by observing the Christlike actions of others. "Discipleship is best learned through the imitation of other disciples."[103]

We have already heard Paul say that he is no longer living, but Christ is living in him (Galatians 2:20). He also expects Christ to come alive in his congregants, as reflected in Christlike love embodied in acts of self-giving for others. Each deliberative assembly is a gathering of Christ-followers being led by the Lord, the Spirit of the risen Christ. They are slowly learning Christ's way of life together by watching each other, face-to-face and action-to-action, as though reflected in a mirror. They see Christ reflected in one another and through one another's Christlike actions. Each time a Christlike action leads to an experience of God's resurrection power for new life—a moment of God's *doxa*—the community takes notice. They see a new glory of the Lord as reflected in a mirror. The more times they see these moments of glory taking place in and through other Christ-followers, the more they are being transformed into that same image of Christ. This comes from the Lord, who is the Spirit leading their discernment (2 Corinthians 3:18).

Paul expects that he and the members of his congregations are being transformed into the image of Jesus Christ by paying attention to each other's faces and actions, as reflected in a mirror, in the contexts of ordinary life. They are being reciprocally formed into Christ's image through their face-to-face encounters at the Lord's Supper and in their moral deliberations in the practice of discernment.

Pilgrims Reflect on Their Experience

After departing from the Corinthian assembly, the pilgrims gather in their customary circle in the hotel meeting room. They are showing some physical signs of fatigue—we've now made four stops in five days—but their enthusiasm hasn't waned a bit. They begin to reflect on what they've heard and to consider what they might want to reclaim for their churches today.

Robert opens the reflections. "I continue to find myself conflicted about what it means to be 'holy.' I was glad to hear that being a 'saint' did not require a level of moral perfection. On the other hand, when we started this pilgrimage, I had no idea that being 'holy' meant being set apart exclusively to serve God in the world. Paul continues to remind us of this point. The bar still seems to be set very high."

"Yes, I agree," says Philip. "How many of us really think of our commitment to Jesus Christ as exclusive? That's a high bar, too."

Gail responds, "I hadn't really thought about Christian formation as a process of being made holy over time. I worship regularly on Sunday, but I'm not sure that I'm any holier today than I was five years ago. I feel like I'm in more of a holding pattern."

"On top of that, Gail, I'm not sure Paul would characterize my church as a deliberative assembly," says Diane. "We don't really engage in what Paul is calling moral deliberations about an event from daily life and how to embody Christ in that situation."

"I agree," responds Jim. "Our modern translation of *ekklēsia* as 'church' certainly obscures the centrality of moral conversation in Paul's deliberative assemblies."

"I was intrigued by the creative potential from the roles of improvisation and lively repartee among participants in these conversations," adds Reynoldo. "I don't see much interaction like that taking place in our churches today."

"I'm glad we heard about the 'logic of the cross' and how it is synonymous with the logic of life we heard about in Philippi," adds Esperanza. "I've had a vague sense of discomfort when I hear people talk about the 'message of the cross.' It always made me think that the gospel involved learning information about Jesus and I knew that wasn't enough. But until this pilgrimage I'd never heard anyone talk about reasoning with the 'logic of life' or the 'logic of the cross.' Those translations sure make better sense, since Paul then talks about having the mind of Christ. Reasoning with logic is what the mind does. We've now heard Paul emphasize that reasoning in two places—Philippi and Corinth."

"I agree," says Reynoldo. "Paul's distinction between talk and power was very enlightening. Power is usually viewed negatively in today's culture. But I think that might change if we talked more about experiences of God's resurrection power for new life. It would help me trust that there really is a living God. And that, in turn, would give me more confidence in entrusting myself to Christ's way of love embodied in self-giving for others."

"I was shocked when that man stood up to ask Sosthenes a question," confides Ann.

"But we were told when he was introduced that he would also answer questions," recalls Dante. "Still, though, I also didn't expect anyone to be that bold. But I'm glad he was, because I needed that background to understand what Paul was saying."

"What really struck a chord with me was Paul's talk about certainty," says Ann. "I spent a lot of years paralyzed to act in some important situations because I wanted to be certain I was making the right choice before I took any action. What a difference it would make in the world today if everyone realized that in earthly life we can only ever know something in part."

"That sounds quite prophetic, Ann," says Esperanza. "I've never thought of myself as a prophet. But the way Paul defines 'prophet' opens up the possibility that we can all be prophets at various times. It's all about affirming someone's Christlike action to build up and encourage that person, while the rest of us learn from that experience, too."

"It also means we have to be open to critique from other prophets," acknowledges Latisha. "I bet that's also why Paul talks about the prophet's role of consoling others. If someone points out my stumble, I hope they will also console me in the process."

"Before I forget," continues Latisha, "I'm glad that Paul addressed that point that Philip and I were discussing at our stop on the road to Damascus. In this letter, Paul affirmed Philip's suggestion that part of discernment ought to be discussing and deciding whether an action has been inspired by the 'spirit of the world' or the 'Spirit from God.'"

"That sounds like messy business," muses Jean, stroking her chin in deep thought. "I can now understand the importance of humility and acknowledging that we can never know anything with certainty. That's the only way discernment can work as an ongoing practice."

"I appreciate the order Paul imposed on the structure of their moral conversations in discernment," offers Robert. "I get tired very quickly in conversations where people start pinging off one another like popcorn. There's no time to reflect on and evaluate what each person is saying. There's very little learning taking place in those situations. Paul expects everyone to learn and be encouraged by these conversations."

"That was helpful to hear how Paul uses the word 'glory,'" says Esperanza. "That makes sense to me. There is a certain radiance that surrounds an experience of new life. And it was very helpful to hear the practice of discernment elaborated in Second Corinthians, where Paul used the word 'glory' again. When we recognize a gospel-event of resurrection power, we often learn what actions led to the experience. That sets us up for acting that way again and, hopefully, experiencing another moment of glory. As Paul says, we are being transformed from glory into glory."

"What's really sinking in for me is the importance of the practice of proof through testing for discernment in the community," says Reynoldo. "We've heard that in every one of Paul's letters. That clearly makes it one of his 'ways in Christ Jesus' that he teaches in every church."

"Yes, me too," agrees Jean. "Connecting actions with consequences. In a way it's so simple."

"And, over time, it leads to practical wisdom," responds Gail. "This is all so simple, but it's sure not easy."

"I love the thought of being in a community where, if one person suffers, we all suffer with that person," adds Sarah. "That's a real sharing of the burdens of life."

"I appreciated the other part of that, too, where we all rejoice if one person is glorified," adds Dante. "That law firm I was in for a while was a workplace where some of our lawyers got jealous when another lawyer in our own firm succeeded. It became not only a cutthroat environment, but it seemed like we were sometimes working against the success of the business."

"Kind of like those people in Corinth who were building the community with actions that Paul depicted as wood, hay, and straw," said Ann.

"Funny you should say that," adds Dante. "That law firm I was talking about had a major falling out of the key partners and it experienced hard times."

"We are learning so much about life and the life of faithfulness," concludes Latisha.

"Speaking of learning," adds Diane, "I hope we learn this much at the next stop!"

"Where is our next stop?" asks Esperanza. "I haven't been looking closely at the itinerary."

"It's Rome," I tell them.

"It's our last stop, right?" asks Reynoldo.

"Yes," I answer. "Let's hit the pause button on this discussion and get ready to go."

CHAPTER FIVE

Discernment in Rome: Under Grace, Not Under Torah

*"Be Transformed by the Renewing of the Mind,
So You Can Prove Through Testing What Is the Will of God,
What Is Good and Well-Pleasing and Mature"*
(Romans 12:2)

We have now arrived in Rome, the last stop on our pilgrimage back to the early Christ-movement. We are preparing to hear the reading of Paul's influential letter to the Romans. There is palpable energy among the pilgrims, knowing they will soon enter a gathering of the faithful in the heart of the Roman Empire. Before joining the assembly, however, pilgrims do some additional preparation to ensure this stop bears fruit for reclaiming Paul's vision of formation, community building, and discernment.

Where Are We?

The history of the Christ-movement in Rome prior to the late 40s CE is shrouded in mystery.[1] Historians and biblical scholars generally agree that the movement had penetrated Rome from a variety of sources in the decades prior to Paul's letter. Neither Paul nor his colleagues played a role in starting these Christ-communities.

The Christ-movement probably began among members of Rome's large Jewish population. Estimates of its size range from 15,000 to 60,000 by the time Paul writes in the late 50s CE. Archaeological inscriptions and non-Jewish writings suggest that many members of the Jewish community were impoverished and relatively uneducated. Most spoke Greek and came to Rome throughout the centuries-long Jewish Diaspora or were brought to Rome as slaves captured during Rome's intervention in Jerusalem in the 60s BCE. Starting with Julius Caesar, the Jewish community in Rome was given permission to follow its own laws and customs. They did not have to worship the emperor or the pantheon of Roman gods. By the time of Paul's letter, historians estimate there were at least eleven Jewish synagogues operating independently of one another.

The Christ-movement in Rome likely emerged from conversations and debates taking place in the various Roman synagogues.[2] The earliest assemblies of Christ-followers were probably led or heavily influenced by Jewish Christ-followers. That means these early Christ-communities focused on the Torah as their exclusive pattern of life, even for the Gentile Christ-followers who participated in these assemblies.

The influence of Torah in these Christ-communities changed with one important historical development that impacted the entire Jewish community in Rome. According to the second-century Roman historian Suetonius, the emperor Claudius issued an edict around 49 CE expelling Roman Jews "who were constantly making disturbances at the instigation of Chrestus."[3] Many historians and biblical scholars interpret this as a reference to conflict arising in the Roman synagogues concerning the identity of Jesus as the Christ, the Jewish Messiah. This edict remained in place until Claudius died and Nero ascended the throne as emperor in 54 CE.

It seems that when the expelled Jewish Christ-followers were finally able to return to Rome, they found their congregations had changed under the leadership of the Gentile Christ-followers. During their five-year absence, these congregations apparently loosened or even discontinued the dietary and worship regulations mandated by Torah and Jewish customs. When the two groups were reunited, conflict erupted over the applicability of these Jewish requirements and expectations for meals and meetings.

According to Acts 18:2, this expulsion included two Roman Jews, Aquila and his wife Priscilla. Paul later met the couple in Corinth during their exile from Rome. By the time Paul writes to the Romans in the late

50s CE, Prisca (as she's known) and Aquila have returned to Rome. We will return shortly to their important role in the early Christ-movement.

Sometimes, we hear people refer to the "early church in Rome," as if it were like the monolithic modern Catholic Church in Rome. It's important to remember that there were different ways of being "church" in early Christianity. As we have discovered on this pilgrimage, in the Gentile Christ-communities founded by Paul, Christ's pattern of life was the exclusive norm for discerning acts of faithfulness. In his communities, Torah's commandments and rules were not the exclusive pattern for life. They were still considered as a resource in discernment, but they were not binding. We know from other letters like Galatians that Paul was involved in acrimonious disputes with outsiders trying to persuade his Gentile congregants to turn to the Torah as their binding pattern of life.

There were other Torah-observant communities of Christ-followers in the early church. These groups may or may not have admitted Gentiles and, when they did, it may have been on different terms from place to place. For instance, many interpreters hypothesize that the Gospel of Matthew emerged from a community comprised primarily of Jewish Christ-followers who observed the Torah, as interpreted by Jesus (see Matthew 5:17–20). This may have been the beginnings of the Torah-observant Christ-communities in Rome, too. At some point, as in Rome, Matthew's community also began to admit Gentiles. By the end of that Gospel, the risen Christ instructs them to "[g]o therefore and disciple all the Gentiles, baptizing them in the name of the Father and of the Son and of the Holy Spirit, and teaching them to obey everything that I have commanded you" (Matthew 28:19–20).

Worship in the Early Christ-Movement

Worship in the earliest decades of the Christ-movement was very different from what we recognize as worship today. When we read the Bible, we should not think that references to worship describe the same things we call worship today.[4]

In the early Christ-movement, the word worship was not used to characterize participation in communal rituals that include prayer, liturgies, or special genres of music.⁵ Worship was "about the body and about service,"⁶ especially *individual* acts of service to others. Andrew McGowan, a scholar of early Christian worship summarizes it this way: "'[w]orship' was not one sort of weekly corporate activity but the devotion to God that filled the whole of life. This included particular bodily expressions of that devotion, performed communally or privately from day to day."⁷

More specifically, the Greek words usually translated as worship in the New Testament are not primarily focused on the conduct of their gathered assemblies, communal rituals, or even communal prayer. Rather, they describe mostly individual acts of reverence toward God or the risen Christ. For instance, the Greek verb *proskyneō* describes the physical act of face-down prostration by one person or a group of individuals before the deity. It is most often simply translated in English-language versions of the New Testament as "worship."⁸

Similarly, the Greek verb *latreuō* and its related noun *latreia* are regularly translated into English as worship. But the context is usually individual acts of service to others on behalf of Christ or God.⁹ As we will soon see in Romans 6 and 12, Paul associates worship with *individual* acts of sacrificial, Christlike service to others.

Why Are We Here?

A Brief History of Interpretation of Romans

Paul's letter to the Romans has created a history that has been both highly influential and at times deeply problematic. One of today's leading Pauline scholars, Michael J. Gorman, opens his recent commentary on Romans, saying "Paul's letter to the Romans is arguably the most influential letter every written. It is certainly the most significant letter in the history of Christianity."¹⁰ The letter prompted the conversion of St. Augustine, challenged Martin Luther to light the fire of the Reformation, inspired Karl Barth to change the landscape of modern biblical studies, and braced Dietrich Bonhoeffer for resisting the oppressive Nazi regime in Germany.

The interpretation of Romans has also proven to be problematic. Luke Timothy Johnson concludes that "the history of theological interpretation [of Romans] has obscured Paul's meaning with layer after layer of subsequent significance discovered or imposed on Paul's composition. Present-day readers find it difficult to cut through these layers in order to encounter what Paul himself wrote."[11] Johnson suggests that to engage Romans as directly and freshly as possible, today's listeners and readers must "exercise a certain amount of historical imagination."[12]

As we have done at every stop, we will join this assembly of Christ-followers to hear the reading of Romans. We will use our historical imagination as we try to hear the letter, not as a theological and doctrinal treatise, but as another one of Paul's pastoral letters. He is seeking to form Christ-followers and build up a community through its practice of discernment in Christ Jesus. We will avoid detours to discuss the deep (and important!) theological ideas that often dominate discussions of Romans but obscure Paul's central focus on formation, community building, and discernment.

The Situation in First-Century Rome

Why did Paul write to the Christ-followers in Rome? What was the social makeup of the Roman assemblies to whom he wrote? There's no consensus about the answers to these questions. I offer the following, tentative conclusions to help us understand Paul's focus on formation, community building, and discernment in the letter.

Romans is the only letter Paul wrote to Christ-followers in communities that he or his close colleagues had no hand in starting. He'd never even visited Rome. In each of Paul's letters we've heard so far, he reminds the recipients of his embodied gospeling (*euanggelizomai*) activity that led to their experiences of resurrection power. In the case of Romans, however, Paul is writing mostly to Christ-followers who neither know him face-to-face nor have experienced for themselves his teaching and the life-giving power of his gospel.

Moreover, these Torah-observant Christ-followers are receiving a letter from Paul, the well-known but controversial apostle to the Gentiles. They probably have doubts about the authority of this former Pharisee who never knew Jesus. Their concerns may be exacerbated by his reputation for provoking opposition—sometimes even violent opposition—from other Jewish Christ-followers, the leaders of Jewish synagogues, and even some Roman officials.

Consequently, Paul can't rely on his customary approach of drawing on shared experiences with his congregants. In Romans he crafts a different kind of pastoral letter. He describes how the power of God can work through his gospel to reconcile their conflicted Christ-communities. He also lays out the structure by which the Christ-communities in Rome might become what Paul calls an *ekklēsia* in Christ Jesus—a deliberative assembly focused on embodying the faithfulness of Jesus Christ.

To bolster his credibility and authority, Paul sends greetings in Romans 16 to twenty-seven colleagues, coworkers, friends, and acquaintances, now resident in Rome. They can recommend him and the power of his gospel. He also sends greetings from eight other named individuals currently working with him in Corinth. Some of them may be known to the Roman Christ-followers, and this, too, might enhance his credibility.

Paul also appears to have knowledge about the conflict that is disrupting the Christ-communities in Rome.[13] Paul addresses directly the two competing groups in 14:1–15:13. Before doing so, however, he introduces himself, the core elements of his teaching on formation, community building, and discernment, and describes the power of God at work through his gospel. Paul anticipates that if the conflicted groups will follow his pastoral guidance, they will experience resurrection power for reconciled, new life together.

Paul is also writing to introduce himself and to encourage their financial support for his planned mission to Spain and delivery of funds for the poor Christ-followers in Jerusalem (Romans 15:24–28). He must persuade them that he is trustworthy. The conflicted situation in Rome opens the door for him to explain the good news of how God reigns through Christ in the embodied actions of those who live "under grace" rather than "under Torah" (6:14).

What Words Matter?

Romans introduces a few new words and phrases in Paul's vocabulary of formation, community building, and discernment. These include:

- the phrase *hypakoē pisteōs* ("obedience of faithfulness");[14]
- the phrase *logikēn latreian* ("reasoned worship") and its related verb *latreuō* ("to worship");[15] and
- the verb *egeirō* ("to raise").[16]

We will also revisit several of the Greek words introduced at earlier stops to see how Paul develops them for the Romans. We continue to build our own vocabularies and imagine how to reclaim these words, phrases, and practices for use in the church today!

Finally, this is another long chapter. Romans is the longest letter Paul wrote. It's also another situation where most of the letter advocates a process of formation, community building, and discernment focused on Christlike faithfulness, rather than Torah, as the community's exclusive moral guide.

Joining the Assembly in Rome

The assembly has gathered in a good-sized hall, joined by our pilgrims. Everyone has taken their seats or reclined at tables. It doesn't look like they're planning to eat the common meal we've seen in the communities founded by Paul. Apparently, they are no longer sharing a meal together because of their disagreements about the role of Torah's dietary laws. Hopefully, Paul's letter will help.

An elegantly-dressed woman enters the hall. A Roman leader introduces her as Phoebe, a deacon in the *ekklēsia* at Cenchreae, one of Corinth's two ports. She has come from Paul, who is currently working in Corinth. Phoebe has been involved in the production of this letter and hints that we will hear more about her later.

Phoebe tells the group that Paul wishes he could be present in person. He looks forward to visiting Rome in the future when the opportunity arises. For now, he has written this letter to introduce himself and his gospel.

She explains that Paul employs letter-writing to stay in touch with all the *ekklēsiai* (plural) in Christ Jesus he started and serves.

Paul Sets the Apocalyptic Framework for His Gospel (1:1–4:25)

Paul Introduces Himself and His Gospel (1:1–6)

Phoebe starts to read. As is his custom, Paul introduces himself and his gospel. He identifies several major themes associated with formation, community building, and discernment he will develop throughout the letter.

> **Romans 1:1** Paul, a slave [*doulos*] of Jesus Christ, called to be an apostle, set apart for the gospel of God, **2** which God promised beforehand through his prophets in the Holy Scriptures, **3** the gospel [*euanggelion*] concerning God's Son, who was descended from David according to the flesh **4** and was designated Son of God in power according to the Spirit of holiness [*hagiasmos*] by resurrection from the dead, Jesus Christ our Lord, **5** through whom we have received grace [*charis*] and apostleship to bring about the obedience of faithfulness [*hypakoē pisteōs*] among all the Gentiles for the sake of his name, **6** including yourselves who are called to belong to Jesus Christ.

Paul introduces himself as "a slave [*doulos*] of Jesus Christ" (1:1; see also Philippians 1:1). Paul participates by analogy in the story of Jesus Christ. He puts himself in obedient service to God by enslaving himself to Jesus Christ as Lord. In Romans, Paul uses various forms of the *doulos* word-group nineteen times, and a whopping twelve times just in Romans 6–7![17] In chapters six and seven, Paul presents his apocalyptic distinction between being enslaved to worldly, destructive powers (Sin, impurity, lawlessness, and the "law of Sin"), and being enslaved to heavenly, life-giving powers (God, justice/righteousness,[18] and the "law of God").

In Romans I refer to "Sin" with a capital "S" and "sins" with a small "s." Sin (capital "S") is Paul's apocalyptic personification of a spiritual power of evil that opposes God's will for the flourishing of the world. Sin influences humans to act in ways contrary to God's will ("sins") that destroy the life promised by God. These distinctions will be important later in the letter.

Some people are understandably hesitant to use the word "slave," given the historical experience of slavery in America and the Western world. We addressed that issue when we stopped in Philippi. I have chosen cautiously to translate *doulos* as slave here because its theological and metaphorical significance is important for Paul. Using the imagery of slavery, Paul makes an important spiritual point that humans are slaves to the one they obey (Romans 6:16). In Paul's apocalyptic perspective, a person must consistently make a choice. They either choose to stay enslaved to Sin, with its "wages" of "death" for Sin-led actions (6:23), or they choose to be enslaved to God for "holiness" and Christlike actions that lead to "eternal life in Christ Jesus our Lord" (6:22–23).

Paul introduces his gospel (*euanggelion*) concerning God's Son, promised through Israel's prophets in the Scriptures. This is their expected Messiah, who, in his earthly life, would be descended from King David. Paul knows Jesus is the Messiah because God designated him as Son by raising him from the dead in power. According to the Spirit of holiness (*hagiasmos*), Jesus was raised and set apart exclusively to serve God as Lord of earthly life. In Corinth, Paul said that Jesus Christ became holiness (*hagiasmos*) for us from God (1 Corinthians 1:30). By virtue of his resurrection and designation as Son and Lord, his pattern of faithfulness became the exclusive guiding norm for human actions.

It is *through* Jesus Christ as exclusive Lord that Paul received "grace [*charis*] and apostleship" (Romans 1:5). God's life-giving power of grace plays a key role in Paul's vision for formation, community building, and discernment in Christ Jesus.

Paul's distinctive call to apostleship had a specific purpose: to bring about the "obedience of faithfulness [*hypakoē pisteōs*] among all the Gentiles for the sake of his name" (1:5). This includes the Gentile Christ-followers in Rome (1:6). This "obedience of faithfulness" includes much more than simply initiating the conversions of Gentiles. It speaks of Christ's way of life Paul teaches to those who entrust themselves to the power of God at work in and through Jesus Christ.[19] Paul does this for the sake of the name of Jesus Christ—his character and nature reflected in his pattern of faithfulness and obedience to God. His is the "name that is above every name," given to him by God when he was raised from the dead (Philippians 2:9–11). Paul's entire ministry is focused on bringing about the obedience of Christlike faithfulness among all the Gentiles.

Paul Addresses the Romans in a Unique Manner (1:7–9)

Paul writes "to all God's beloved in Rome, called to be holy ones [*hagiois*]" (1:7). As we know, *hagiois* (plural) signifies a community of individuals set apart from the surrounding culture to serve the living God. Individually and collectively, "holy ones" publicly embody and bear witness to God's life-giving reign and healing presence in their lives.[20] By addressing the Romans as "holy ones," Paul acknowledges that they, too, have set themselves apart exclusively to serve God. They do this, however, through their observance of Torah as interpreted by the Messiah Jesus.

Paul's address to the Romans is unique among all his letters. When writing to congregations he founded, Paul always addresses them as the *ekklēsia* (deliberative assembly) in a particular location and/or as a community that is "in Christ Jesus."[21] The absence of the word *ekklēsia* or the phrase "in Christ Jesus" in 1:7 provides an important clue to Paul's view of the Christ-communities in Rome and how their structure contributes to their conflict.

In Romans, Paul uses the word *ekklēsia* five times, but not until Romans 16, near the end of the letter. There, he asks the Romans to greet for him several of his coworkers in the gospel formerly associated with congregations he founded. These are congregations structured according to Paul's "ways in Christ Jesus" he teaches in every *ekklēsia* (see 1 Corinthians 4:17).

First, in 16:1–2, he commends Phoebe to the Romans. She is a deacon in the *ekklēsia* in Cenchreae. She has been a patron to many Christ-followers and provides support for Paul's ministry in Corinth. Next, Paul greets the married couple, Prisca and Aquila. These two Jewish Christ-followers have now returned to Rome from their exile during the edict of Claudius. Paul describes them as "fellow workers with me *in Christ Jesus*, who risked their necks for me" (16:3–4). Paul tells the Romans that he and "all the *ekklēsiai* [plural] of the Gentiles" give thanks for their daring work on Paul's behalf (16:4). Paul also asks the Romans to greet the *ekklēsia* that now meets in their house in Rome.

Prisca and Aquila served with Paul for several years, first in Corinth and later in Ephesus.[22] They probably learned from Paul his structure for a Gentile *ekklēsia* in Christ Jesus that involves a meal followed by the practice of discernment. They are now back in Rome and have gathered a group to meet in their home for worship the way they learned it from Paul. Apparently, only Prisca and Aquila convene a group of Christ-followers in Rome who gather in a way that qualifies for Paul as worthy of the name/term *ekklēsia* in Christ Jesus.

Paul's use of *ekklēsia* only in Romans 16 demonstrates that, other than the *ekklēsia* meeting in the home of Prisca and Aquila, the Christ-followers in Rome do not structure their worship as an *ekklēsia in Christ Jesus*. As a Torah-observant community, they do not gather as a deliberative assembly that practices the discernment of *Christlike* faithfulness. The conflict in Rome presents Paul with an opportunity to explain some of his crucial "ways in Christ Jesus." Paul seems convinced that the conflicted groups in Rome could be reconciled if they replaced their exclusive commitment to Torah-observance with a structure focused on discerning Christlike faithfulness as it is practiced in Paul's other communities.

Paul expands his personal introduction in 1:9. Knowing he is writing to Torah-observant Jewish and Gentile Christ-followers, he uses Jewish cultic language that is also unique in his letters. He describes himself as one who worships (*latreuō*) God "with my spirit in the gospel of God's Son" (1:9). He speaks of worship as his individual action in serving the gospel. As we've seen, worship in the first-century Christ-movement was very different from what we call worship today. Paul will also use Jewish cultic language at key spots throughout the letter.[23]

Paul Introduces Charisma—Crucial for His Gospel of New Life in Christ (1:11–15)

Paul hopes to visit Rome, so they might be mutually encouraged by one another's faithfulness (1:12). For his part, Paul desires to share with the Romans "some spiritual *charisma*" to "strengthen" them (1:11). Paul introduces them to the word *charisma*, which will play an important role in Romans 5 and 12. We often think of *charisma* as a special sort of magnetism that draws us to someone. *Charisma* is hard to put our finger on, but it's what causes us to take notice or pay attention to someone.

Paul uses *charisma* in 1:11 and throughout his letters, however, with more theological grounding. Rooted in *charis*, *charisma* is the embodiment of God's life-giving power of grace (*charis*) given to each Christ-follower. This life-giving power is activated and transmitted through acts of Christlike self-giving to benefit others.[24] Christ-followers do not possess grace, even though a *charisma* is often characterized as a "spiritual gift." They receive gifts of God's life-giving power of grace *in stewardship for others* as part of Paul's vision for formation and building up the Body of Christ.[25]

Paul hopes to "strengthen" the Romans by sharing some embodiment of grace (*charisma*) in an act of self-giving to them. He uses the verb "strengthen" in the passive voice, indicating that it will be God who strengthens them through Paul's embodiment of grace (*charisma*) and act of self-giving. Just as he does in every congregation, Paul desires to give the Romans their *own experience* of God's resurrection power transmitted through Paul's embodied *charisma* and act of Christlike self-giving to them. He hopes that if they experience this life-giving power of grace, they will turn to his gospel and become a community "under grace" rather than "under Torah" (see 6:14). In this way, he might "reap some fruit" among the Romans, just as has done "among the rest of the Gentiles" (1:13).

Paul also tells the Romans in 1:15 that he is eager to gospel (*euanggelizomai*) them. As we first saw in our stop on the road to Damascus and at other stops, Paul employs the Greek verb *euanggelizomai* to highlight how he heralds the good news of God's powerful reign through his words and embodied acts of Christlike ministry. His embodiment of Jesus Christ demonstrates Isaiah's proclamation that "your God reigns" in power in Paul's new life in Christ.

Paul uses *euanggelizomai* in this same way in Romans 1:15. He hopes through his anticipated face-to-face time with them to create gospel-events of God's saving power. He is confident that, through his embodiment of Christlike faithfulness, they will experience persuasive moments of God's powerful and life-giving reign on earth. Paul seeks to gospel Christ so the Romans can see for themselves that Christ is living in Paul and comprehend how God reigns through Christ in the world.[26] Paul's goal is for the Romans to entrust themselves to the power of God at work through Christ's pattern of faithfulness—his love embodied in acts of self-giving for others.

Paul Introduces His Apocalyptic Gospel
of God's Saving Power (1:16–17)

Having just told the Romans he is eager to gospel them, Paul offers a succinct description of his apocalyptic gospel of God:

> **Romans 1:16** I am not ashamed of the gospel; it is the power of God for salvation to everyone trusting [*pisteuō*], to the Jew first and also to the Greek. **17** For in it [the gospel] the justice/righteousness [*dikaiosynē*] of God is being revealed from faithfulness [*pistis*] for faithfulness [*pistis*]; as it is written, "The one who is just/righteous [*dikaios*] will live from faithfulness [*pistis*]."

Paul boldly claims he is not ashamed of this gospel, even though a crucified Messiah does not meet Jewish messianic expectations.[27] Paul has confidence in this gospel because he has experienced gospel-events, starting with his own experience of the revelation of the risen Christ in himself.[28] Paul knows from firsthand experience that the gospel is the power of God for salvation to everyone, whether Jewish or Gentile, who entrusts themselves to the resurrection power of God at work through the faithfulness of Jesus Christ.

This gospel is not a verbal or spoken message *about* God's power, nor is it information *about* Jesus. The gospel is God's powerful reign for new life and peace on earth. It is, as Katherine Grieb says, "the event of God's power that has brought about salvation,"[29] inaugurated in the death and resurrection of Jesus Christ. This power Paul attributes to the gospel "is deeper and more pervasive than any words exchanged between humans."[30]

Paul's gospel is about experiences of God's creative and life-giving power, a power so great that it created the world, raised Jesus from the dead, and continues to effectuate experiences of salvation in human relationships.[31] This gospel of divine power can be seen and experienced as salvation for humanity and the entire creation. Paul puts it this way in First Corinthians: "the kingdom of God does not emerge by talk, but by power."[32]

In Philippi we discussed Paul's understanding of salvation. Throughout the first-century culture, salvation characterized this-worldly experiences of peace, prosperity, guidance, and protection provided by the emperor, the forces of the empire, and the pantheon of Roman gods they worshiped.[33] Salvation was a distinctively present and earthly experience.

The same is true for Paul. Salvation is experienced collectively in earthly life. It is a social rather than individual experience. But for Paul, the source of salvation is God, not the emperor or those who support him. Salvation is for everyone who entrusts themselves to God and God's promise of resurrection power through the risen Jesus Christ for both Jewish and Gentile Christ-followers.[34] The Jewish people were first to hear the post-resurrection proclamation of the gospel, probably because God was faithful to their preexisting relationship.[35] But now, in the death and resurrection of Jesus, Gentiles also have access to this divine power for salvation by entrusting themselves to God and God's promises of new life through Jesus Christ.

Paul continues explaining his crisp thesis statement in 1:17. God's justice/righteousness (*dikaiosynē*) is being revealed from acts of faithfulness to inspire responsive acts of faithfulness. As we saw and discussed on the road to Damascus, Christ's resurrection from the dead began a new history of God's power and kingdom breaking into earthly existence in a never-ending series of gospel-events.[36] In these gospel-events of God's power, God's justice/righteousness continues to be revealed.

As previously noted, the Greek word *dikaiosynē* is polyvalent. It reflects two sides of one coin.[37] The "righteousness of God" is God's will to "do justice" on earth by "intervening in human affairs to establish right relationships where they do not yet exist."[38] This is precisely how Paul interprets the gospel-event of Christ's resurrection from the dead in Romans. Paul regularly refers to God as faithful.[39] The faithful God intervened to demonstrate God's justice/righteousness by raising the faithful and obedient Jesus from the dead. The one God of Jews and Gentiles put all people back into right relationship with God and with one another through the faithfulness of Jesus Christ.[40]

The ongoing revelation of God's justice/righteousness in gospel-events involves three parties: God, Jesus Christ, and Christ-followers. Just as Jesus entrusted himself to the faithfulness of God, Paul and Christ-followers entrust themselves to the pattern of Christ's faithfulness and the power of God that raised him from the dead. This revelation of God's justice/righteousness continues in gospel-events taking place from faithfulness for faithfulness.

By now we have seen examples of how the power of the gospel spreads. The faithfulness of Jesus Christ became the pattern of faithfulness Paul embodies in his own life.[41] Paul's Christ-patterned faithfulness becomes the channel of grace for conversion by the Corinthians, Thessalonians, and Philippians. The faithfulness of the Thessalonians, in turn, became a conduit for faithfulness in Macedonia and Achaia.[42]

As a scriptural warrant for Paul's understanding that gospel-events continue "from faithfulness for faithfulness," he quotes Habakkuk 2:4. Paul probably intends to communicate several things with this quotation.[43] The person who is "just/righteous" (*dikaios*) will live "from faithfulness." Paul builds his case on this association, later concluding that no human is "just/righteous" (3:10), that God is "just/righteous" (3:26), and that, through the one obedient and righteous act of Jesus Christ, many people are rendered as "just/righteous" (5:19).

I picture this progression from faithfulness for faithfulness in my own mind based on a childhood experience. I loved to set up a long line of dominoes and then tip over the first one in the line. It was thrilling to watch as one domino tipped over the next one and started an energizing and unstoppable sequence. This illustrates metaphorically what Paul means by the phrase "from faithfulness for faithfulness."

There is a long and complex conversation in Pauline scholarship involving the uses and meanings associated with the "righteousness of God" in his letters and in the Scriptures of Israel. These discussions include various Greek words rooted in *dik-*, such as *dikaiosynē*, *dikaios*, and *dikaioō*,[44] translated as "justice," "righteousness," "justification," "justified," "just," etc. In Romans, Paul uses examples from this *dik-* word group over sixty times. Some interpreters also read Romans as suggesting that God may be "on trial." The "justice" of God may be in question, especially among the Jewish Christ-followers, who are now seeing that Gentiles are freely accepted into the people of God without conversion to Judaism or commitment to live exclusively by the Torah. These interpreters all raise and discuss important theological questions and issues. Because we are focused on Paul's vision for formation, community building, and discernment in this letter, and how we might reclaim that vision for today, however, we don't have the time or space to engage all of these important issues.

God Shows No Partiality—All Humanity Has Sinned (1:18–3:20)

In 1:18–3:20 Paul takes a two-pronged approach to interpret and characterize the issue of universal human transgression through his apocalyptic lens.[45] He explores the apocalyptic power of Sin that enslaves all human beings—Jewish and non-Jewish people alike. "Both Jews and Greeks are 'under Sin'" (3:9).

In 1:18–32 Paul specifically addresses Gentile Christ-followers and the larger issue of Gentile sinfulness. Sin's power is evidently at work in the idolatry and licentiousness among Gentiles who do not know God's Torah.[46] Paul describes the Gentiles as futile in their moral reasonings and uncomprehending hearts (1:21). They venerated and worshiped (*latreuō*)[47] the creature rather than the creator (1:25). All Gentiles who have sinned apart from the Torah will perish apart from the Torah (2:12).

In 2:1–24 Paul challenges hypocrites in the communities of Jewish people and Jewish Christ-followers. They judge Gentiles for their disobedient actions, while also transgressing the Torah themselves (2:17–24). All who have sinned under the Torah will be judged by the Torah (2:12).

Paul tells both groups that God will repay every person according to their actions—Jew and Gentile alike (2:6). To those who are selfishly contentious, obedient to unrighteousness, and do evil, there will be anguish and distress—to the Jew first and also to the Gentile (2:8–9). For those who are doing good, however, God will give glory, honor, and peace (2:10), and eternal life (2:7)—to the Jew first and to the Gentile. For God shows no partiality (2:11).

God Restores Right Relationships Through the Faithfulness of Jesus Christ (3:21–26)

Romans 3:21–26 serves as the climax of Paul's presentation about how all Jewish and Gentile people fall short of God's expectations for humanity. In 3:21–22, Paul reprises part of his thematic statement from 1:16: apart from Torah, God's justice/righteousness has been manifested through the faithfulness of Jesus Christ for all who are trusting. Through God's Son, raised from the dead, sinful humanity has been delivered from the power of Sin and put back into right relationship with God (3:22–24).

More specifically, Paul continues to level the playing field between the two groups of Jewish Christ-followers and Gentile Christ-followers in the Roman assemblies. He wants to make sure that neither group can claim to be superior in God's sight. He picks up this thread again when he suggests particular actions in response to the situation in Romans 14:1–15:13.

Paul filters three Jewish cultic metaphors through his apocalyptic lens to interpret the unexpected death and resurrection of Jesus, the Jewish Messiah. Paul dares to say in 3:21–26 that what the Roman world called a justified execution, God received as an acceptable sacrifice of atonement—a Yom Kippur sacrifice for Gentiles—because it was the obedient faithfulness of God's anointed one that brought him to his death. What Rome intended as punishment, God chose to receive as a sacrifice of atonement.[48] The proof is God's raising of Christ and the ongoing power of his life in Paul's communities.

God accepted Christ's unjust crucifixion as a sacrifice to atone once for all human sinfulness and to set humanity back in right relationship with God. Having been liberated from Sin and set back in right relationship with God, humans must now join themselves to this revelation of God's justice by aligning their faithfulness with the faithfulness of Jesus Christ.[49]

The grace at work in 3:21–26 is that God's gift of new life extends beyond Christ's resurrection for the restoration of a right relationship with God for all people. All those who *receive* this grace put their trust in the power of God at work for new life through the pattern of the faithfulness of Jesus Christ.

Abraham Models Faithfulness Because He Entrusted Himself to God (4:1–25)

As he does in Galatians, Paul uses the story of Abraham from the Jewish Scriptures to support his argument that justice/righteousness depends on faithfulness, not on Torah. He presents Abraham as a model of faithfulness for both Jews and Gentiles. Abraham trusted God's promise of descendants to him and Sarah, who were both "as good as dead" in their advanced age (4:19). Abraham was fully convinced that God was able to do what God promised (4:21). His trust was reckoned to him as righteousness/justice (4:5, 9). This all took place before God gave the Torah and before Abraham was circumcised as the seal of his relationship with God (4:10–11).

This sequence of events makes Abraham the ancestor of everyone who trusts the power of God without regard to their Jewish or Gentile status. God's promise of life to all of Abraham's descendants depends on faithfulness and is grounded in God's grace (4:16). By specifying that Abraham trusted the God who gives life to the dead and calls into existence things that do not otherwise exist (4:17), Paul even connects the *content* of Abraham's faithfulness to those whose trust is now grounded in the God who raised the Lord Jesus from the dead (4:24).[50]

God's grace has been given to all of Abraham's descendants without regard to the ethnic, cultural, or moral worth of the recipients. God gives this gift of grace on the same basis to Jew and Gentile alike. Paul came to understand this through experiences in his own life and what he saw taking place in his Gentile mission.[51]

Formation Under Grace in Paul's Apocalyptic Gospel (5:1–8:39)

Paul is not writing to the Romans to convert them. They were first converted by Jewish Christ-followers and were turned over to a type of teaching that presented the gospel in Jewish categories and was Torah-observant (see Romans 6:17).[52] In Romans 1–4 Paul connected with them by summarizing the gospel in the Jewish terminology, symbolism, and cultic language they shared.

Now, in Romans 5–8, Paul sets out the essential components of formation according to his own apocalyptic gospel. He lays the foundation for new life "in Christ Jesus" (6:11, 23; 8:1, 2, 39)—that physical space where Jewish and Gentile Christ-followers gather to share a meal and deliberate in discernment focused on the person of Jesus Christ. In this way, Paul anticipates the Spirit-led practice of discernment that drives Romans 12–15, with its hope of Christlike actions through which God might work to reconcile the Roman divisions.

At this point in the letter, though, Paul is not so concerned with the specific norms, practices, or actions he suggests in Romans 12–15. He is focused here on the "ethic-structuring orientations, allegiances, and dispositions"[53] we characterize today as Christian formation.

God's Gift of Grace and the Gift in Grace of Jesus Christ Abound for New Life (5:1–21)

Phoebe continues to read Paul's letter. We hear a complex theological argument unfold in Romans 5. At the heart of Paul's argument is the love (*agapē*) of God and of Jesus Christ embodied *for* others—for the benefit of humanity and the world.[54] In God's time, while humanity was still weak, Christ died *for* the ungodly (5:6). God shows God's own love (*agapē*) *for* humanity in that, while humans were still sinners, Christ died *for* humanity (5:8). Moreover, as a gift of God's grace (*charis*) *for* humanity, God accepted Christ's unjust death as an atoning sacrifice *for* all humanity (3:21–26). Then, God once again acted *for* humanity by pouring God's divine love (*agapē*) into the hearts of Christ-followers through the Holy Spirit (5:5).

This interpretation of divine love *for* the world reflects what Paul said at our stop on the road to Damascus. Based on his experience of the risen Christ, Paul died to the Torah so that he might live to God. "I am no longer living, but Christ is living in me. The life I now live in the flesh, I live by the faithfulness of the Son of God, who loved me, indeed, who gave himself *for me*" (Galatians 2:19–20).

Divine love is embodied in acts of self-giving for others. This is Paul's foundation for the moral life in Jesus Christ. Since humanity is now reconciled to God by Christ's death (3:21–26), humanity is also positioned to be saved in/by Christ's life (5:10).[55] Paul explains how this salvation happens through the life-giving power of God's grace (*charis*). Grace works in and through Jesus Christ (5:12–21), who is God's "gift in grace" to the world (5:15).

In 5:15–16 Paul returns to the Greek word *charisma* introduced in 1:11. He incorporates it into an apocalyptic, typological interpretation. He compares the effects of Adam's one act of disobedient transgression with Christ's one act of obedient righteousness.

Adam's one act of disobedience was eating from the tree of the knowledge of good and evil. This act opened the door for Sin and death to enter the world. His one act of disobedience brought the divine judgment of condemnation on everyone (5:16, 18).

Jesus Christ's one obedient act was his embodiment of grace (*charisma*) in an act of self-giving for others. By raising Jesus from the dead, God judged Christ's one obedient act to be "just/righteous." Christ's one obedient act opened the door for God's just decree of life (*dikaiōma*)[56] for everyone (5:15–16). Through Christ's one act of obedience, the many will be rendered "just/righteous" (*dikaios*; 5:19). Just as Sin reigned in death, so grace will reign for eternal life through the Lord Jesus Christ (5:21). Paul reaffirms this conclusion in Romans 6:23: "the wages of Sin is death, but the embodiment of God's gift of grace [*charisma*] is eternal life in Christ Jesus our Lord."

God's gift of grace and God's gift in grace of Jesus Christ are abounding for life among the many (see 5:15). How is this happening? According to the logic of Paul's argument, God has gifted the world with new life in two interconnected ways. First, God has given the world this divine gift of grace—God's life-giving power. Second, as God's gift in grace, Jesus Christ dispenses this life-giving power of grace to each member of his earthly body. Christ gives this grace without regard to the ethnic, cultural, or moral worthiness of the recipients (5:6–11).[57] Grace then abounds for eternal life through the many new embodiments of grace (*charismata*) in Christlike acts of self-giving by the members of Christ's earthly body.

This foundation for the moral life in Christ Jesus introduces what can be called Paul's "circle of grace."[58] Grace flows from God into the world in Jesus Christ. Then grace flows through Christ to his followers. They, in turn, become channels or conduits of that grace to others through their own embodiments of grace in acts of Christlike self-giving. Through these acts of Christ-patterned faithfulness, Christ-followers become links in the metaphorical "domino effect" I mentioned earlier. It's the way one act of Christlike faithfulness leads to new acts of faithfulness by those who receive God's gift of life-giving grace and channel it to others through their own acts of self-giving (see 1:16–17). Paul's "circle of grace" is finally completed each time someone who receives and benefits from an experience of life-giving grace offers thanksgiving (*eucharistia*) back to God. This circle of grace is repeated endlessly in human life. It is the way grace abounds and reigns for life eternal through Jesus Christ our Lord (5:21).

Paul also tells the Romans in 5:1–2 that they now live in a new location where they have access to God's grace through Jesus Christ.[59] This location is the inbreaking of God's new age in Christ Jesus, which includes the actual assembly of Christ-followers who gather in his name. This is the place where Christ-followers are led by the Spirit of the risen Christ, who shapes the direction of their earthly lives in the practice of discernment.

This new location "in Christ Jesus" is also essential to Paul's strategy for community building. Through embodiments of grace (*charisma*) in Christlike acts of self-giving, God builds up each local assembly into a distinctive Body of Christ. For this to happen, Paul's congregants must be formed as people who know how to discern and embody grace (*charisma*) in acts of Christlike self-giving in their daily lives. This formation starts with baptism into Christ, which Paul now addresses in Romans 6.

Baptism Into Christ Liberates a Person from Sin to Walk in Newness of Life (6:1–23)

Paul continues to set out his apocalyptic approach to formation in Romans 6. Baptism into Christ Jesus reorients the lives of Christ-followers. Baptism is not just a ritual of initiation, but a powerful participation in the death and resurrection of Jesus (6:3–4).[60] Baptism delivers Christ-followers out of the territory where Sin lords over people and leads them to death.[61] Baptism relocates them *into* the physical space of the Christ-assembly, where they "must imagine" themselves "dead to Sin and alive to God in Christ Jesus" (6:11). This is both the spiritual Body of Christ *and* the assembly of Christ-followers who gather and call on his name for guidance.[62] This assembly is the location where their new lives are "sourced, established, and upheld" by the risen Christ.[63] This assembly is the location of God's new age, where grace reigns for eternal life under the direction of the risen Lord Jesus Christ.

More specifically, Paul emphasizes that Christ-followers are baptized into Christ's death and buried with him (6:3–4). Their metaphorical death and burial symbolically align them with Christ, who literally died to Sin (6:10). In baptism they participate by analogy in Christ's crucifixion, which frees them from their slavery to Sin and reconstitutes their human nature (6:6–7). They become, like Christ, truly human.

The ritual of baptism in early Christ-communities probably involved an immersion into water that metaphorically reenacted being crucified with Jesus and buried with him.[64] Christ-followers probably disrobed before immersion to signify the death of their old self.[65] This physical act reinforces the symbolic nature of baptism into Christ's death.

Baptism into Christ's death also serves a life-giving purpose. Although Christ died to Sin, in the risen life he is now living, he lives to God (6:10). Christ-followers are baptized into his death so that, just as Christ was raised from the dead by God, they, too, "might walk in newness of life" (6:4). The very same resurrection power of God that raised Jesus from the dead empowers baptized Christ-followers to walk in Christlike ways in their new life in Christ Jesus. This new life can only be lived in "[p]ractice, action, and obedience."[66]

After emerging from the water in the ritual of baptism, Christ-followers were probably clothed with a white robe to signify their new identity in Christ. Recall our time beside the road to Damascus, where we heard Paul say, "I am no longer living, but Christ is living in me" (Galatians 2:20). Those who are baptized into Christ Jesus have clothed themselves with Christ (Galatians 3:27; Romans 13:14). Clothing themselves with the new white robe symbolized putting on the new pattern of life in Christ to which they committed in baptism.

Walking in newness of life is imaginative work. How to clothe oneself with the Lord Jesus Christ in concrete actions changes with every new situation and context. There are no binding rules or absolute prescriptions to follow for how to walk in Christlike ways. As we saw in Corinth, "all things are permissible," but discernment is required, because "not all things bind people together" and "not all things build up" (1 Corinthians 6:12; 10:23). This imaginative work requires moral deliberation and discernment among all those who gather in the name of Christ Jesus.

Paul reminds the Roman Christ-followers that this imaginative process is still apocalyptic warfare. Each moment of earthly life requires a choice. They are slaves of the one they obey, either of Sin, which leads to death, or God, which leads to righteousness and life (Romans 6:16). The language of slavery appears twelve times in Romans 6 to emphasize this point. So, they must imagine themselves dead to Sin, but living to God in Christ Jesus (6:11). Paul stimulates their moral imaginations for this process: "present yourselves to God as ones who have passed from death to life and present your members"—the parts of their physical bodies—"to God as weapons of righteousness" (6:13). By making this choice, Sin will not lord over them, since they are not "under Torah" but "under grace" (6:14).

Paul is not primarily directing this guidance to individuals but to the community assembled in Christ Jesus. The Romans must use their imaginations as they reason together in discernment, deliberating on ways to walk in newness of life. They deliberate together on how to serve God by offering their hands, arms, feet, and minds in daily life. Every part of their bodies becomes a weapon of righteousness in God's apocalyptic holy war against the spiritual forces opposing God's will for the world.

By encouraging the Romans to "present" themselves and the members of their bodies to God, Paul anticipates Romans 12:1–2. There, he introduces his crucial practice of communal discernment and offers specific suggestions for how the Romans might participate in God's cosmic holy war. He opens that section of the letter with an echo of 6:12–23, urging the Romans to "present your bodies as a sacrifice, living, holy, and well-pleasing to God, which is your reasoned worship" (12:1). Throughout Romans 12–15, he suggests concrete actions by which they might present their bodies in the service of God.

Paul ends this discussion on the implications of baptism with more encouragement. Now that they have been metaphorically freed from the power of Sin and "enslaved to God," Christ-followers have the fruit of holiness (*hagiasmos*). Recalling that Jesus Christ became holiness (*hagiasmos*) from God (1 Corinthians 1:30), the fruits of holiness are earthly experiences of resurrection power through Christlike actions. The end or goal of their Christ-patterned holiness is eternal life (6:22). For the wages of Sin is death, but the embodied grace of God [*charisma*] activated in self-giving for others, is eternal life in Christ Jesus our Lord (6:23).

Baptism Discharges Christ-Followers from Torah for New Life in Christ (7:1–25)

In 7:1–6 Paul turns to "those who know the Torah" (whether Jewish or Gentile Christ-followers). He describes the implications of their baptism into Christ Jesus. Drawing on an analogy from a legal principle in the culture, he concludes that their metaphorical death in baptism frees them from the Torah for new life in the Spirit. "Now we are discharged from the Torah, dead to that which held us captive, to enslave us in newness of Spirit and not to an obsolete written code" (7:6). Paul seeks to liberate all Christ-followers in the Roman communities from their exclusive commitment to Torah as their pattern of life, since Torah-observance is leading to division and conflict.

In the rest of Romans 7, Paul explains why their exclusive commitment to Torah should be relinquished. Whether his presentation is autobiographical or reflects the use of a rhetorical device with the fictive "I" does not matter for our purposes.⁶⁷ He acknowledges that the commandments of Torah are holy and good (7:12) and the Torah itself is holy (7:12), spiritual (7:14), and good (7:16). The Torah even promises life (7:10), an allusion to LXX Leviticus 18:5: "You will keep all my commandments and all my decrees and you will do these things; the ones doing these things will live in them."

The problem, says Paul, is that Sin seized an opportunity in the various members—the limbs—of a person's mortal physical body,⁶⁸ which had been sold into slavery under Sin (7:14). This enslavement under Sin causes a person to do the very things they do not want to do under the Torah. It is not the person doing these things, says Paul, but the power of Sin managing and directing (*oikeō*)⁶⁹ a person's actions (7:17–18). Paul describes this conflict (whether Paul or the fictive "I") clearly in 7:25: "on the one hand, I myself am enslaved to the Torah of God in my mind [*nous*], but on the other hand, with my flesh [his bodily limbs] I am enslaved to Sin." With a plaintive cry in 7:24, Paul asks the question every listener and reader is asking by now: "[w]ho will rescue me from this body of death?" He then provides the answer: "[t]hanks [*charis*] be to God through Jesus Christ our Lord!" (7:25)

It is the Lord Jesus Christ who rescues people from their enslavement to Sin. Paul expresses a similar understanding in 1 Thessalonians 1:10 (Christ delivers his followers from the coming wrath) and Galatians 1:4 (Christ delivers his followers out of the present evil age). The inner conflict Paul decries here in Romans 7 is resolved in the new life of freedom from Sin and enslavement to God in the Body of Christ. Paul further illuminates this divine rescue in Romans 8:1–17.

The "Law of the Spirit of Life" Guides Moral Reflection "In Christ Jesus" (8:1–39)

In Romans 8 Paul gives a more complete introduction to the Spirit, who is vital to and inseparable from the gospel he proclaims.⁷⁰ Since the Gentile Christ-followers in Paul's audience were converted by Jewish Christ-followers, it is quite possible they do not know the critical connection between the Spirit and the gospel of Christ's death and resurrection.⁷¹

Thus, in Romans 8, Paul more fully illuminates the role of the Spirit, poured into hearts of Christ-followers (Romans 5:5), that made his work for God on behalf of Gentiles so distinctive.[72]

Paul uses vivid apocalyptic imagery to address the conflict between the law of God and the law of Sin with which he wrestled in Romans 7. He builds on his earlier descriptions of the new territory where Christ-followers gain access to God's grace (5:1–2) and where their baptized bodies that were once under the wrongful rule of Sin are now reclaimed by God (Romans 6).[73] Paul contrasts the realms of Christ/Spirit and Adam/Flesh that symbolize two different sovereignties that govern a Christ-follower's life. He identifies Spirit and Flesh as "two opposing spheres of action" where "one's thoughts and actions" are shaped by their allegiance to one or the other of these two warring apocalyptic powers.[74]

The role of this apocalyptic *spatial* language must not be missed. Paul is highlighting a key apocalyptic distinction. On the one hand is the physical location where Christ-followers gather "in Christ Jesus," God's new age governed by the Spirit of the risen Lord. On the other hand is the rest of the physical world—the present age—governed by the power of Sin at work corrupting human flesh.

In the opening verses of this crucial section of the letter, Paul makes one of the most important contributions to moral reflection contained in the Scriptures:

> **Romans 8:1** Therefore, there is now no condemnation for those who are in Christ Jesus. **2** For the law of the Spirit of life in Christ Jesus has freed you from the Torah of Sin and of death. **3** For what the Torah was powerless to do, weakened through the human flesh, God has done by sending his own Son in the likeness of sinful flesh, and concerning Sin, condemned Sin in the flesh, **4** so that the just decree of the Torah might be fulfilled among us, who walk not according to the Flesh but according to the Spirit.

Paul opens this passage on moral reflection by telling the Romans that for those "in Christ Jesus" there is freedom from "condemnation." In God's new age in Christ Jesus, God has created a place where the divine judgment that brought condemnation into the world through Adam's one disobedient act (5:16, 18) no longer applies.

With this declaration of "no condemnation," Paul makes a profound moral statement. God's new age is the new place of freedom for discerning Christlike actions. The process does not start with a consideration of what is good and what is evil. Those who are "in Christ Jesus" are now free to deliberate and discern together regarding whether a wide range of possible actions align with the "the law of the Spirit of life" (8:2). These are actions analogous to the pattern of the faithfulness of Jesus Christ—love embodied in acts of self-giving for others. These are actions that demonstrate "faithfulness working through love" (Galatians 5:6). They are embodiments of grace (*charismata*) in Christlike acts self-giving for others. They are actions that please God and bear fruit in the community.

For those in Christ Jesus, there is still "no condemnation," even when particular actions fail to meet God's approval and do not bear fruit. This is because Christ died once, for all (6:10). Christ-followers simply return to the gathered assembly to discern new actions in the same or similar contexts that may yet meet with God's approval and bear fruit. As we saw when we visited the assembly "in Christ Jesus" in Corinth, the risen Lord was present in the gathered community and judged at least one action as displeasing to God. In that case, the Lord disciplined them so they could correct their misguided and destructive actions to avoid condemnation on the day of final judgment (1 Corinthians 11:32).

Freedom from condemnation is the key to moral discernment and action in Paul's congregations (see also Galatians 5:1, 13). This freedom undergirds the structure for the discernment of new life "in Christ Jesus" that Paul is commending to the Romans. As long as they stay focused on discerning Christlike actions, experiences of resurrection power, or experiences of stumbling and judgment, there is no fear of condemnation. There is true freedom for moral discernment and action in Christ Jesus!

As Paul said earlier, the Torah promised life (Romans 7:10). But weakened by Sin at work in the members of each human body, Torah was powerless (8:3) to deliver on its promise of life. God stepped into this power vacuum and sent God's Son into the world in the form of earthly human flesh to condemn Sin in the flesh (8:3; see also Philippians 2:7).

In this action of sending Christ into the world, God revealed a new pattern of living by which God's people could fulfill Torah's just decree for life (Romans 8:4). By raising Jesus to eternal life through resurrection power, God affirmed Christ's faithfulness—his embodiment of grace (*charisma*) in self-giving for others—as the exclusive pattern of living for Christ-followers in the new age.

God has also empowered Christ-followers to live in this new Christlike way. By pouring God's love into their hearts through the Holy Spirit of God's Son (5:5; 8:9; cf. 1:4), God has given them freedom and insight into Christ's pattern of faithfulness that leads to Christlike actions. God's desire for flourishing human life is now being fulfilled among Christ's followers—"the ones walking not according to the Flesh, but walking according to the Spirit" (8:4; see also Galatians 5:16, 25). "In other words, as a result of God's condemning sin in the flesh, sin the resident preventer is replaced by the Spirit, the new resident enabler."[75]

What does moral reflection and discernment in the Spirit require for those gathered "in Christ Jesus?" Paul addresses this in 8:5–17. He contrasts the structure of those "walking by the Flesh" with the structure of those who walk by the Spirit. Those who live according to the Flesh have a mindset (*phronēma*) and pattern of reasoning (*phroneō*) hostile to God and focused on earthly values, norms, and customs (8:5–7). They are unable to submit to the law of God or please God (8:7–8). Actions resulting from this mindset lead to death.

In contrast, those who are baptized into Christ Jesus live according to the Spirit and have a mindset (*phronēma*) and pattern of reasoning (*phroneō*) focused on life and peace (8:5–6). According to 8:9, Christ-followers are "in the Spirit," since the Spirit "manages and directs your household [*oikeō*]."[76] Two verses later, in 8:11, Paul uses the same metaphor even more emphatically, saying "if the Spirit of the one who raised Jesus from the dead manages and directs your household [*oikeō*], the one raising Christ from the dead will also give life (*zōopoieō*)[77] to your mortal bodies, through the Spirit that dwells [*enoikeō*] in/among you." The Spirit's goal is twofold: (1) creating new life in the mortal bodies of each Christ-follower; and (2) managing and directing the assembly of Christ-followers to lead them to new life from God by showing them the connections between Christlike actions and experiences of resurrection power.

We can more fully appreciate the brilliance of Paul's metaphor using the verb *oikeō* because we understand the physical dimension of a Christ-community that gathers "in Christ Jesus." This community is very much the physical incarnation of the "household of God" (Ephesians 2:19). Christ-followers there are "members of the household [*oikeoi*] of the faithfulness" (Galatians 6:10). This physical household "in Christ Jesus" is the new territory, or realm, or sphere of action[78] where the Spirit of the risen Christ guides the community to walk in newness of life. It is where they work out their own salvation by connecting Christlike actions to experiences of God's resurrection power (see Philippians 2:12–13).

The Spirit guides them in their moral deliberations when they gather "in Christ Jesus":

> **Romans 8:14** For all who are led by the Spirit of God are sons of God. **15** For you did not receive a spirit of slavery to fall back into fear, but you have received the Spirit of adoption. When we cry, "Abba! Father!" **16** it is that very Spirit bearing witness with our spirit that we are sons of God, **17** and if sons, then heirs, heirs of God and joint heirs with Christ—if, in fact, we suffer with him so that we may also be glorified with him.

God created a relational religious experience of sonship by pouring the Holy Spirit—this Spirit of adoption (8:15)—into the hearts of Christ-followers (5:5).[79] The practice of discernment "in Christ Jesus" is the place where this Spirit of adoption leads Christ-followers. This Spirit "manages and directs" their household (8:9, 11) by guiding their deliberative conversations in discernment. As we saw in Corinth, revelations of the Spirit from God reveal to individuals and the assembly the "things graced to them by God" (1 Corinthians 2:12). These revelations occur during the process of moral discernment (1 Corinthians 14:30). In the midst of their discussions, Christ-followers are prompted by the Spirit toward actions that cultivate communal strength and prevent division. Paul will demonstrate this practice of "reasoned worship" in Romans 12:1 and give examples of suggested actions to the conflicted groups in 12:9–15:13.

Paul sets out a similar sequence in Galatians 5:16–26. Those who are "led by the Spirit" are not "under Torah" (Galatians 5:18). In Galatians, as in Romans, Paul contrasts life in the Spirit with life under Torah. These are two distinctive and exclusive patterns of life that stand in opposition to one another (Galatians 5:17).

I translate this passage at Romans 8:14–17 as Paul wrote it, addressing the Gentile Christ-followers as adopted "sons of God." This is another rare case where using inclusive language ("children of God" in the NRSV) potentially masks Paul's two important points.

First, Paul is drawing on the cultural custom in antiquity regarding the responsibility of a "son" to continue with the business of the father. Christ-followers, whether female or male (see Galatians 3:28), continue their Father's business by participating actively in God's mission of reconciling the world to God and all humans to one another. Paul will address this major theme directly by suggesting specific actions to the conflicted Jewish and Gentile Christ-followers in Romans 14:1–15:13.

Second, Christ-followers have received the Spirit of adoption—the Spirit of Jesus Christ—so that Christ the Son comes alive in them and they share aspects of his life as "sons of God." This "Spirit of adoption" inspires Christ-followers to cry, "Abba, Father!" (8:15) As sons they commit to carry out God's divine mission of reconciliation (see also 2 Corinthians 5:16–21). Thus, concludes Paul in Romans 8:9, "anyone who has the Spirit of Christ belongs to him."

Paul employs a similar line of reasoning in his letter to the Galatians. The Galatians are all "sons of God through the faithfulness in Christ Jesus" (Galatians 3:26). They are "all one in Christ Jesus" (3:28) and belong to Christ (3:29). And because they are "sons," God sent the Spirit of God's Son into their hearts crying, "Abba, Father" (4:6). In Galatians, as in Romans, Paul is trying to reconcile conflicted groups of Christ-followers. In both Galatia and Rome, the Christ-followers must decide whether to live by an exclusive commitment to Torah or to use the Torah only in an advisory role as one set of resources when it comes to discerning Christlike actions.

Paul also describes the Spirit as the "first fruits" of future resurrection life for Christ-followers (Romans 8:23). This statement confirms again that Paul is primarily focused on formation, community building, and discernment. The Spirit that pours God's love (*agapē*) into the hearts of Christ-followers creates new life (*zōopoieō*) in their mortal bodies (8:11). This resurrection power of God for new life enables Christ-followers to walk in newness of life (6:4). This same Spirit leads them collectively in discernment to Christlike acts of self-giving for others and experiences of resurrection power for new life in the community (8:14–17). The experiences provide Christ-followers with hope that bridges the present and the future, when there will be complete redemption of their bodies and eternal, resurrection life (8:24–25).[80]

These experiences have also persuaded Paul that nothing can separate Christ-followers from the love (*agapē*) of Christ and the love (*agapē*) of God in the Lord Jesus Christ (8:35–39). Even in hardships, says Paul, "we are more than conquerors" through Christ, "the one who loved [*agapaō*] us" (8:37; see also Galatians 2:20). For Paul, the foundation of moral life "in Christ Jesus" is divine love (*agapē*) embodied and demonstrated in acts of self-giving for others.

The key, then, for embodying these acts of self-giving is discernment. Christ-followers must come together "in Christ Jesus" to reflect on their actions and experiences to discern future actions that are pleasing to God and bear fruit in the community. Paul explains this practice of discernment in Romans 12:1–15:13.

Discernment Under Grace in This Apocalyptic Gospel (12:1–15:13)

Paul shifts his focus from formation to discernment and community building in the letter's climactic section in 12:1–15:13. First, he describes his distinctive practice of discernment: the heartbeat of his apocalyptic gospel of formation and community building through the saving power of God. Paul explains how this practice guides congregations to new life. He amplifies the role of *charisma* for the moral life in Christ Jesus.

Then, Paul suggests specific Christlike actions and attitudes through which he anticipates God's resurrection power for new life will work to reconcile the conflicted Christ-followers in Rome. His discerning approach will be crucial for the Romans to determine through testing which actions are effective in reconciling the divided community. In these chapters we see clearly emerging the overall goal of Paul's apocalyptic gospel and ministry: the formation of discerning moral communities in Christ Jesus.

With a Renewed Mind, Christ-Followers Prove Through Testing God's Will (12:1–2)

In Romans 12:1–21, Paul describes the process for this crucial practice of discernment. He echoes the Jewish cultic metaphor of sacrifice from 3:21–26 and the cultic language from Romans 6. He explains how the community must evaluate the consequences of past actions for guiding the discernment of future acts. As we've seen in the Pauline congregations of Gentiles, the "proof through testing" (*dokimazō*) of God's will represents an essential aspect of moral deliberations in discernment. It is part of helping Christ-followers decide whether a contemplated action—a Christlike embodiment of grace (*charisma*) in an act of self-giving for others—will be well-pleasing to God (12:2) and bear fruit in the community. Paul opens this pivotal section of the letter by challenging both groups of Christ-followers:

> **Romans 12:1** Therefore, brothers and sisters, through the mercies of God, I urge you to present [*parastēmi*] your bodies as a sacrifice—living, holy, and well-pleasing to God—your reasoned acts of worship [*logikēn latreian*]. **2** Do not be conformed to this present age, but let yourselves be transformed [*metamorphoō*] by the renewing of the mind [*nous*], so that you may prove through testing [*dokimazō*] what is the will of God—what is good and well-pleasing and mature.

Because of the conflicts bedeviling the community, Paul strongly exhorts the Christ-followers to "present" their bodies to God as a living sacrifice.

He uses the same verb *parastēmi* as in Romans 6. Now, instead of presenting their bodily limbs, they are to present their individual bodies as a sacrifice that is living, holy, and well-pleasing to God (12:1).

By using metaphors drawn from the Jewish cultic setting in the temple,[81] Paul once again communicates his gospel to Torah-observant Christ-followers using the symbolic framework of Judaism. Unlike the obedient, sacrificial act of Jesus that led to his death, however, each Christ-follower must offer themselves as a "living" sacrifice. This softens the shocking cultic metaphor of a Jewish sacrifice, which would involve placing the bodies of each Christ-follower on the temple's altar.[82]

These individual acts that constitute "living" sacrifices continue regularly in daily life. The actions are discerned not under Torah but under grace. They are discerned under the lordship and direction of the risen Christ.[83]

As a "holy" sacrifice, their bodily actions reflect they are "living to God in Christ Jesus" (6:11). They are serving only God and God's mission of reconciliation in the world. These actions should also be "well-pleasing" (*euarestos*) to God. Paul always uses this adjective to describe actions that find favor with God.[84] He uses a similar verb (*areskō*) to designate human actions that are pleasing to God[85] or to other humans.[86] For Paul, the goal of all human action is to please God, so that the actions bear fruit for new life in the community.

Paul characterizes these sacrificial bodily offerings as "your reasoned acts of worship" (*logikēn latreia*). The noun *latreia* means "worship,"[87] understood as individual action. In antiquity, *logikēn* was consistently applied to human acts to signify that they were rational and aligned with the principles of reason.[88] The pronoun "your" is plural. So, in 12:1, Paul clearly indicates that these individual, sacrificial acts are the result of "reasoning well" in the whole community.[89] The actions constitute sacrificial offerings of individual bodies that are the result of rational moral deliberation during discernment in the Christ-community.[90]

Romans 12:1 highlights the dramatic difference between worship in the early church and worship today. For Paul, "bodily self-giving to God is an act of worship."[91] In that sense, Paul understands *every aspect* of a Christ-follower's embodied earthly life as a "sacrament"—an "outward and visible sign of inward and spiritual grace, given by Christ as sure and certain means by which we receive that grace."[92] Christ comes alive in every Christ-follower through their Christlike love, embodied in acts of self-giving for others. Paul anticipates that through these actions they, too, will say that "I am no longer living, but Christ is living in me."

Romans 12:2 clearly highlights the apocalyptic and communal nature of discerning these individual, sacrificial acts. Using the plural form of the subject and verb, Paul says they must collectively reorient their lives from "this present age" to "the will of God."[93] This requires a mindset (*phronēma*) and pattern of reasoning (*phroneō*) focused on the Spirit, life, and peace (8:5–6), rather than a mindset (*phronēma*) always looking to earthly norms, values, customs, and experiences for guidance (8:6). Discernment calls for the community to look back to identify specific actions that have led to life and peace. Because they still live a mortal human life, where Sin still seeks to influence their actions, they must support and encourage one another in their deliberations. The strength to resist the temptations of the power of Sin comes from their mutual acts of support in their common life together (see Philippians 2:1).

To reorient their focus, they must, together, "be transformed [*metamorphoō*] by the renewal of your mind." Paul uses the decisive verb *metamorphoō* that we examined in connection with 2 Corinthians 3:18. Both times Paul uses the verb to describe the process of transformation underway for Christ-followers who participate in the practice of discernment in God's new age.

While the subject and verb in 12:2 are in the plural form, the "mind" (*nous*) is singular. Paul emphasizes that only the one mind and one pattern of reasoning revealed in Jesus Christ guides all communal discernment. We heard Paul explain Christ's mindset and moral reasoning in Philippians 2:1–11. This renewed human mind of Christ replaces the undiscerning mind Paul challenged in Romans 1:28. As Christ-followers mature, their confidence and spiritual discernment deepen through shared deliberation, allowing them to embody Christ's mindset and moral framework.

As their powers of communal discernment grow, the Christ-community must "prove through testing [*dokimazō*] what is the will of God." The "will of God" characterizes actions that God desires for individuals and communities in specific situations and contexts.[94] As we have seen, Paul consistently uses the verb *dokimazō* in his letters to define the practice of "proof through testing" that is crucial for discernment (Philippians 1:10; 1 Thessalonians 2:4, 5:21; 1 Corinthians 3:13, 11:28; and Ephesians 5:10).

This practice of proof through testing is *not* about the community acquiring information from an established body of knowledge like the Torah or the Jesus tradition.[95] Instead, the practice involves what Victor Furnish calls "a process of inquiry, critical appraisal, and reasoning."[96] This is the work of the whole congregation—the *ekklēsia* in Christ Jesus—the deliberative assembly of Christ-followers in a local setting.

The specific goal of proof through testing is to distinguish which actions are well-pleasing to God and, therefore, good and mature. This requires Christ-followers to reflect on past actions and the consequences of those actions. They must determine whether specific actions were well-pleasing to God by recognizing how they bore discernible fruit in the community. The practice requires that they recognize experiences of resurrection power for new life and link them to specific actions. They are to hold fast to actions that bear fruit and abhor actions that do not (12:9; see also 1 Thessalonians 5:21–22).

For instance, the Gentile Christ-followers might reflect on their inclusion of non-kosher food at their common meal and how that is preventing Jewish Christ-followers from joining them in the Lord's Supper. They might easily determine that this practice is not pleasing to God since it is dividing the community. On the other hand, these same Gentile Christ-followers might offer a leadership position in their community to one of their recently returned brothers or sisters who is a Jewish Christ-follower. If the action pleases God, it may result in an experience of resurrection power that starts to bind the members of the community together again.

For Paul, there is no certainty involved with knowing the "will of God." There is no certainty achieved in advance of taking an action that it will be well-pleasing to God and bear fruit. That's why "proof through testing" is the *definitive* component of discernment in Paul's communities. In this practice, over time, Christ-followers become more confident in discerning God's will and more mature in Christ. Proof through testing in discernment is one of Paul's most important "ways in Christ Jesus" he teaches to all his congregations. The practice also leads, over time, to the formation of practical moral wisdom as we saw earlier in Philippians 1:9–11 and Colossians 1:9–10. The primary goal of Paul's ministry is to proclaim Christ, admonishing and teaching everyone in all wisdom, "so that we may present everyone mature in Christ" on the day of Christ's final return (Colossians 1:28).

Paul Offers Moral Advice to Influence Romans Walking Under Grace (12:9–13:10)

The community's transformed consciousness, through which they discern God's will, is the foundation for everything that follows in Romans 12:3 onward. Throughout this next section, Paul identifies specific actions and attitudes to guide the Romans' responses to their conflict. He does not offer these as rules that must be followed. They are only suggestions for possible actions.[97] His instructions in 12:1–2 strongly imply, however, that whatever actions they decide to take, they need to reflect on the consequences of the actions to prove through testing whether God's will has been done. These chapters reveal the clear goal of Paul's apocalyptic ministry: to form a discerning moral community that participates in God's new age in Christ Jesus.

In 12:3–8 Paul expands his discussion of *charisma* introduced in Romans 5. Paul now illustrates how Christ-followers might embody God's gift of grace (*charisma*) and activate that life-giving power in Christlike acts of self-giving that abound for life in the Christ-community:

> **Romans 12:3** For by the grace [*charis*] given to me, I say to everyone among you not to think of yourself more highly than you ought to think, but to reason [*phroneō*] with sober reasoning, each according to the specific portion of Christlike faithfulness [*pisteōs*] God has distributed. **4** For as in one body we have many members, and not all the members have the same practice, **5** so we, who are many, are one body in Christ, and individually we are members one of another. **6** We have embodiments of grace [*charismata*] that differ according to the grace given to us: prophecy, by analogy to the faithfulness; **7** ministry, in ministering; the teacher, in teaching;

8 the encourager, in encouragement; the giver, in generosity; the leader, in diligence; the merciful, in cheerfulness.

Paul's moral life in Christ Jesus is founded on his understanding that Jesus Christ, God's unique gift in grace (5:15), dispenses this life-giving grace to the members of his body.

Each member of the body receives gifts of grace. Each gift becomes an active power for new life when the recipient of grace embodies that grace (*charisma*) in an act of self-giving for others. The various *charismata* only exist because of the existence of the *one* overarching *charisma* from which all others derive: eternal life in Christ Jesus (6:23). All these other subordinate *charismata* represent human participation in the eternal life of Jesus Christ that becomes manifest in earthly reality through Christlike acts of self-giving to others.[98]

Thus, as Christ's "bodily limbs,"[99] individuals present their bodies to God as a living sacrifice—as "weapons of righteousness" (see 6:13)—who embody grace and activate that life-giving power in Christlike acts of self-giving to others. Each person, gifted by grace, contributes to the community through a unique act of self-giving (12:4). That unique act depends on the specific portion of Christ's faithfulness (*pisteōs*) distributed to that person by God (12:4). Awareness of these connections is the fruit of moral deliberations in the community's discernment.

In 12:6–8 Paul gives examples of different *charismata*—different embodiments of grace by different members of the community—that become channels of God's life-giving power to others through Christlike acts of self-giving. Among these are the Christlike acts of prophecy, ministry, teaching, encouragement, giving, leadership, and mercy. In every example described by Paul in Romans 12:6–8, those receiving the Christlike act of self-giving experience the life-giving power of grace, which the giver embodies and channels to them through their acts.

The Greek word *charismata* is often translated as "spiritual gifts." This translation is deficient because it implies that the "gifts" are given to and for the benefit of the individual. We often hear someone who has taken a spiritual-gifts inventory say things like, "I am gifted in teaching," or "I am gifted in pastoral ministry." As I have shown, however, *charismata* are rightly understood as embodiments of God's gift of grace given to individuals *in stewardship for others*. The gift of life-giving power (grace) is intended to bring new life to the community through an act of self-giving. It is not just a gift intended for the individual. Instead, the individual who receives the gift of grace activates and channels that life-giving power to others through actions that reflect, by analogy, the faithfulness of Jesus Christ (12:3–4).

This mirrors what Paul said to the Corinthians in 1 Corinthians 12:4–6. A gift of grace blossoms into the power for new life only when it is expressed through acts of Christlike self-giving to others. Some individuals might be frequent vehicles and channels of God's grace to others, but this does not mean they possess the gift or the power. This understanding of *charisma* ensures that no one thinks more highly of themselves than is necessary (12:3).

This understanding of *charismata* also illuminates our earlier discussion of Paul's circle of grace. Each member of Christ's body receives grace dispensed by the risen Lord (who is God's original gift in grace). Each gift of grace is useless and received in vain unless and until it is embodied in a Christlike act of self-giving to others. The gift of grace then becomes active power for new life. Hopefully, the act of self-giving will channel the life-giving power of grace to create new life among those who are served. The circle of grace is completed each time the recipients of that grace give thanks (*charis* or *eucharistō*) to God for their experience of new life through God's power.

We can now look more closely at 12:3 to see how the practice of proof through testing in discernment and the proper understanding of *charisma* play key roles in the way grace abounds for life in Christ Jesus (5:15). Paul uses an important phrase associated with the discernment of Christlike actions: "By the gift of grace given to me, I say to everyone among you not to think of yourself more highly than you ought to think, but to reason with sober reasoning, each according to the specific portion of Christlike faithfulness God has distributed."

In this case, Paul has received a gift of grace for communicating practical wisdom. But that power for new life does not become active until Paul puts the practical wisdom into words and speaks it to a congregation.

If received by the Romans in this case, the grace he channels empowers them to assess *realistically* their own gifts of grace and how best to embody them in acts of Christlike self-giving. The community can only know this through their own practice of proof through testing in their moral deliberations.

This practice of proof through testing in discernment fuels the knock-on effect of the domino example I've used earlier. The resurrection power of God continues to be revealed "from faithfulness for faithfulness" (1:16–17). Acts of Christlike faithfulness in self-giving lead to experiences of new life in the community. This, in turn, inspires the recipients of this gift of new life to become channels of grace through their own acts of Christlike faithfulness to benefit even more people. Grace abounds for new life in the Christ-community and in the world.

Similarly, Paul passes on these words of wisdom because they have already been proven through testing to be a channel of life-giving power for others in different contexts. Christ-followers in other communities have already experienced God's life-giving power through Paul's words of practical wisdom. Thus, Paul confidently offers them to the Romans in the anticipation they will bear fruit for them, too.

What kinds of new life might be channeled through Paul's words of wisdom? If the Romans can hear his words, they will be realistic about two important aspects of life in Christ Jesus. They will realistically assess how much or how little God has empowered each member of the group and how that empowerment might best be put into concrete Christlike actions that benefit the congregation. They must reflect on their lives together in discernment to make these determinations.

Acts of Christlike faithfulness are always contextual to each individual and their diverse settings in the world. That's what makes *communal* discernment of the will of God in each person's life so important. The group serves as a sounding board for someone considering whether a particular action will be analogous to Christ's pattern of faithfulness. The group helps the individual determine whether the proposed action has proven through testing to be life-giving for others in the past. Based on these deliberations, the individual decides how to act in the particular context in view.

As Christ-followers now "under grace" rather than "under Torah," the practice of proof through testing in communal discernment becomes the key that empowers them to walk in newness of life. The community, united "in Christ Jesus" as "one body," becomes the place for discerning and embodying the life-giving power of grace (*charisma*), activating it through Christlike acts of self-giving, which channel resurrection power for new life to others.

Throughout 12:9–21 Paul encourages believers to live humbly, identifying with the needs of others: "rejoice with those who rejoice and weep with those who weep" (12:15; see also 1 Corinthians 12:26) and "love one another dearly as family, preferring to honor one another" (Romans 12:10). That means placing the interests of others ahead of one's own interests (see Philippians 2:4, 6–11).

These commitments to mutuality are not simply emotional, but practical as well. In Romans 12:13 Paul encourages them to "partner with the needs of the holy ones, pursuing hospitality" to community members and to strangers. He thereby promotes the radical, self-giving act of sharing possessions in the community as need arises (compare Acts 2:42–47). From other letters we know that Paul was actively involved in taking up a collection from his Gentile communities for the poor Jewish Christ-followers in Jerusalem (see 2 Corinthians 8:1–15).

Similarly, Paul encourages the Christ-followers in Rome not to seek retribution: "do not repay anyone evil for evil" (Romans 12:17) and "bless those who persecute you" rather than cursing them (12:14). They are never to avenge themselves (12:19). He even suggests that Christ-followers feed and give drink to their enemies (12:20). He implores them to do everything within their power to live peaceably with everyone (12:18; see also 2 Corinthians 13:11; 1 Thessalonians 5:13). Paul recognizes that living peacefully with others requires all parties to participate.

Finally, Paul even includes suggestions that relate directly to their moral deliberations in the practice of discernment. "Reason [*phroneō*] the same way with one another; do not reason [*phroneō*] proudly, but associate with the humble, and make no claim to be wiser than you are" (Romans 12:16). To "reason the same way" is an essential dimension of moral deliberations in the practice of discernment. We saw Paul emphasize this three times in

Philippians 2:2 and 2:5 and in 1 Corinthians 1:10. Christ-followers are to reason the same way together, using the one mind of Christ during their deliberations in Christ Jesus. In the closing paragraphs of Romans, Paul makes the same crucial point: "may the God of steadfastness and encouragement grant you to *reason the same way among one another according to Christ Jesus*" (Romans 15:5).

Interpreters often contend that 12:9–21 is standard moral instruction that has little continuity of thought or connection to the issues challenging the Christ-followers in Rome. Yet, many of these suggested attitudes and actions appear in other letters by Paul. I suggest that Paul has proven through testing that these proposed attitudes and actions have been pleasing to God and have borne fruit in other contexts. As a result, they reflect some of Paul's most important "ways in Christ Jesus" that he teaches to all his congregations (1 Corinthians 4:17).

Thus, Paul has been persuaded from past experience of three things. First, these suggested attitudes and actions demonstrate the transformation that results from the Romans having reasoned with a 'renewed mind' (Romans 12:2), which is the mind of Christ. Second, by embodying the gift of life-giving grace in these actions, they will partner with God in "conquering evil" rather than being "conquered" by evil (12:21). Third, through their Christlike reasoning and acting, God will deliver them from their conflicts and unite them in a community that Paul will recognize as an *ekklēsia* in Christ Jesus.

"Clothe Yourselves with the Lord Jesus Christ" to Walk in God's New Age (13:8–14)

Paul told the Romans in 13:7 to "pay to all what is owed them." Paul thus concludes his practical advice in 13:1–7 on avoiding conflict with governing authorities. In 13:8, he takes up this theme of indebtedness, shifting the focus to another direction.

What they owe is acting in love (*agapaō*) for one another (13:8). Love embodied in acts of self-giving fulfill "the *other* Torah" (13:8), referring to the Jewish law. Remember that in 8:2, Paul told the Romans that the "law of the Spirit of life in Christ Jesus" frees Christ-followers from the "Torah of Sin and death." In 13:8 Paul is entering a first-century debate in Judaism that seeks to find the heart of Torah in fewer commandments. He concludes that all the essential commandments of Torah are summarized or fulfilled in the one commandment to love one another (13:10) embodied in acts of self-giving (see also Galatians 2:20; 5:14).

For Paul, this conclusion means the Jewish Torah remains authoritative, but its specific commandments are not absolutely binding unless they embody love in acts of self-giving for one's neighbor. We have seen this same pattern since our first stop on the road to Damascus. Christlike love is embodied in acts of self-giving for others (Galatians 2:20). The Torah's full significance for Paul can be found only with reference to its completion or goal which, according to Romans 10:4, is Christ.[100]

Paul interprets the situation in Rome through his apocalyptic lens in 13:11–14 (recall 1 Thessalonians 5:1–11). God's time (*kairos*)—the new age—has already arrived (Romans 13:11). It is already the time for the Romans "to be raised [*egeirō*] from sleep" (13:11). Paul uses the same verb (*egeirō*) that he has used *eight* times before in this letter to describe God's act of raising (*egeirō*) Jesus from the dead.[101] It is high time for the Romans to wake up! It is time for them to rise to new life—to "walk in newness of life"—through the resurrection power of God (6:4)!

For now, says Paul, "salvation is nearer" than when they first had enough trust and confidence to become Christ-followers. But the Romans have yet to awake to the fact that they've all been reconciled to God through the death of Christ Jesus, and they will all be "saved in/by his life" (5:10). Paul's gospel is the power of God for salvation to all the ones who trust—to both Jewish and Gentile Christ-followers (1:16). They will all be saved *together* by living *in*, and *by*, the pattern of the "faithfulness of Jesus Christ" (see 1:16–17; 3:21–26).

Thus, in 13:13, Paul encourages the Romans to "walk honorably...without quarreling and jealousy."[102] "Clothe yourselves [*enduō*] with the Lord Jesus Christ" (13:14; see also Galatians 3:26–28). Paul forcefully directs them to specific Christlike actions that address their conflict. He directs them, as participants in God's new age, to *wake up*—to turn away from their exclusive commitment to Torah, which is dividing them. It's time for them to focus on Jesus Christ as their community's exclusive norm for moral reasoning and discernment. Paul is echoing his apocalyptic instructions in Romans 12:2: do not be conformed to this present age, but be transformed by the renewal of your mind, so that you can prove through testing what is the will of God—what is good, well-pleasing to God, and mature. They are to live Christ in their daily lives. By reasoning together with the one mind of Christ, they will discern Christlike actions that lead to experiences of resurrection power for new life in God's new age in Christ Jesus.

"Welcome One Another as Christ Welcomed You for the Glory of God" (14:1–15:13)

Some members of the Christ-communities in Rome still follow the Torah by refusing to eat any meat, since most meat in that culture had been sacrificed to another god or idol (see 1 Corinthians 8 and 10). Similarly, some of the Jewish Christ-followers still observe traditional Jewish holy days. These are sources of friction among the Romans.

But Paul, instead of focusing on these sources, concentrates instead on the attitudes displayed by community members toward those who have made different behavioral choices.[103] One group "despises" those who refrain from eating certain foods, while those who refrain from eating apply Torah to "judge" those who do (Romans 14:3). In 14:6 Paul encourages them to recognize that both groups are trying to honor the same Lord with their different practices. Paul relativizes the importance of the actual decisions. He contends that Christ-followers are just as accountable to God for their *attitudes* toward other Christ-followers as they are accountable for their *decisions* and *actions* on the issues dividing them.[104] This is the same logic of the cross we saw Paul employ in 1 Corinthians 8:1–13.

Paul is candid with those involved in this conflict (see Romans 15:15). He tells one group to welcome the ones who are "weak in trust" without quarreling over opinions (14:1). In 14:5 he says, "let each person be fully convinced in their own mind" that their actions embody God's will. This lack of "trust" or "confidence" (another possible translation of *pistis* in 14:1) about the propriety of an action can often cause a person to fall back on the strict observance of rules for determining appropriate behavior. This, in turn, can lead them to "judge" those who do not strictly follow the rules (see Romans 14:3, 4, 5, 10, 13, 22).[105]

Conversely, people who are "fully convinced" in their own minds about something often act with freedom and creativity, responding to situations that arise without needing the strict guidance of rules and precedence. Those who act with this freedom and confidence, in turn, sometimes express contempt for those they deem to be confined by rules and conventions.

Paul reminds both groups that God alone is the judge. When actions are pleasing to God, they will bear fruit. God will also hold them all accountable for failing to welcome one another into the new community shaped by the death and new life of Jesus Christ. Christ, alone, has been appointed to rule over both the living and the dead (14:9).

On the matter of food, Paul offers his own view that all foods are clean (14:14, 20). "I know and am persuaded in the Lord" (14:14). His conviction probably results from participating in moral deliberations among members of his own community "in Christ Jesus."[106]

"Being right" on the issue, however, is not the point of his argument! For those who are not fully persuaded, the food is still "unclean" and should not be eaten (14:14). The perceived Christlike character of the action lies in the intention of the actor. Paul is shifting the decision on whether to take a particular action away from the character of the action itself (is it "right" or "wrong"/"good" or "evil"?). He is placing responsibility for the decision to act in the conscience of the individual actor, following the community's moral deliberations on the issue in their practice of discernment.[107]

This is another creative aspect of Paul's approach to moral reasoning and discernment. In God's new age in Christ Jesus, Christ-followers need not know, distinguish, or consider whether any proposed action is good or evil. Instead, as we saw in Corinth, "all things are permissible, but not all things bind people together." Paul imagines a kind of freedom where Christ-followers are solely engaged with focusing on past actions and consequences to help them discern future actions that will please God and lead to new experiences of resurrection power that build up their community.

Paul's focus throughout this passage (and the whole letter, for that matter) is not on the rightness or wrongness of a particular action or attitude, but its impact on other members of the community. If a person's action causes another brother or sister to stumble in their own walk, then the action should not be taken (14:21). This is what it means to live by the faithfulness of Jesus Christ, "who loved me, indeed, who gave himself for me" (Galatians 2:20). A Christ-follower must be willing to place limits on her or his own freedom for the sake of others. To "clothe yourselves with the Lord Jesus Christ" requires aligning one's actions with the pattern of the faithfulness of Jesus Christ, who set aside his own self-interest and died for others (see Romans 14:15; Philippians 2:6–11; Galatians 3:22–28).

Readers must also be clear about what Paul is *not* saying in this passage. He is not saying that one should refrain from eating any and all food simply because another person *disagrees* with that decision. Moral deliberations in Christ Jesus do not require that unanimity or even a consensus be reached before an individual acts in a specific way. In 14:1, Paul encouraged the Romans to welcome the "weak in trust," but not for purposes of arguing about opinions. If a person who refrains from eating "unclean" food is fully convinced in his or her own mind not to do so, that person is not at risk from being adversely influenced by those who eat anything. Paul is only concerned about the person who might be persuaded to act, contrary to their own conscience, by seeing another person eating indiscriminately. Thus, he says, a Christ-follower should not act in ways that cause others to stumble in their own walk (14:13).

The logic of Paul's argument is once again the same as in 1 Corinthians 8:1–13. He does not want a Christ-follower who eats all food to serve as a model for anyone who is not fully convinced that all food is "clean." He does not want those who are fully convinced to cause another Christ-follower to eat that food and, by doing so, experience themselves as defiled before God because their own conscience does not approve the action.

According to Paul, being enslaved to Christ is doing what is "well-pleasing to God" and has human approval (Romans 14:18). The phrase "well-pleasing to God" echoes 12:2. New life in Christ Jesus is not about following a predetermined set of moral rules. The key to walking in newness of life under grace is the practice of discernment. The assembly reflects on past actions and consequences—proof through testing—to anticipate imaginatively what future Christlike actions might be "pleasing to God." In 14:19 Paul identifies two criteria to help guide these deliberations. The community must seek and identify Christlike actions which have resulted in peace and built up the community. By making the connection, they can act with confidence that God will approve.

Paul encourages Christ-followers to be confident in their faithfulness before God when they take actions that have proven through testing (*dokimazō*) to reflect God's will (14:22). They are blessed and have no reason to judge themselves for taking such actions (14:22). Conversely, he discourages anyone from taking an action when they are wavering and questioning whether the action will meet with God's approval. Any action that is not grounded in a person's confident, discerned faithfulness is an act of sin! (14:23)

In 15:1–6 Paul summarizes his presentation in Romans 14. He directs those who have power in their Christ-communities to bear the burden of the weaknesses of those who are powerless.[108] He is probably addressing the Gentile Christ-followers who assumed leadership roles in the Roman Christ-communities when the Jewish Christ-followers were expelled under the edict of Claudius. They have now returned to Rome and find themselves to be powerless in their old Christ-communities.

Using Jesus Christ as the example, Paul tells those with power to refrain from actions that please themselves and, instead, to act in ways that are pleasing to their neighbors and build them up in a truly good life (15:1–3). This closely follows what Paul told the Philippians in 2:4: put the interests of others ahead of one's own interests. It's also an action analogous to the faithfulness of Jesus Christ, "who loved me, indeed, who gave himself for me" (Galatians 2:20). Paul supports this suggested action by quoting from the Scriptures in Romans 15:3–4. He continues to use the Torah as "written for our teaching" and to provide encouragement and hope (15:4). Torah remains as a contributing voice and influential guide for the community's moral deliberations.

Paul prays that the God of perseverance and encouragement would grant all the Roman Christ-followers the skill to "reason [*phroneō*] the same way among one another according to Christ Jesus" (15:5). With this counsel,

Paul again echoes the story of Christ and his pattern of moral reasoning in Philippians 2:1–11. The purpose of reasoning this one way, says Paul, is so that the Romans might, with one accord and with one mouth, glorify the God and Father of the Lord Jesus Christ (15:6).

For this reason, concludes Paul, they must "take in one another" just as Christ "took in" them for the glory of God (15:7). The Greek verb *proslambanō* in 15:7 is often translated simply as "welcome" one another.[109] But that translation obscures the predominant sense of *proslambanō* as taking in something extra, multiplying what already exists, or adding something by apposition.

Clearly, Paul is insisting that Gentile Christ-followers, who are now in the power positions of leadership, "take in" the returning Jewish Christ-followers (Paul yet again echoes Philippians 2:6–11). He suggests that, like Jesus Christ, these Gentiles empty themselves of their power and status to serve those with less power. Only then, says Paul, will both groups become one *ekklēsia* in Christ Jesus, speaking with one voice, to glorify the God who has reconciled all humanity to God and to one another through Jesus Christ the Lord.

Paul has laid out in detail his apocalyptic gospel of the power of God for salvation to Jewish and Gentile Christ-followers. He set out for the Romans his approach to formation and its structure for those who are baptized into Christ Jesus. He encourages them to walk in newness of life through resurrection power under grace. They must discern Christlike actions as they are led by the Spirit in their assembly that comes together "in Christ Jesus." He explained his practice of proof through testing that grounds this crucial practice of discernment. And he has suggested many concrete actions, proven through testing in other Christ-communities, through which he confidently trusts God will work to reconcile the conflicted Christ-followers in Rome.

Despite never having been to Rome, Paul has written to them boldly on some issues through the grace of God given to him (15:15). He hopes that he has begun to gospel the Romans in ways that at least bring the Gentile Christ-followers there into the orbit of his ministry among the Gentiles. As final encouragement, Paul recounts the success of his gospeling activity that he one day hopes to complete among the Romans, too:

Romans 15:18 I will not dare to speak of anything except what Christ has achieved through me for the obedience of Gentiles, by word and deed, **19** by the power of signs and wonders, by the power of the Spirit of God, so that from Jerusalem and as far around as Illyricum I have fully proclaimed the gospel of Christ. **20** Thus I earnestly endeavor to gospel [*euanggelizomai*] not where Christ has already been named, so that I do not build on someone else's foundation, **21** but as it is written, "Those who have never been told of him shall see, and those who have never heard of him shall comprehend."

After finishing the letter, Phoebe offers a few closing comments. "Paul hopes you Romans have understood from his letter that Christ lives *in* Paul. He hopes you now comprehend how God reigns in resurrection power for new life in the world. He hopes that after hearing this letter all of you—or at least you Gentile Christ-followers—will entrust your lives to Christ's pattern of faithfulness and the saving power of God at work in Christ through all those who embody his pattern of faithfulness. May God's peace be with all of you, my friends!"

Pilgrims Reflect on Their Experience

Before getting back to the hotel, the pilgrims strolled through the ruins of the Roman Forum to experience the grandeur and power Rome displayed to its citizens and visitors. It gave the pilgrims a real dose of how the empire imposed itself on the people. After taking a short time to refresh themselves, the pilgrims reconvene on the veranda of our hotel to reflect on what they've heard in Paul's letter to Rome. They are still tired from hearing such a long and intense letter. But they are also energized, as their conversation reflects.

"I'm really impressed with the stamina of those folks," says Esperanza. "That letter was so dense and long, but they stayed attentive to the end!"

"Thankfully, Phoebe needed some short breaks," adds Robert. "Otherwise, I wouldn't have made it. I'm not accustomed to listening so closely for so long!"

Ann turns in a different direction. "All that slavery language was hard to hear! I'm glad that slavery is no longer an issue for us today."

"It's not?" asks Dante. "I know some people who are enslaved to social media and others to their cell phones. It looks to me like that fellow Sin is still having lots of success with people who are so consumed with communicating through social media or cell phones rather than face-to-face."

"Yes," says Latisha. "And there's no community like Paul's 'deliberative assembly in Christ Jesus' to hold people accountable for posting false or misleading information or hateful personal attacks."

"I used to be enslaved to my job," Jim confesses. "The idol I served was not money but the affirmation I craved from my colleagues. Paul's letters have inspired me to think about the 'faithfulness of Jesus Christ' as a pattern of life. I see no evidence in Paul, the Gospels, or other Scriptures, that Jesus craved or sought affirmation from his colleagues."

"And what about those poor workers in foreign countries who work for small wages in brutal conditions just so we can buy cheaper shirts and phones," adds Esperanza. "That is another contemporary version of how slavery continues and it makes us complicit as slave owners because we participate in—no, we insist on—the fruit of that slavery."

"That's hard to hear, Esperanza," says Robert. "I've always heard that those workers are now doing better economically than before. Doesn't that justify the situation?"

"Maybe we should ask them," responds Esperanza provocatively.

"I've never heard anyone say that we're slaves of the ones we obey," says Jean. "I need to ponder that some more. I do seem to respond to lots of cultural influences that Paul might designate as idols."

"I hear you on that," adds Philip. "And I've been thinking about Paul's point: we're either hearing and obeying God's will for our lives or we're hearing and responding in obedience to the idols that surround us in the culture."

"I agree," says Sarah. "There's no middle ground here. From Paul's point of view, we're either walking in one direction or the other."

"I resonated with Paul's description of his gospel," offers Reynoldo. "I learned my path of Christlike faithfulness from watching how my mother lived her life. She was a wonderful model of Jesus for me. As Paul said, 'from faithfulness for faithfulness.' I can't get that image of the dominoes falling one after the other out of my head."

"That's exactly what we heard when we visited the Christ-community in Thessalonica, too," responds Jim. "Their examples of Christlike faithfulness led to the spread of faithfulness throughout Macedonia and Achaia. Another domino falls in the sequence."

"I can now see more clearly how Paul's circle of grace also contributes to the spread of faithfulness," says Gail. "I'm now more conscious about recognizing experiences of new life through someone else's Christlike act of self-giving and thanking God for the experience. It creates a mindfulness about the importance of channeling the grace we receive."

"Paul's explanation of *charisma* gives me a new understanding of 'spiritual gifts,' too," says Ann. "I've always assumed a gift of grace was personal. I never considered that it was a gift given to me in stewardship for others. That point has reshaped how I will see the gift of grace going forward."

"Well, wait a minute," says Jim. "The gift of grace is for you, too. It's how the Spirit inspires and energizes you to 'walk in newness of life.' It's a both/and situation."

"Good point. Thank you Jim," Ann replies.

"I've always misunderstood the apocalyptic perspective," Jean confesses. "I thought it was just about the catastrophic end of the world. I realize now that it expresses the reality that there are spiritual forces trying to influence us to act in ways that oppose God's will for life and peace. That rings very true for me as a description of reality."

"Me, too," says Dante. "It gives me a completely different mindset for seeing and interpreting the world."

"Yes, I think Paul would say you've had a transformation of your mind over the course of this pilgrimage," Diane adds encouragingly. "We've all got to focus on life and peace, rather than the norms, values, and expectations of the culture."

"In my experience, I've waited for certainty that an action is 'right' so often," says Ann. "Many times that desire for certainty created paralysis and inaction. Certainty never comes; Paul seems to be clear about that."

"Yes, and he's also clear that discernment does not require unanimity or consensus in the group before an individual takes a particular action," Reynoldo suggests. "Paul said we simply need to be persuaded and confident in our own mind that the action is faithful."

"That's right," adds Jean. "But don't forget that the persuasion and confidence Paul is talking about comes through the deliberations in the community and not just from individual reflection! We're not free to be persuaded and confident without hearing from others."

"Paul also says that we should *not* take a contemplated action when we're wavering about whether the action will be pleasing to God and bear fruit," Philip reminds the group.

"That's also why it's so important to know that there is no condemnation in Christ Jesus—there is no condemnation in taking an action when we've discussed and discerned it in a community," Latisha concludes. "Even if it doesn't bear fruit or even has a harmful effect. That's why it's important for the rest of us not to say, 'I told you so!'"

"I heard very clearly that moral certainty about the rightness of an anticipated action can be destructive to the community," Robert says insightfully.

"Yes, I heard that, too," adds Gail. "Moral certainty is arrogance, the opposite of Christlike humility which Paul frequently lifts up."

"Did you pick up on Paul's allusion to Adam eating from the tree of the knowledge of good and evil?" asks Latisha. "Was Paul implying that in God's new age in Christ we now live in a space where we don't need to know the difference between good and evil?"

"That's what I think he was implying," says Robert. "That's a frightening thought, on one hand, but completely freeing, on the other hand."

"I think we must take Paul seriously, even if it's a daunting task," adds Gail. "Paul makes it sound like the crucial key to freedom in discernment is that we stay in touch with the risen Lord through his Spirit that leads us in discernment. Without his divine guidance and direction showing us new life or the chaos of judgment, it sounds like we'd be dead in the water."

"It's a humbling insight that God gives us that freedom and trusts us to stay in touch," adds Ann. "Freedom brings a corresponding responsibility, too."

"Your comments, Latisha, remind me that I got a little nervous when Paul talked about no rules for behavior," says Diane. "Is he saying that we are free to do anything? I'm a teacher and my students need rules for the classroom."

"That's a different issue, I think," responds Gail. "He's saying that, for Christ-followers, the strict enforcement of rules potentially impairs our imaginations and keeps us from seeing and discerning all kinds of actions that might meet with God's approval and bear fruit for new life in our communities."

"Yes, I agree, and that also confirms the crucial role of proof through testing in the practice of discernment," adds Jean. "I can't tell you how many times in my life I have taken some action and never thought about reflecting on its consequences. It's embarrassing."

"We've all been there, Jean," says Esperanza consolingly. "There have been many times when it never consciously occurred to me to reflect on past actions and their consequences to anticipate what might result from a future action. I may have done that subconsciously, but Paul is insisting that we make proof through testing a high priority for consciousness in the community."

"I've been hearing that throughout our pilgrimage," offers Reynoldo. "I'm also beginning to appreciate how looking back on our past actions and projecting forward in the discernment practice can lead over time to practical moral wisdom. Until this pilgrimage, I would have never believed I'd be discussing a practice connected to Aristotle or even Paul!"

"What I've come to realize on this pilgrimage is that discernment was the centerpiece of worship in the early church," says Reynoldo. "It's not even a regular practice in my church."

"I can't wait to get home and figure out where and how to start practicing discernment in a group," Sarah says with excited enthusiasm.

"That's a great idea, Sarah," says Dante. "I'm wondering, John, whether we could get some more information from you about St. Benedict's Workshop and their practice of discernment. I'd love for us to keep meeting together. I've made new friends and want to continue building our relationships."

"Of course," I tell the group. "When we get home, I'll follow up by sending you a letter by email that summarizes some of what we've learned and spells out for you how to set up your group and the general rules for an orderly meeting. After hearing all of these letters from Paul together, I've even got a thought about how I might put that letter together in a way you would recognize from our time together."

"That sounds great," says Sarah.

"Yes, I think we're all in on this," adds Diane. "I know we will all be eagerly expecting to hear from you, John!"

With that, the members of the group toast their time together on this pilgrimage. They then travel home, anticipating the letter from me and St. Benedict's Workshop.

CHAPTER SIX

Discernment in Christ Jesus Today

"By the Grace of God Given to Me, I Say to All of You. . ." (Romans 12:3)

"We've received John's letter from St. Benedict's Workshop!" Dante texts to all the pilgrims. "Let's set up a meeting on Zoom so we can all hear the letter read at the same time."

"Great idea," responds Gail. "I'll set it up."

A few days later, the group assembles on their Zoom screens at the designated time. Gail facilitates the meeting.

"I think we're all here," says Gail. "Reynoldo has agreed to read the letter. Reynoldo, why don't you go ahead."

"Wait a minute," says Esperanza. "I haven't seen Robert on the screen yet. I think Paul's advice to the Corinthians was 'wait for everyone.'"

"Good point," says Gail. "Let's wait a few more minutes."

Robert's face pops up on the screen. "Sorry I'm late," he says, "I had trouble with my internet connection."

"No problem," says Diane. "We've all been there. Reynoldo is going to read the letter."

Reynoldo begins to read:

To the Deliberative Assembly of Pilgrims in Christ Jesus

Grace to you and peace from God our Father and the Lord Jesus Christ. I, John, bring you greetings from all the beloved holy ones at St. Benedict's Workshop.

I give thanks to God always in my prayers for you pilgrims. For your joy in life and your Christlike care for one another on our recent pilgrimage.

And I thank God for the many ways God has enriched you in all kinds of new knowledge and new ways of talking about, and acting on your trust, faith, and faithfulness in God and Christ during our time together.

I give thanks for the Spirit of the risen Christ who worked among you during your reflections at each stop on the pilgrimage. That the Spirit revealed to you Paul's goal of forming moral communities in Christ Jesus, where, over time, you are transformed into the image of Jesus Christ and formed as the Body of Christ in your local setting. I give thanks that the Spirit has called you to form and build your own community of accountability in Christ Jesus, just as you are now doing.

I also give thanks that the Spirit has revealed to you the importance of reasoning with the logic of the cross as you clothe yourselves with Christ and embody his love in your acts of self-giving for others, just as you are doing. I give thanks that you have come to know Christ in more meaningful ways through your Christlike practices. I give thanks that you are now using the logic of the cross to imagine new ways to clothe yourselves with Christ in all the contexts of your daily lives. I pray that you will continue to entrust yourselves to Christ's pattern of faithfulness as participants in the circle of grace that defines God's new age and mission of reconciling relationships in a broken world.

I also thank my God that, from the first day of our pilgrimage until now, you have continued to grow in practical wisdom and moral understanding, so that your Christlike love for others has become an established disposition and practice among you. I pray that your love might continue to abound more and more, so that you may prove through testing the will of God as you walk worthily of the Lord, who continues to call you into God's kingdom and glory, just as you are already doing.

Continue to walk in ways that please God and bear fruit in your community. Hold fast to Christ's logic of life and your self-giving actions through which God is working with resurrection power to give new life to you and your communities.

Now, concerning the things about which you have written, sisters and brothers, do the following things before you come together in your deliberative assembly of pilgrims in Christ Jesus:

Set a regular time and place to meet for no more than seventy-five minutes and strictly enforce the time limits set for each meeting. This builds your confidence in the trustworthiness of the process and availability of your partners in Christ Jesus.

Agree to the confidentiality of all discussions and hold one another strictly accountable to the agreement. This builds your confidence in sharing everything germane to the discussion, including what might otherwise be sensitive or even embarrassing.

Agree that Scripture and your individual imaginations are the only resources you use to interpret, analyze, and respond to each situation presented. The topics selected for discussion must be appropriate to the occasion and simple enough so that everyone can take part in the discussion. This means that more complex analytical frameworks like psychology or medicine are not appropriate for this practice. That's not to say those areas are unimportant, but people often defer to the expert, and that hinders the participation of everyone in the conversation. Agree to build a circle of trust, which means that your goal is not to fix the presenter's problem or to direct the presenter about how to resolve the situation. When a group member offers a biblical passage for consideration, however, let that person identify the rhyme or analogy they see between the passage and the presenter's situation. The analogy should be presented as an "I" statement by the one offering the passage ("here's the rhyme I see between the passage and the situation").

Therefore, when you do come together in the deliberative assembly of pilgrims in Christ Jesus, let all things be done in love through acts of self-giving for building up one another.

Choose someone in advance to facilitate each meeting. This person bears the responsibility to make sure the prior agreements and timeline are enforced and to keep the space safe for everyone to participate.

Open with a prayer, inviting the Spirit to guide your deliberations and open you to revelation and new insights.

Let the facilitator remind everyone of your confidentiality agreement.

Let the facilitator remind everyone that the group reasons only with the mind of Christ and the logic of the cross to offer possible interpretations and responses to the situations presented from daily life, not to fix a person's particular problem.

Let the facilitator remind everyone that the group only uses the canon of Scripture and the analogical imaginations of group members to reflect together on the situations presented.

Let the facilitator remind everyone that there is not just one right action God wills for any given situation. There are many possible faithful responses to any situation. The responsibility of the group is to imagine possible responses, grounded in one or more readings from Scripture.

Let the facilitator remind everyone that the Scriptures offered may not, and do not need to agree with each other. This is a good thing! Different possibilities give the presenter different choices to consider before deciding how to respond. Ultimately, the presenter decides on what action to take and that decision usually comes later.

Let the facilitator invite one person to share an event in their life. The event should be current, specific, and ask a question for discernment. Events can be small or large, mundane or potentially life-changing. We all learn from and are encouraged by deliberations associated with each event. The process remains the same for all events.

Let the group take a few minutes of silence to consider clarifying questions to the presenter that may be necessary for identifying additional layers of facts or issues.

Let the group then take a few more minutes to go to the Scriptures to find analogous passages that rhyme with some aspect of the situation and issues presented. Remember that no passage will ever align completely with the situation presented. Remember also that there is no "right" or "wrong" in suggesting a particular biblical passage. We use the biblical stories to discover patterns of action that imaginatively align with some pattern in the contemporary situation presented.

Let the facilitator invite group members to offer their passages, one by one. The passages should be read from the biblical text. This avoids unintentional mischaracterization, misinterpretation, or oversimplification of the passage offered. The person offering a passage should identify the rhyme or analogy they see between the passage offered and the situation presented. Responses might be, "I chose this Scripture because. . ."; or "The rhyme for

me is…"; or "The possible faithful action I glean from this passage is…."
All comments and questions associated with a particular passage should be discussed. The group may identify other rhymes or other faithful responses suggested by the passage. The presenter of the event should also offer any reflections before the group moves to hear the next passage being offered.

Let the facilitator remind the presenter to come back at a future gathering of the group to report on the action taken and any known consequences of the action. At a subsequent meeting, let the group follow the same process to analyze and respond to the updated report: asking clarifying questions, presenting more passages, discussing the rhymes/analogies of the new passages, and suggesting new possibilities for faithful actions in response to the unfolding situation.

Let every comment, insight, or passage be offered in a spirit of gentleness.

Let every prophetic comment or insight be offered to encourage, console, or build up the original presenter and the members of the group.

And, if time permits, let the facilitator invite a second person to share a current life event. Let the process be repeated in order, step by step.

Let the facilitator close the gathering with a prayer.

My brothers and sisters, I know that your deliberative assembly of pilgrims in Christ Jesus will soon be discussing my letter and, more importantly, considering current situations in the lives of your fellow pilgrims. I offer this closing prayer:

May the God of peace make you holy, and keep your spirit, soul, and body blameless in the continuing presence of the Lord Jesus Christ. The God who is calling you is faithful and will do this!

The grace of our Lord Jesus Christ be with you in your time together!

The assembled group of pilgrims on Zoom are silent for several minutes after Reynoldo finishes reading the letter.

"Wow! We've got our work cut out for us," says Gail. "Since we all live in the same town, though, let's meet in person to start our deliberative assembly. The pilgrimage showed us the importance of learning the moral life in-person, through face-to-face conversations, and modeling the life of Christlike faithfulness for one another. We can use the conference room in my office if you like."

After thirty minutes of conversation, the group agrees on the ground rules for their assembly. They also decide to accept Gail's offer of hospitality. To accommodate everyone's schedule, they agree to meet in the conference room in her office once a week on Thursday mornings at 7 a.m. They choose Ann to facilitate the first meeting next week.

Gail makes the arrangements and confirms the meeting for next Thursday.

The Deliberative Assembly of Pilgrims in Christ Jesus... First Meeting

The following Thursday, the pilgrims begin to gather at 7 a.m. in the conference room at Gail's office. It's still dark outside. People enter one or two at a time through the side door of the building that gives direct access to the conference room. Everyone arrives with Bibles in hand and some anxiety about starting something so new and unfamiliar.

Ann opens with this powerful prayer inspired by her church's tradition and sets people at ease right away:

> O God, by whom those with open hearts are guided in their discernment, and light rises up in darkness for the godly: Grant us, in all our doubts and uncertainties, the grace to ask what you would have us to do, that the Spirit of the risen Lord might guide us in all wisdom to fruitful choices and save us from all destructive choices, and that in your light we may see light, and may walk along your straight path without stumbling; through Jesus Christ our Lord. *Amen*.[1]

"Ann, you just created a gospel-event for me!" says Dante. "I was pretty nervous when I came through that door this morning. But now, I'm relieved."

"Amen," says the group in unison.

After reminding everyone of the agreed-upon ground rules, Ann asks whether anyone has an event they want to present.

"I do," says Sarah.

"So do I," adds Robert.

"Let's take them one by one," says Ann. "I'll make sure we have time to consider both events. Sarah, why don't you go first?"

"Thank you, Ann. As most of you know, I own a business in town. It was started by my grandfather more than fifty years ago. I'm the third member of my family to serve as CEO. Here's my situation.

"The work of my lead in-house accountant has not met my expectations for more than a year. I've had several sit-down meetings with him and shared my frustrations with his performance. Each time he promises to improve, but his work hasn't gotten any better. He's been with the company for quite some time, so I don't really want to terminate his employment. But I don't know what else to do. I'd love some input from this group about how I might clothe myself with Christ in my next conversation with him."

After thanking Sarah, the group spends some time in silence followed by some clarifying questions. Ann then invites the group to look for some Bible passages that rhyme with some part of Sarah's event. After a few more minutes of silence, she asks for responses.

"I have one," says Esperanza, jumping into the discussion. "Luke 13:6–9, the parable of the owner of the fig tree." Pages rustle as everyone turns to the passage in their Bibles. Some find it faster than others, who don't yet know the Bible's order of books.

Esperanza reads the passage and then explains the rhyme she sees between Sarah's story and the passage. "The owner of the fig tree is frustrated that the tree hasn't produced fruit for three years. I see a rhyme there with Sarah's situation. The owner instructs the gardener to cut it down, since it's wasting the good soil. To me, the owner's decision would mean that Sarah terminates the employee.

"The gardener, however, suggests giving the tree one more year and says he will dig around it and fertilize it with manure. Then, if it doesn't bear fruit next year, the owner can cut it down. So, I also see a rhyme between Sarah and the gardener. She doesn't really want to terminate the employee. What this parable suggests to me is the possibility that Sarah gives the accountant one more opportunity to bear fruit in his work. She might tell the accountant firmly that he's got one more chance, but there's a limit on the time in which he must turn things around."

"Thank you, Esperanza," says Ann.

"Three years is a long time for a fig tree not to bear fruit," says Philip. "A year is a long time for an important employee not to be very productive. The owner of the vineyard seems to get it right if you ask me."

"I agree," says Jean. "There's already been a high cost for the owner to bear."

"I have another passage," offers Dante. "It's the Gospel of John 8:1–11, the woman caught in adultery." A pained look crosses the faces of several pilgrims, but they remain silent. Everyone finds the passage. Dante reads it and then explains why he thought there was a rhyme with Sarah's situation.

"Let me get one thing straight right way," says Dante. "I'm not suggesting the accountant is committing sin. Here's the rhyme I hear. Most business leaders would probably conclude that the accountant needs to be terminated at this point. Like the scribes and Pharisees, who think this woman should be stoned.

"But Sarah is hesitant about terminating this longtime employee. So, after Jesus defuses the nearly tragic situation, he says firmly to the woman, 'go your way and sin no more.' What this passage suggests to me is that Sarah might consider telling the accountant firmly, 'it's time for your work to improve, immediately.' Much like what Esperanza suggested from her passage."

"Thank you, Dante," says Ann. "Does anyone else have one for Sarah to consider?"

"I do," responds Diane. "It's Philippians 2:6–11. We heard Epaphroditus read this from Paul's letter when we stopped in Philippi on our pilgrimage." Once again, everyone starts turning to the passage, although some don't know where to look to find Philippians in their Bibles.

Diane reads the passage and then says, "Here's the rhyme I see between Sarah's situation and the passage. As the CEO and business owner, Sarah is clearly the person with status and power in this relationship. Just like Jesus in the passage. Given Sarah's position, she clearly has the power to terminate the accountant. From my emerging apocalyptic perspective"—Diane pauses to smile—"I think that's what leaders in this present age would do under these circumstances.

"But that's not what Jesus did. He emptied himself of his status and power to become a servant to others. He was obedient to God, even to the point of death on a cross. The possible action this passage suggests to me is that Sarah imagine an action that would be analogous to Jesus emptying himself of status and power and putting herself in the service of the accountant."

"Whoa," says Jim. "That's exactly the kind of thing I was worried about when we were in Philippi. I'm not sure that works in the business world. The spiritual world and business world are two separated compartments of life. Sarah, what do you think?"

"I need to go home and pray about this. I'll give you an update on my situation when there is something to report."

Ann looks at her phone to check the time. She confirms that there is time for another event. "Robert, would you like to go ahead with your event?"

Jim interrupts. "Wait a minute. I'm frustrated. I don't know the Bible well enough to pull up passages like this and I don't know where to find them when someone else offers one."

"I completely understand," responds Sarah. "I've been there. But let me encourage you, Jim. First, the more we do this reflection, week in and week out, I promise that you will realize you know more than you think, and you'll learn even more in this process. Second, there are all sorts of apps for your phone or handy, printed tools that let you look up topics or key words and find passages quickly. You'll be amazed how fast you grow into this."

"Thanks, Sarah, I'll get more details from you after we finish, today."

"That was helpful for everyone. Thank you Jim and Sarah," says Ann. "Robert, why don't you present your event."

"Thank you," says Robert. "I'm a high school teacher. I've only been at my school for three years. But I've already had several contentious conversations with a much older, more experienced teacher, about how I manage my classroom, especially my leniency to students who are late turning in their work. She rules her class with strict discipline and no mercy. She reflects the teaching style and discipline of a number of the more experienced teachers at the school. And she frequently criticizes my more lenient approach in front of our colleagues.

"Now, she's gotten more and more vocal in opposition to my approach. She recently went to the principal to complain about my poor class management. I'm worried that she could jeopardize my job. I like teaching at this school, and I need the job. Like Sarah, I'd like some help to imagine how Jesus might come alive in me to engage my colleague with how I feel about her involving the principal in our disagreement and why I manage my classroom the way I do."

Ann goes through the process of getting the clarifying questions answered, gives people time to look for biblical passages, and then asks for responses.

"I have one," says Reynoldo. "It's Mark 8:22–26. It's that unique story where it takes Jesus two touches on a man's eyes to heal his blindness." Reynoldo reads the passage to the group and then explains where he sees the rhymes with Robert's situation. "I think Robert's older colleague may have a spiritual blindness. She seems very certain in her rules-based, strict discipline that she imposes on her class. She's analogous to the blind man in the village. I'd also add that she's like those Corinthians who were certain about their positions on food sacrificed to idols and were acting in ways that encouraged others to take the same action, resulting in them feeling terribly remorseful and guilty for what they had done. In this passage, Jesus takes the man out of the village to heal him.

"That suggests to me that the village is somehow contributing to the man's blindness. I think there's an analogy here between the village and the school. The groupthink of the older teachers may be blinding Robert's colleague to different ways of managing a classroom and to the potential harm she's doing by reporting him to the principal. What this suggests to me is that Robert might consider taking his colleague 'out of the village' before talking to her. Maybe he should consider taking her to a nearby restaurant for lunch or a coffee shop after school to visit with her, outside the village that might be the problem."

Before Ann can ask for comments or for another passage, Philip jumps in. "I have another passage. Micah 6:6–8. It says. . ."

"Wait a minute, Philip," cautions Ann. "Let's wait until everyone finds the passage and then you can read it to us."

Philip pauses for everyone to find the passage. He reads it and then says, "What God requires is to do justice, love kindness, and walk humbly with your God. I think the rhyme with the passage involves Robert's colleague. She's coming from the place of justice for the other students. Justice requires the imposition of a penalty for those who don't turn their work in on time. Otherwise, it's not fair to the majority of the class who work hard and probably make sacrifices to meet deadlines and turn work in on time."

"Thank you, Philip," says Ann. "We're short on time. We can continue this conversation next week. Are you OK with that, Robert?"

"Yes, that's fine. Thank you," he says.

Ann offers a concluding prayer, and dismisses the group, saying, "This has been a great start to our discernment group. I look forward to seeing everyone next week, same time, same place."

The group agrees that Ann will facilitate the meeting again next week.

The Deliberative Assembly of Pilgrims in Christ Jesus . . . Second Meeting

The group gathers the following Thursday, eagerly waiting to hear whether Sarah or Robert have updates on their situations. Ann is facilitating and offers an opening prayer. Then she asks Sarah and Robert if they have any updates to offer on their respective situations and also asks whether anyone else has an event to discuss.

"Yes," answers Robert.

"I'm not ready to report yet," Sarah responds.

"I have an event I'd like to present," says Gail.

Ann quickly responds, "OK, great. Robert, why don't you give us an update on your situation and then we'll hear Gail present her event."

Robert jumps right in. "After praying about it, I decided to do what Jesus did in that passage Jim offered about the blind man. I invited my colleague to coffee after work. She was surprised, but accepted. We went to the local coffee shop down the street.

"I learned that she was upset with her daughter, who had just reconciled with her husband after a long period of separation. Apparently, her son-in-law had been unfaithful and the couple had been separated for many months. My colleague was upset with her daughter because she had forgiven her husband, and the couple had just gotten back together again. I just listened patiently.

"When the time seemed right, I finally got around to explaining why I was showing mercy to my students. I told her that it was part of my practice of Christian discipleship. Mercy was one of the central teachings of Jesus. And I told her there was way too little mercy in the world today. I wanted my students to see a model for what mercy looked like in action.

"She paused, then thanked me for sharing my reasons for running my classroom that way. After a few minutes of small talk, we shook hands. As we were leaving, she simply said, 'you've given me a lot to think about. Thank you.' These last few days, she's been seeking me out for more conversation in the faculty lounge. We'll see what happens!"

Ann offers an interpretation. "That's an amazing story, Robert. Based on the language of the letters we've heard on our pilgrimage, it sounds like the action you took was pleasing to God and bore the fruit of resurrection power for new life in your relationship with your colleague. Thank you for trusting us with your circumstances and sharing what happened."

"There's more to this story," injects Sarah. "Robert may have created a gospel-event in the life of his colleague. She may have heard the good news that God reigns when someone shows mercy. It will be interesting to hear whether her attitude toward her son-in-law changes."

Philip paused, then said, "Robert, your event has also given me something to think about. Mercy does not come naturally to me, as I'm guessing most of you have figured out. I've always been a strict rule-follower. But on our pilgrimage, I was wrestling with the lack of rules that Paul seemed to impose on people. And I was resistant. Now, you come here with this story, and I see how you've created a gospel-event that I would never have seen coming until recently. Thank you for being courageous in the face of your colleague's opposition. There's a lot of divine revelation that seems to be going around!"

Ann then turns to Gail and asks, "Are you ready to present your event?"

"Yes, I'm ready to go," responds Gail. "My mother is ninety-four years old and lives in another state. She still resides in the house where she and my father lived for more than fifty years before he died. She's lived alone in the house for several years now. She hasn't driven for at least ten years. She has multiple myeloma, which requires regular medical appointments, and she takes oral chemotherapy, when she remembers to take it.

"I have one brother who lives about three hours from her house. He helps her out from time to time as he's able, but he's not in a position to give her regular attention. He visits her every couple of weeks to help with groceries, doctor appointments, and a few minor house maintenance items.

"I've been trying for several years to convince her to sell the house and move to an assisted living facility where she would have access to meals, transportation, and regular attention from the staff. She adamantly refuses and insists on staying in the house. I'm inclined to force her to move for her own well-being. But I would like to hear from the group about Scriptures to help me imagine how Jesus might respond."

After handling clarifying questions and giving the group some time to look for biblical passages, Ann invites the group to offer and explain what they've come up with.

Jean speaks up first. "I turned to Mark 10:46–52. It's the story of Jesus and Bartimaeus." Everyone knows where Mark is located and they quickly flip to the passage. Jean reads it to the group and then explains why she presented this story. "Here's the rhyme I see between Gail's story and the passage. It's obvious what Bartimaeus needs—he's blind. Just like it's pretty obvious that Gail's mother needs to move to a facility that can offer her more care than her family can provide.

"But instead of just healing Bartimaeus, Jesus asks him, 'what do you want me to do for you?' Jesus gives Bartimaeus the responsibility for expressing his need. So many of us today think we know what other people need. And we act on our assessment of their needs. Gail, I wonder if the first thing you should do is ask your mother what she wants you to do for her."

"That's very interesting, Jean, thank you," says Gail. "You're right about one thing. I'm one of those people who regularly thinks I know what's best for others. Ann, if it's OK with you, I want to follow up with what Jean has suggested. We're nearing the end of our time, so why don't we break and I'll follow up next week?"

"That sounds good," says Ann. She offers a concluding prayer and the group agrees that Dante will facilitate next week. Most of the group lingers for a short while as they share what's happening in other parts of their lives. Then they depart.

The Deliberative Assembly of Pilgrims in Christ Jesus... Third Meeting

Dante opens the meeting with a prayer and calls on Sarah to give her update.

Sarah begins, "After prayerfully considering the passages from two weeks ago, I heard Philippians 2:6–11 speaking the loudest to me. I decided to empty myself of my status and power as the owner and CEO. I knew that if I called him to my office for a meeting, he would probably think I was about to fire him. Instead, I went downstairs to his office, sat down, and here's what I said, 'I know you've been a loyal employee for many years here at the company. I also know—and have told you this more than once—that I've not been happy with your work for more than a year now. Is there something going on in your life that I should know about?

"He sat there quietly for a several minutes, thinking about my question. Tears formed in his eyes, and he responded, 'my aging mother was diagnosed with a debilitating condition about eighteen months ago. She lives alone, can't afford home health services, and I'm an only child. So, on many evenings, I've been leaving my family to go prepare dinner for her and make sure she has what she needs. I often don't get home until late and still have responsibilities at home to fulfill. For the past eighteen months, I've been getting far less sleep than is healthy for me.'"

"To make a long story short," Sarah continued, "I offered to provide my employee with some additional help for his mother. We're in the process of sorting out the details. I don't know whether his work will get better soon or not. It doesn't matter right now. I feel very good about the next step we're taking."

"That's nothing short of a miracle," says Esperanza. "Now you, too, have created a gospel-event. And it's directly connected to your reasoning with the pattern of Christ we heard Paul tell us about on the pilgrimage in his letter to Philippi. Sarah, Paul could have included you, too, in the paragraph where he lifted up Timothy and Epaphroditus as analogous examples of moral reasoning like Christ."

"It's clear to me," says Diane, "that if we keep helping one another this way, we will continue to grow in confidence that God's resurrection power for new life is real and that Christlike acts of self-giving help those gospel-events take place!"

Dante now turns to Gail and says, "Gail, do you have an update?"

"Yes, I do," she responds. "I did just what we talked about last week. I asked my mother what she wanted me to do for her. To make matters worse from my point of view, she insisted that I move back home to live with her. She says I owe it to her after all that she and my dad did to help me get through college and graduate school.

"While I'm single and work remotely, I don't want to leave this city where I've lived for decades. My kids and friends are here. And I love my job—it's a calling that brings me lots of joy and it's what I spent my graduate education preparing to do. What's my next step?"

"Oh, I'm so sorry," offers Jean. "I thought that passage I suggested might be healing in some way. I guess this just proves there's no certainty. We can only ever know in part, as we heard Paul tell us in his letter to Corinth."

"Thank you, Jean," says Gail. "I think this is all helpful, even if I didn't get the response I had hoped to get."

After inviting further clarifying questions to Gail and giving people time to search for biblical passages, Dante asks people for responses.

"Honor your father and mother," says Jim. "That's what came to my mind. What that suggests for me, if I were in your shoes, is that I would feel pretty responsible for moving back to take care of her."

"I think the passage I have suggests otherwise," says Reynoldo. "It's Matthew 25:1–13." Pages turn in Bibles as they find their way there.

Reynoldo reads the passage and then offers why he thinks it applies to Gail's situation.

"In that passage, ten bridesmaids are waiting for the arrival of the bridegroom, who has been delayed. Five bridesmaids are wise because they've kept oil in their lamps in the event the bridegroom arrives in the middle of the night. The five who are foolish haven't kept any oil. Sure enough, when the bridegroom comes in the middle of the night, the five wise bridesmaids have brightly lit lamps and go out to meet him. The foolish ones ask them to share their oil. The wise ones refuse, go out to meet the bridegroom and enter into the celebration with him. By the time the foolish ones go to buy some oil and get to the celebration the door is shut and the bridegroom won't let them in. 'I don't know you,' he says, and then Jesus tells the point of the parable, 'keep awake,' because you don't know the day or hour when the Son of Man will come again.

"Gail, I think that means you should continue with your calling in your work. Your light is burning brightly now and if you move to live with your mother, I'm not sure your lamp will burn so brightly."

"But isn't Gail supposed to put the interests of her mother ahead of her own interests?" asks Jim. "That's what I heard when we were in Philippi."

"I need more time to pray about this," says Gail. "Thank you. I'll give an update when I have more clarity."

Dante wraps up the conversation, offers a closing prayer, and the group disperses until next week.

The Deliberative Assembly of Pilgrims in Christ Jesus... Months Later

"This has been a remarkable nine months," says Robert, who is facilitating. "This practice of discernment is life-giving and life-changing in so many ways."

"I know there have been stumbles along the way," adds Philip. "But I have already discovered that someone who values mercy as much as Robert has become an encouraging and consoling friend in my time of need. Thank you, Robert."

"You're welcome," says Robert.

"Yes, thank all of you for this powerful start to our practice of discernment," adds Ann. "I am really excited and look forward to seeing everyone every week. Who knows what will come next!"

"I'm already growing more agile in how I use Scripture," says Latisha.

"Me, too," says Jim. "And I'm growing more confident from listening to everyone's events that I'm also growing in practical wisdom. I have a slightly better feel for what a Christlike response to a situation looks like now than I did six months ago."

"And to think that before we went on that pilgrimage, most of us didn't even know each other," offers Gail. "Although we don't really socialize together, even now, I feel like I know more about the eleven of you than I know about most of my friends and even my family members. By doing this work together, week in and week out, God and the Spirit have knit us together into a unique body of Christ."

"What I really love," says Esperanza, "is that I have now learned to recognize God at work in my own life by listening to the stories you tell of God at work in your lives. I now know what it means to have an experience of resurrection life. It happens often when one of you encourages or consoles me in all sorts of ordinary situations. I would have never guessed this possible a year ago!"

"To use Paul's words," says Diane, "we've become more effective proclaimers of the good news of God's reign in the world by word and deed in our daily lives!"

"I now know the Scriptures are crucial for my daily life," responds Reynoldo. "I have learned to interpret my life through the lens of the Scriptures *and* I've learned to interpret the Scriptures through my experiences in daily life!"

"You know what may be the most amazing thing of all?" asks Sarah. "I don't even know much about any of your political views. We just stay focused on living Jesus, proving through testing our embodied actions and connecting them with experiences of new life."

"That's a miracle!" cries Dante jubilantly. "And they happen every day for those of us with eyes to see!"

Jean closed the group with a prayer modified from the Episcopal tradition:

> Blessed Lord, who caused all holy Scriptures to be written for our learning:
> Grant us so to hear them, read, mark, learn, inwardly digest and embody them, that we may embrace and ever hold fast
> the logic of life and the gift of resurrection life
> that leads us to the blessed hope of eternal life, which you have given us
> in our Savior Jesus Christ; who lives and reigns
> with you and the Holy Spirit, one God, for ever and ever.[2]

And they all responded, "Amen! Amen!"

EPILOGUE
Where Have We Been? Where Are We Going?

This epilogue works a lot like the practice of discernment in Paul's early churches. First, we look back and reflect on our pilgrimage to summarize what we've learned from hearing Paul's letters. Then, we look forward and imagine ways we might reclaim Paul's vision for formation, community building, and discernment to bring new life to the church today.

Where Have We Been?

At each stop on this pilgrimage, we heard Paul prioritize moral formation of congregants and building up local congregations of care and accountability through the practice of discernment. We also learned that worship in Paul's *ekklēsia* in Christ Jesus started with a shared meal followed by moral deliberations in the practice of discernment. These transformative conversations served three crucial functions. They focused individuals on ways to embody Jesus Christ in daily life. They empowered diverse Christ-followers to develop the capacity for group decision-making through shared moral agency. And they added a level of trustworthiness to the evaluation of their shared experiences that grounded the practice of discernment.

Discernment was the heartbeat of the flow of God's life-giving power of grace that gave life to each community. The practice was the centerpiece of Paul's "ways in Christ Jesus" that he taught "everywhere in every *ekklēsia*" (1 Corinthians 4:17).

Our journey together began with a stop on the road to Damascus. Paul described in his own words the life-changing experience when the gospel and the risen Christ were revealed *in* Paul. In that event, Paul metaphorically died to his old way of life under the Torah so he could live to God in Christ Jesus. From that moment forward, Paul proclaimed that "I am no longer living, but Christ is living in me." Christ's pattern of life became the exclusive foundation for how Paul walked his path of earthly life in Judaism: "the life I now live in the flesh, I live by the faithfulness of the Son of God, who loved me, indeed, who gave himself for me."

Through this experience of the risen Christ, God called Paul to proclaim Christ among the Gentiles. Henceforth, through his words and embodied, Christlike actions, Paul gave Gentiles their own experiences of the crucified and risen Christ. Through his embodied proclamation of Christ crucified and risen, Paul demonstrated how "your God reigns!" through experiences of resurrection power for new life.

As a result of these ongoing gospel-events, Gentiles were baptized into Christ Jesus and became active participants in God's new age. They entered not just a new, ethereal spiritual realm in Christ. They became active participants in Christ Jesus—a local, physical assembly of Christ-followers who met regularly for a meal and after-dinner discernment.

In baptism, these Gentiles metaphorically died to their old ways of living by the norms, values, and customs of the Greco-Roman world. They dedicated themselves to serving God through Jesus Christ. They entrusted themselves to Christ's way of life by clothing themselves with Christ and committing to live exclusively by his pattern of faithfulness in daily life. God poured the Spirit of the risen Christ into their hearts to empower them to walk in newness of life through the resurrection power of God.

The risen Christ also guided their Spirit-led practice of discernment. In this practice, the congregation reflected on actions and their consequences. They determined whether the Spirit from God or the spirit of the world was influencing a person's motives and actions. They connected Christlike acts of faithfulness—Christlike love embodied in acts of self-giving for others—with experiences of new life in the community. They came to know God through these experiences of resurrection power. And, through their own Christlike practices in daily life, Paul's congregants came to know Christ deeply within themselves.

Paul laid this foundation of Jesus Christ in every congregation, teaching and modeling how to embody Christ in acts of self-giving for others. He taught them how to employ Christ's pattern of moral reasoning—what he called the logic of the cross and the logic of life—in their discernment. Like Christ, they are to empty themselves of status and power to become humble servants of others in obedience to God. Paul emphasizes that this is the *only* pattern of moral reasoning they are to use in discerning Christlike actions in the distinctive contexts of their own lives.

Paul also taught these Gentiles the practice of proof through testing that was a key to discerning future Christlike actions. The assembly looked back to see earlier connections between Christlike actions and experiences of resurrection power. By making these connections, the congregation was better able to predict which future actions might be pleasing to God and lead to new experiences of resurrection power in the community.

Finally, our pilgrimage introduced us to God's gift of life-giving power called grace. We learned that Jesus Christ—God's unique gift in grace—dispenses grace to each Christ-follower in the Body of Christ. The Spirit of the risen Christ leads the community to discern how each distinctive gift of grace should be embodied (*charisma*) in a Christlike act of self-giving for others. The hope is that each embodiment of grace will be pleasing to God and become a channel for new life in the community. We also saw how Paul's circle of grace flowed from God to Christ, then from Christ into Christ-followers, who then embodied that grace (*charismata*) in acts of self-giving that lead to new life in the community. The circle of grace is completed each time those who experience the life-giving power of grace give thanks back to God.

In less than two centuries, Paul's practice of communal discernment lost its place as a crucial, transformational dimension of congregational gatherings. Several factors contributed to this change that evolved over time. The appearance of the written Gospels toward the end of the first century CE signaled the early stages of this transition. The church was already moving away from the shared oral discourses and prophecies we saw in Paul's assemblies and toward the normative reading of authoritative texts. This movement coincided with a shift to a more scholastic and textual emphasis in Christian gatherings.

The mid-second-century emergence of the popular Christian leader Marcion (characterized as a heretic for his views) caused the church to double down on its process for deciding which readings would be authoritative in churches. This effort to establish a canon of Scripture (which continued for at least two more centuries), coupled with the emergence of leaders authorized to interpret the Scriptures, doomed the deliberative conversations of discernment in Paul's churches. By the time Emperor Constantine designated Christianity as the religion of the Roman Empire around 325 CE, which swelled attendance at worship services, the practice of discernment in worship became completely impractical.

The important role of communal discernment resurfaced in the Benedictine monastic movement starting in the sixth century CE. But it never returned as a key discipline in the worship of the church. Consequently, theological reflection to discern God's will in daily life and to recognize experiences of resurrection power has become a lost art for many modern Christians. This is a major dilemma confronting today's church and adversely impacting the wider culture.

Where Are We Going?

The wisdom of the early church's commitment to moral formation and community building through discernment can transform life in today's church. For this to happen, though, *there must be a transformation of the imaginations of not only church leaders and pastors, but entire congregations*. For today's churches to become communities of accountability and resurrection life, we must reclaim early church wisdom and reimagine our practices of discernment and pastoral ministry. What might be a first step?

Acknowledge the Challenges

Surveys in America regularly show that participation in church and "organized religion" have steadily declined in recent decades. Churches have contributed to this decline. Our contemporary understanding and structure of worship has helped to undermine the moral transformation of congregants and their mutual practices of Christlike care for one another.

Many models of Sunday worship in the church today do not adequately prioritize Christian formation in ways that lead disciples to maturity in

Christ. These churches are not built to practice discernment, which is grounded in experiential learning. This learning happens through deliberative moral conversations, as disciples reflect together on their individual, Christlike actions and connect them to experiences of new life in the community.

Instead, services of worship usually include the reading of Scripture encountered as passive listening events. While sermons often focus on Scripture contextualized for daily life, they are usually delivered as a monologue. The preacher seldom engages congregants in conversation. Many churches even make oral preaching the primary vehicle for Christian formation. This places an unfair burden and unachievable goal on those who are designated as church leaders.

Many churches do offer teachings on Scripture and Christian formation outside of worship. But these presentations are often made in the form of a lecture. Passive learners receive information about a topic, rather than engaging Scripture or formation in more active and participatory ways. This approach to Christian formation does not create effective opportunities for experiential learning. As a result, Luke Timothy Johnson concludes that "[t]he teaching of children, youth, and adults alike ought to share an explicit commitment to transformation rather than simply information."[1]

The failure of Christian formation contributes to the reign of individualism, political partisanship, and moral certainty in our culture. It leads to impaired relationships in families, churches, workplaces, and local communities, and disrupts our search for the common good.

We are having trouble building communities of accountability, where there is mutual care and trust, as envisioned by Paul. Christians must reclaim the crucial practice of communal discernment to build these communities of resurrection life and to form individual disciples as participants in God's mission to reconcile a broken world.

Discernment in the Early Church and Today suggests a biblically grounded road map for achieving these goals. Through regular participation in this practice of communal discernment developed at the Workshop and adapted from its use in Paul's churches, present-day disciples can: (1) become more knowledgeable and agile in their use of Scripture as they discover its relevance for shaping embodied faithfulness in daily life; (2) learn to recognize experiences of the living God's saving power; (3) be knit together into unique, discerning bodies of Christ; (4) become proclaimers of the good news by word and deed in their daily lives; and (5) develop Christian practical wisdom, learning the moral life by sharing and deliberating together on their experiences in daily life.

This practice of communal discernment helps people from diverse backgrounds bridge today's social, political, denominational, and economic divisions and discord by deliberating together to interpret and embody the Scriptures—discerning and doing God's will as active participants in the divine transformation of the world. From more than thirty years of experience in biblical studies and teaching, pastoral ministry, and Christian formation shaped by discernment in community, I am persuaded that reclaiming the early church's wisdom will promote healing, peace, and reconciliation, not only in churches but also in local communities and the wider world.

So, where do we go from here?

Implementation in Church Planting

Paul and his colleagues were church planters. They started building Christ-communities from scratch in each new city. While they may have attracted curious Gentile "God-fearers" from a local Jewish synagogue, they nevertheless immediately set about to form their new converts in the ways of Jesus Christ. At first, this took place in Paul's own workshop. Over time, as a Christ-community began to form, the regular meetings shifted to the home of one of the congregants. There was never a church building associated with Paul's ministry.

This background makes church planting today the perfect setting for incorporating what we've learned about Paul's commitment to moral formation and community building through discernment. Today's church planters have the unique opportunity to establish the practice of discernment as the community's principal spiritual discipline from its very beginning (with or without a shared meal). They do not labor under the added burden of trying to change the ethos of an established congregation.

Church planters in Christian denominations with a liturgical tradition may need to negotiate with their leaders about how to establish discernment as a key practice for the startup community. This is a situation where the transformation of the imaginations of church leaders and pastors will be crucial for the success of this adaptive change to historical patterns of worship.

Implementation in Smaller Churches

Small churches today provide a rich environment for incorporating what we've learned on this pilgrimage. In many ways, they most resemble the early churches Paul encouraged to become communities of accountability and resurrection life. Those first churches did not have professionally trained leaders and only rarely enjoyed a visit from their apostle Paul or one of his experienced church-building colleagues. This is also true for many small churches today. They either have no designated and trained pastoral leader or have one who is only available to them on a part-time basis.

Paul taught his small churches a simple practice of discernment—a decision-making process for the whole group—that empowered them to be self-sustaining in the absence of Paul or one of his coworkers. Jesus Christ was the focus and empowering presence of this practice, where every voice was heard and considered. As participants learned how to embody Christ in their relationships with one another, God built them up into a Body of Christ.

The implementation of this practice could be accomplished in two different ways. The practice might easily take place as an aspect of regular weekly worship in smaller churches. As part of the ministry of the Word (even in denominations with a liturgical tradition), and in lieu of a sermon, congregants could engage with one another in deliberative moral conversations about how that day's Scripture readings might shape their daily lives. Over time, congregants would learn how to interpret their lives through the lens of the Scriptures and how to interpret the Scriptures through the lens of their life experiences.

If that approach presents too great a challenge to the comfort level of congregants in worship, a separate time could be set for interested congregants to gather and learn the practice. This is how the Workshop's practice of discernment first began. The problem that often emerges with this approach in smaller churches is one of time constraints. Many small churches can only count on seeing their congregants for a few hours on Sunday morning. Which leads us back to the practice of communal discernment in place of a sermon.

Implementation in Larger Churches

In larger churches, where moral conversation in lieu of a sermon might prove to be disruptive, a more practical approach is to establish small groups who meet on other days and times to practice discernment as supplemental to their worship. This was the genesis of the Workshop's introduction of the practice at St. Mark's Episcopal Church in San Antonio, Texas.

What we saw happen over time at St. Mark's offers encouragement to larger churches. Over time, as more congregants participated in this practice, they not only became more faithful pastoral ministers to one another and their local communities, but they also became evangelists for the practice. They persuaded the clergy leaders at St. Mark's to incorporate this practice of discernment as the framework for meetings and decision-making of the church's leadership team. As the practice took root among the church's leaders, it also spread to other congregational committees and ministries.

This same practice of theological decision-making in community that nurtured the courage and spiritual growth of disciples and ministry in the early church, has also strengthened the practices of formation and community building in contemporary churches.

Implementation in Seminaries and Local Schools of Formation

We must reclaim Paul's emphasis on moral formation and community building through discernment to transform the imaginations of pastors, leaders, and congregations. One step toward accomplishing this goal is to highlight moral formation and discernment in the curricula of seminaries and schools of local formation. These topics could be presented as important aspects of pastoral ministry, which is the responsibility of every member of the congregation. Similarly, our understanding of Christian formation would be broadened to emphasize the integrated proclamation of Jesus Christ in word and deed inside the church and out in the wider world. This would also include, as suggested by Luke Timothy Johnson, putting a greater emphasis on the importance of personal witness, above all the witness to God's working in human lives. This would help pastors, leaders, and congregants make the crucial connections between experiences of resurrection power and Christlike acts of self-giving for others.

Moving forward

I am not alone in calling for the church to reclaim Paul's focus on moral formation.[2] What is unique about this book, however, is my contention that reclaiming Paul's focus on moral formation is not just the responsibility of pastors, but the work of the whole congregation. The practice of communal discernment in Christ Jesus points the way forward for more effective moral formation in today's church.

Discernment in the Early Church and Today offers the small group practice of discernment at St. Benedict's Workshop, adapted from Paul's churches, as one tried and true way to reclaim Paul's vision for formation and community building. I hope readers will experiment with this practice in your own distinct contexts.

I leave you with the same exciting challenge Paul gave to the Philippians: *Y'all work out your own salvation. . .for God is the one working among you, enabling y'all both to will and to work in ways that are well-pleasing to God!*

BIBLIOGRAPHY

The Book of Common Prayer. New York: Church Publishing, Inc. 1979.

Banks, Robert. *Paul's Idea of Community.* 2d ed. Peabody, MA: Hendrickson, 1994.

Barclay, John M. G. "Under Grace: The Christ-Gift and the Construction of a Christian *Habitus.*" In *Apocalyptic Paul: Cosmos and Anthropos in Romans 5–8*, edited by Beverly Roberts Gaventa. Waco: Baylor University Press, 2013.

Barclay, John M. G. *Paul and the Power of Grace.* Grand Rapids: Wm. B. Eerdmans, 2020.

Bass, Dorothy C., Kathleen A. Cahalan, Bonnie J. Miller-McLemore, James R. Nieman, and Christian B. Scharen, *Christian Practical Wisdom: What Is It, Why It Matters.* Grand Rapids: Wm. B. Eerdmans, 2016.

Betz, Hans Dieter. *Galatians.* Minneapolis: Fortress Press, 1979.

Bolsinger, Tod E. *It Takes a Church to Raise a Christian: How the Community of God Transforms Lives.* Grand Rapid: Brazos Press, 2004.

Brower, Kent E. and Andy Johnson. "Introduction: Holiness and the *Ekklēsia* of God." In *Holiness and Ecclesiology in the New Testament*, edited by Kent E. Brower and Andy Johnson. Grand Rapids: Wm. B. Eerdmans, 2007.

Brown, Alexandra R. *The Cross and Human Transformation.* Minneapolis: Fortress Press 1995.

Byrne, Brendan. *Romans.* Sacra Pagina Series, vol. 6. Collegeville, MN: Liturgical Press, 1996.

Cherry, Natalya A. *Believing Into Christ: Relational Faith and Human Flourishing.* Waco: Baylor University Press, 2021.

Copan, Victor. *Saint Paul as Spiritual Director.* Colorado Springs: Paternoster Press, 2007.

Cosgrove, Charles H. *The Cross and the Spirit: A Study in the Argument and Theology of Galatians.* Macon, GA: Mercer University Press, 1988.

Dunn, James D. G. *The Theology of the Apostle Paul.* Grand Rapids: Wm. B. Eerdmans, 1998.

Eastman, Susan Grove. *Recovering Paul's Mother Tongue: Language and Theology in Galatians*. Grand Rapids: Wm. B. Eerdmans, 2007.

———. "What Did Paul Think God is Doing in Christian Communities." In *The New Cambridge Companion to St. Paul*, edited by Bruce W. Longenecker, 210–24. Cambridge: Cambridge University Press, 2020.

Engberg-Pedersen, Troels. "The Gospel and Social Practice According to 1 Corinthians." *New Testament Studies* 33 (1987): 557–84. https://doi.org/10.1017/S0028688500021007.

———. *Paul and the Stoics*. Louisville: Westminster John Knox Press, 2000.

———. "Justice, Love, and the Gift: The Logic of Soteriology." In *The New Perspective on Grace: Paul and the Gospel after Paul and the Gift*, edited by Edward Adams, Dorothea H. Bertschmann, Stephen J. Chester, Jonathan A. Linebaugh, and Todd D. Still. Grand Rapids: Wm. B. Eerdmans, 2023.

Fee, Gordon D. *The First Epistle to the Corinthians*. Grand Rapids: Wm. B. Eerdmans, 1987.Eerdmans, 1987).

Fowl, Stephen E. *The Story of Christ in the Ethics of Paul*. Sheffield: JSOT Press, 1990.

———. *Engaging Scripture: A Model for Theological Interpretation*. Eugene, OR: Wipf & Stock Publishers, 1998.

———. *Philippians*. Two Horizons New Testament Commentary Series. Grand Rapids: Wm. B. Eerdmans, 2005.

Fredriksen, Paula. "Paul and Augustine: Conversion Narratives, Orthodox Traditions, and the Retrospective Self." *Journal of Theological Studies* 37, no. 1 (April 1986): 16. https://doi.org/10.1093/jts/37.1.3.

Furnish, Victor Paul. "Living to God, Walking in Love: Theology and Ethics in Romans." In *Reading Paul's Letter to the Romans*, edited by Jerry L. Sumney. Atlanta: Society of Biblical Literature, 2012.

Gaventa, Beverly R. "Galatians 1 and 2: Autobiography as Paradigm." *Novum Testamentum* 28, no. 4 (October 1986). https://doi.org/10.2307/1560586.

Gombis, Timothy G. *Power in Weakness: Paul's Transformed Vision for Ministry*. Grand Rapids: Wm. B. Eerdmans, 2021.

Goodrich, John K. "'Standard of Faith' or 'Measure of a Trusteeship'? A Study in Romans 12:3." *Catholic Biblical Quarterly*, 74 (2012): 753–772.

Gorman, Michael J. *Cruciformity: Paul's Narrative Spirituality of the Cross.* Grand Rapids: Wm. B. Eerdmans, 2001.

———. *Apostle of the Crucified Lord: A Theological Introduction to Paul and His Letters.* 2d ed. Grand Rapids: Wm. B. Eerdmans, 2017.

———. *Romans: A Theological and Pastoral Commentary.* Grand Rapids: Wm. B. Eerdmans, 2022.

Grieb, A. Katherine. *The Story of Romans: A Narrative Defense of God's Righteousness.* Louisville: Westminster John Knox Press, 2002.

———. "'The One Who Called You...': Vocation and Leadership in the Pauline Literature." *Interpretation* 59, no. 2 (April 2005). https://doi.org/10.1177/002096430505900205.

Hays, Richard B. *First Corinthians.* Interpretation: A Bible Commentary for Teaching and Preaching. Louisville: Westminster John Knox Press, 1997

Hooker, Morna. "A Partner in the Gospel: Paul's Understanding of His Ministry." In *Theology and Ethics in Paul and His Interpreters*, edited by Eugene Lovering Jr. and Jerry L. Sumney. Nashville: Abingdon Press, 1996.

Horrell, David G. "Theological Principles or Christological Praxis? Pauline Ethics in 1 Corinthians 8:1-11:1." *Journal for the Study of the New Testament* 67 (1997): 83-114.

———. "Restructuring Human Relationships: Paul's Corinthian Letters and Habermas's Discourse Ethics." *The Expository Times* 110, no. 10 (July 1999): 321–325.

Jervis, L. Ann. "The Spirit Brings Life to Life." In *Reading Paul's Letter to the Romans*, edited by Jerry L. Sumney. Atlanta: Society of Biblical Literature, 2012.

Jewett, Robert. *Romans: A Commentary.* Hermeneia Series. Minneapolis: Fortress Press, 2006., Jipp, Joshua W. *Pauline Theology as a Way of Life: A Vision of Human Flourishing in Christ.* Grand Rapids: Baker Academic, 2023.

Johnson, Andy. "The Sanctification of the Imagination in 1 Thessalonians." In *Holiness and Ecclesiology in the New Testament*, edited by Kent E. Brower and Andy Johnson. Grand Rapids: Wm. B. Eerdmans, 2007.

———. *1 & 2 Thessalonians.* Grand Rapids: Wm. B. Eerdmans, 2016.

Johnson, Luke Timothy. *Scripture and Discernment: Decision-Making in the Church.* Nashville: Abingdon Press, 1996.

———. "Edification as a Formal Criterion of Discernment in Church." *Sewanee Theological Review* 39, no. 4 (1996): 362–72.

———. *Religious Experience in Earliest Christianity: A Missing Dimension in New Testament Studies.* Minneapolis: Fortress Press, 1998.

———. *Reading Romans: A Literary and Theological Commentary.* Macon, GA: Smith & Helwys Publishing, Inc. 2001.

———. *The Revelatory Body: Theology as Inductive Art.* Grand Rapids: Wm. B. Eerdmans, 2015.

———. *Miracles: God's Presence and Power in Creation.* Louisville: Westminster John Knox Press, 2018.

———. *Constructing Paul: The Canonical Paul.* Vol. 1. Grand Rapids: Wm. B. Eerdmans, 2020.

———. *Interpreting Paul: The Canonical Paul.* Vol. 2. Grand Rapids: Wm. B. Eerdmans, 2021.

———. *Imitating Christ: The Disputed Character of Christian Discipleship.* Grand Rapids: Wm. B. Eerdmans, 2024.

Käsemann, Ernst. "Ministry and Community in the New Testament." In *Essays on New Testament Themes*, translated by W. J. Montague. London: SCM Press, 1964.

———. "Worship in Everyday Life: A Note on Romans 12." In *Essays on New Testament Themes*, translated by W. J. Montague. London: SCM Press, 1964.

Keck, Leander. *Romans.* Nashville: Abingdon Press, 2005.

Klinghardt, Matthias. "A Typology of the Communal Meal." In *Meals in the Early Christian World: Social Formation, Experimentation, and Conflict at the Table*, edited by Dennis E. Smith and Hal E. Taussig. New York: Palgrave MacMillan, 2012.

Lewis, John G. *Looking for Life: The Role of "Theo-Ethical" Reasoning in Paul's Religion.* London: T&T Clark/Continuum, 2005.

Malherbe, Abraham J. *The Letters to the Thessalonians.* The Anchor Yale Bible Commentaries, vol. 32B. New York: Doubleday, 2000.

Marshall, Molly T. *1 & 2 Thessalonians.* Belief: A Theological Commentary on the Bible Series. Louisville: Westminster John Knox Press, 2022.

Martyn, J. Louis. *Galatians*. The Anchor Yale Bible Commentaries, vol. 32A. New York: Doubleday, 1997.

McGowan, Andrew B. "Rethinking Eucharistic Origins." *Pacifica: Australasian Theological Studies* 23, no. 2 (June 2010): 173–91. https://doi.org/10.1177/1030570X1002300204.

———. *Ancient Christian Worship: Early Church Practices in Social and Historical Perspective*. Grand Rapids: Baker Academic, 2014.

McNight, Scot. *Pastor Paul: Nurturing A Culture of Christoformity in the Church*. Grand Rapids: Brazos Press, 2019.

Meeks, Wayne A. *The First Urban Christians: The Social World of the Apostle Paul*. New Haven: Yale University Press, 1983.

———. *The Origins of Christian Morality*. New Haven: Yale University Press, 1993.

———. "The Polyphonic Ethics of the Apostle Paul." In *In Search of the Early Christians: Selected Essays*, edited by Allen R. Hilton and H. Gregory Snyder. New Haven: Yale University Press, 2002.

———. "The Man from Heaven in Paul's Letter to the Philippians." In *In Search of the Early Christians: Selected Essays*, edited by Allen R. Hilton and H. Gregory Snyder. New Haven: Yale University Press, 2002.

Mitchell, Margaret M. *Paul and the Rhetoric of Reconciliation: An Exegetical Investigation of the Language and Composition of 1 Corinthians*. Louisville: Westminster John Knox Press, 1991.

Moberly, R. W. L. *Prophecy and Discernment*. Cambridge: Cambridge University Press, 2006.

Morgan, Teresa. *Being "In Christ" in the Letters of Paul: Saved Through Christ and in His Hands*. Tübingen: Mohr Siebeck, 2020.

———. *The New Testament and the Theology of Trust*. Oxford: Oxford University Press, 2022.

Nanos, Mark D. *The Mystery of Romans: The Jewish Context of Paul's Letter*. Minneapolis: Fortress Press, 1996.

———. "To The Churches Within The Synagogues of Rome." In *Reading Paul's Letter to the Romans*, edited by Jerry L. Sumney. Atlanta: Society of Biblical Literature, 2012.

Newman, Carey. *Paul's Glory Christology: Tradition and Rhetoric*. Supplements to Novum Testamentum, vol. 69. Leiden: E. J. Brill, 1992.

Patterson, Jane Lancaster. *Keeping the Feast: Metaphors of Sacrifice in 1 Corinthians and Philippians*. Atlanta: SBL Press, 2015.

Plutarch. *Quaestiones Convivales*. In *Moralia*, vol. 8. Translated by P. A. Clement, H. B. Hoffleit. Loeb Classical Library 424. Cambridge, MA: Harvard University Press, 1969.

Purvis, Sally B. *The Power of the Cross: Foundations for a Christian Feminist Ethics*. Nashville: Abingdon Press, 1993.

Sanders, Boykin. "Imitating Paul: 1 Cor 4:16." *Harvard Theological Review* 74, no. 4 (1981): 353–363. https://www.jstor.org/stable/1509566.

Ramsaran, Rollin A. "'In Christ' and 'Christ in' as Expressions of Religious Experience: Testing the Waters in Galatians." In *Experientia, Volume 2: Linking Text and Experience*, edited by Colleen Shantz and Rodney A. Werlne. Atlanta: Socieity of Biblical Literature, 2012.

Rowland, Christopher, and Jonathan Roberts. *The Bible for Sinners: Interpretation in the Present Time*. London: SPCK, 2008.

Schmidt, Ulla. "Practicing as Knowing: The Epistemological Significance of Practices, Exemplified with Funerary Practices." *Studia Theologica: Nordic Journal of Theology* 75, no. 1 (April 2021): 32. http://dx.doi.org/10.1080/0039338X.2021.1916289.

Scott, Ian W. "'Your Reasoning Worship': ΛΟΓΙΚΟΣ [LOGIKOS] in Romans 12:1 and Paul's Ethics of Rational Deliberation." *Journal of Theological Studies* 69, no. 2 (October 2018): 500–532. https://www.jstor.org/stable/48548543.

Smith, Dennis E. *From Symposium to Eucharist: The Banquet in the Early Christian World*. Minneapolis: Fortress Press, 2003.

———. "The Greco-Roman Banquet as a Social Institution." In *Meals in the Early Christian World: Social Formation, Experimentation, and Conflict at the Table*, edited by Dennis E. Smith and Hal E. Taussig. New York: Palgrave MacMillan, 2012.

Spohn, William C. *Go and Do Likewise: Jesus and Ethics* (New York: Continuum, 2007).

Stendahl, Krister. "The Apostle Paul and the Introspective Conscience of the West." *Harvard Theological Review* 56, no. 3 (July 1963): 199–215. http://www.jstor.org/stable/1508631.

Sumney, Jerry L. "Paul's Weakness: An Integral Part of His Conception of Apostleship." *Journal for the Study of the New Testament* 16, no. 52 (October 1993): 71–91.

Taussig, Hal. *In the Beginning Was the Meal: Social Experimentation and Early Christian Identity*. Minneapolis: Fortress Press, 2009.

Thiselton, Anthony C. *The First Epistle to the Corinthians*. Grand Rapids: Wm. B. Eerdmans, 2000.

Thompson, James W. *Pastoral Ministry According to Paul: A Biblical Vision*. Grand Rapids: Baker Academic, 2006.

———. *Apostle of Persuasion: Theology and Rhetoric in the Pauline Letters*. Grand Rapids: Baker Academic, 2020.

Wagner, J. Ross. "Working Out Salvation: Holiness and Community in Philippians." In *Holiness and Ecclesiology in the New Testament*, edited by Kent E. Brower and Andy Johnson. Grand Rapids: Wm. B. Eerdmans, 2007.

Wanamaker, Charles A. *The Epistles to the Thessalonians*. Grand Rapids: Wm. B. Eerdmans, 1990.

White, L. Michael. "Regulating Fellowship in the Communal Meal: Early Jewish and Christian Evidence." In *Meals in a Social Context*, edited by Inge Nielsen and Hanna Sigismund Nielsen. Aarhus: Aarhus University Press, 2001.

Wright, N. T. "Putting Paul Together Again." In *Pauline Theology, Vol 1: Thessalonians, Philippians, Galatians, Philemon*, edited by Jouette Bassler. Minneapolis: Fortress Press, 1991.

———. *Galatians*. Grand Rapids: Wm. B. Eerdmans, 2021.

Discernment in the Early Church and Today:
Reclaiming Paul's Vision for Formation and Community Building

ACKNOWLEDGMENTS

This book, like all ministries with and for the church, the Body of Christ, came into being with the assistance and insights of many faithful companions.

The genesis of this book lies in my theological education. I've had the privilege of being formed by four extraordinary biblical scholars dedicated to serving the church. They've showed me in various ways how to clothe myself with Christ in my role as a priest, biblical scholar, and teacher serving God in the church. My deep thanks go to the Rev. A. Katherine Grieb, PhD, Ellen Davis, PhD, the Rev. Robert Morgan, and the Rev. Christopher Rowland, PhD.

I also want to thank biblical scholar, Luke Timothy Johnson, PhD, whose writings, especially *Scripture and Discernment*, first introduced me to the crucial role of discernment in the early church. He stimulated my imagination for how we might reclaim that practice for today's church. And special thanks to Kathleen Cahalan, PhD, a scholar and practical theologian from whom I've learned so much about the practice of discernment.

To these six faithful scholars I owe a great deal. I also know, of course, they would strenuously debate and even oppose some of the interpretations I've offered here. For that I accept complete responsibility.

In late 2001 my wife Pat and I moved back to our adopted home of San Antonio, Texas. We had spent the previous four years in England, where I did research and writing on my New Testament doctoral dissertation at the University of Oxford. We returned to San Antonio for me to enter a partnership with St. Mark's Episcopal Church to create a new ministry to people in the workplace in the city's downtown area.

The new ministry launched in late 2001. Originally called the St. Mark's Center for Faith in the Workplace, the ministry soon became an ecumenical, nonprofit entity known today as St. Benedict's Workshop or, simply, the Workshop. My deepest thanks to the Rev. Michael Chalk, rector of St. Marks, and to the church's vestry, the new ministry steering committee, the Rev. Mary Earle, and the members of St. Marks who have joined us in this remarkable journey. I am also grateful to the current rector at St. Mark's, the Rev. Elizabeth Knowlton, and her leadership team, who continue to support the Workshop's ministry and provide us with office space at the church.

In 2005 the Rev. Jane Lancaster Patterson, PhD, joined me as a codirector of the Workshop. Jane and I have continued to share leadership of the Workshop and collaborate in ministry ever since, despite the twists and turns of our respective callings. My profound thanks to Jane for her abiding friendship, creative and brilliant scholarship, commitment to mutual accountability, trust in the Spirit's guidance, and flexibility during twenty-plus years of ministry together, guided only by the vision of sowing seeds and following up on the ones that seemed to take root in good soil. I have learned a great deal from Jane about the Bible and its interpretation, as well as how to be a faithful follower of Jesus.

I also give thanks to the Episcopal Seminary of the Southwest, especially the Very Rev. Cynthia Kittredge, ThD, and Scott Bader-Saye, PhD, for the privilege of teaching there over these past twenty-five years and for entrusting me with leadership of the Iona Collaborative at the seminary from 2016 to 2022. My heartfelt thanks also go to the Collaborative's current leaders, the Rev. Nandra Perry, PhD, and Rebecca Hall, MSF, who have encouraged me every step of the way in this writing project that, hopefully, will benefit their growing network of dioceses and congregations in the Iona Collaborative.

This book first began to take shape and then got wings during three short-term residencies at the Collegeville Institute in Collegeville, Minnesota. Thanks go to the members of the 2024-25 seminar of resident scholars for their creative input and affirmation of my project. I'm especially grateful for the generosity and gracious Benedictine hospitality of the Institute's staff, along with all they provide for writers: a beautiful setting, access to an excellent library, comfortable accommodations, and the opportunity to worship regularly with the brothers at St. John's Monastery.

This book owes its life to the participants in the Workshop. For twenty-five years, hundreds of friends in Christ have participated in our many different Workshop reflection/discernment groups and retreats. Jane and I have worked collaboratively with them as we learned together how to interpret our lives through the lenses of Scripture and to interpret the Scriptures through the lenses of our lives. Special thanks to our longtime Workshop administrative assistant Katherine Buzzini and board members Christiana Lopez, Jill Vassar, Jane Patterson, and Drew Cauthorn, who have wholeheartedly supported this project in so many ways.

I want to express my deep appreciation to the vast network of Workshop financial supporters over the past twenty-five years. They are the lifeblood of the Workshop. Special thanks go to several early and continuing Workshop champions who have been with us from the beginning and without whose support the Workshop and this book would still only be a dream: Mollie and Bartell Zachry, Elizabeth and Cliff Waller, the Dooley Family Foundation, and the Woodbury Foundation. Thanks also to Cliff Waller and Drew Cauthorn, faithful mentors and cheerleaders.

I am also grateful to the staff of the Bishop Dena A. Harrison Library at Seminary of the Southwest. Special thanks go to Alison Poague, library director, who joyfully fielded my numerous requests for access to electronic resources. This book would not have been possible without the library's generous support over these past three years.

I owe a great deal of thanks to Church Publishing and, especially, to my editor Carl Bromley. He has provided wise guidance, and many valuable and creative suggestions for ways to improve this book and make it more readable.

Three people stand out for special thanks in the development of this book. The Rev. Andrew Terry, an area missioner for the Episcopal Diocese of Texas, has read and commented on countless drafts of chapters and provided sage advice on how to make this book accessible to the widest possible audience.

Jane Patterson has been indirectly helping me write this book for the twenty years we've worked together. Over the course of a thousand conversations, we have imaginatively entered the world of Paul the apostle and worked out many details of his pastoral and teaching ministry that show up in this book. This is as much her book as mine (though she, too, will not agree with everything I've written).

Finally, a very special thanks to the Rev. Amy Richter, PhD. Amy has spent countless hours over the past six months offering many insightful, brilliant, and practical suggestions, as well as enthusiastic and generous encouragement and support.

Finally, I would not have completed this project without the sacrificial efforts of my wife, Pat Bridwell. She's read and commented on so many drafts that we've both lost count. She has continued to encourage me throughout, during times of inspiration and during times of doubt.

This book is dedicated to Pat and to the entire community of St. Benedict's Workshop.

NOTES

Foreword

1. See John G. Lewis, *Looking for Life: The Role of "Theo-Ethical Reasoning" in Paul's Religion* (London: T&T Clark International/Continuum, 2005).

Introduction: An Invitation to Pilgrimage

1. Luke Timothy Johnson, *Scripture and Discernment: Decision Making in the Church* (Nashville: Abingdon Press, 1996), 112.
2. Dennis E. Smith, *From Symposium to Eucharist: The Banquet in the Early Christian World* (Minneapolis: Fortress Press, 2003), 173–217. Paul addresses both stages of the dinner-party in 1 Corinthians 11–14.
3. According to Susan Grove Eastman:

> [W]hile the Christian community is to embrace great diversity in backgrounds, gifts, and practices, it also is to develop a capacity for group decision-making grounded in the self-giving love of Christ. Paul's goal is the formation of shared moral agency through the interpersonal bonds of love in the body of Christ. The theme of mutual discernment grounded in love runs through 1 Corinthians, as Paul exhorts his fractious congregations to grow up into maturity in Christ... Rather than setting down formulaic guidelines for behavior, Paul thinks God is transforming fellowships of believers into communities of shared moral agency—a moral agency that is both grounded in Christ's other-regarding love and sourced continually by the movement of the Spirit in their midst.

Susan Grove Eastman, "What Did Paul Think God is Doing in Christian Communities," in *The New Cambridge Companion to St. Paul*, Bruce W. Longenecker, ed. (Cambridge: Cambridge University Press, 2020), 215–16.
4. See 1 Corinthians 4:17. Paul does not refer directly to discernment in 4:17. But our stop in Corinth will show that the church's failure in its practice of discernment is a central theme in the letter.
5. The phrase "communities of resurrection life" comes from Timothy G. Gombis, *Power in Weakness: Paul's Transformed Vision for Ministry* (Grand Rapids: Wm. B. Eerdmans, 2021), 10.
6. Luke Timothy Johnson, *Miracles: God's Presence and Power in Creation* (Louisville: Westminster John Knox, 2018), 284. See also Andy Johnson,

"The Sanctification of the Imagination in 1 Thessalonians," in *Holiness and Ecclesiology in the New Testament*, Kent E. Brower and Andy Johnson, eds. (Grand Rapids: Wm. B. Eerdmans, 2007), 275–92, at 291; Tod E. Bolsinger, *It Takes a Church to Raise a Christian: How the Community of God Transforms Lives* (Grand Rapids: Brazos Press, 2004), 130–32.

7. Michael J. Gorman, *Apostle of the Crucified Lord: A Theological Introduction to Paul and His Letters*, 2d ed. (Grand Rapids: Wm. B. Eerdmans, 2017), 554, n. 7.

8. Luke 10:4–9 (my translation).

9. Christopher Rowland and Jonathan Roberts, *The Bible for Sinners: Interpretation in the Present Time* (London: SPCK, 2008), 8–9.

Chapter 1 Experiencing Resurrection Power on the Road to Damascus

1. Acts 13:9. There is no explanation in Scripture for the change of Saul's name to Paul. Paul never mentions the name Saul in any of his letters.

2. Acts of the Apostles 9:1–19; 22:6–16; 26:12–18.

3. There is scholarly consensus on this point.

4. I am translating the Greek connective *kai* applying its emphatic dimension. For Paul, Christ's active loving proceeds in acts of self-giving for others.

5. Troels Engberg-Pedersen, *Paul and the Stoics* (Louisville: Westminster John Knox Press, 2000), 95.

6. Joshua W. Jipp, *Pauline Theology as a Way of Life: A Vision of Human Flourishing in Christ* (Grand Rapids: Baker Academic, 2023), 5.

7. For a helpful discussion of the connection between divine love and acts of self-giving for others in Paul's letters, see Troels Engberg-Pedersen, "Justice, Love, and the Gift: The Logic of Pauline Soteriology," in *The New Perspective on Grace: Paul and the Gospel after Paul and the Gift*, Edward Adams et al., eds. (Grand Rapids: Wm. B. Eerdmans, 2023), 7–21.

8. Morna Hooker, "A Partner in the Gospel: Paul's Understanding of His Ministry," in *Theology and Ethics in Paul and His Interpreters*, Eugene Lovering Jr. and Jerry L. Sumney, eds. (Nashville: Abingdon Press, 1996), 100.

9. For some other references in Paul to "the faithfulness of Jesus Christ" or "the faithfulness," see, e.g., Romans 3:22, 26; 4:12, 16 (Abraham); 2 Corinthians 1:24; 13:5; Galatians 1:23; 2:16, 20; 3:22, 23, 25, 26; Ephesians 4:13; Philippians 1:27; 3:9; Colossians 1:23; 2:7.

10. Teresa Morgan, *The New Testament and the Theology of Trust* (Oxford: Oxford University Press, 2022), 4.

11. I call this translation "now-traditional," because the King James Version (1611) translates Galatians 2:20 as "the faith *of* Jesus Christ."
12. Morgan, *Theology of Trust*, 5.
13. According to Rollin A. Ramsaran, for Paul:

> The "I" has died ("been crucified"), but it returns transformed ("the life I now live") on a different footing ("live by faith"). What now drives and gives life to the "I" is taking on the "pattern of Christ."

Rollin A. Ramsaran, "'In Christ' and 'Christ in' as Expressions of Religious Experience: Testing the Waters in Galatians," in *Experientia, Volume 2: Linking Text and Experience*, Colleen Shantz and Rodney A. Werline, eds. (Atlanta: Society of Biblical Literature, 2012), 175.

14. See also Colossians 3:10, 12–17; Romans 13:12, 14; Ephesians 4:24; 66:11, 14; 1 Thessalonians 5:8.
15. See Ramsaran, "'In Christ,'" 168, n. 8 ("in Paul's mind, Gal 2:20 refers not only to Paul's religious experience but also to the religious experience of every believer").
16. Morgan, *Theology of Trust*, 5, n. 23.
17. Troels Engberg-Pedersen, "The Gospel and Social Practice According to 1 Corinthians," *New Testament Studies* 33, no. 4 (1987), 557–58, https://doi.org/10.1017/S0028688500021007.
18. We know Paul used the LXX because most of his biblical quotations track nearly word for word from some version of the Septuagint's Greek texts.
19. J. Louis Martyn, *Galatians*, The Anchor Bible (New York: Doubleday, 1997), 129–30.
20. See Martyn, *Galatians*, 130–31.
21. This reflects Paul's Jewish apocalyptic perspective, which is discussed below.
22. Luke Timothy Johnson, *Reading Romans: A Literary and Theological Commentary* (Macon, GA: Smith & Helwys Publishing, Inc. 2001), 28.
23. L. Johnson, *Reading Romans*, 28.
24. See Martyn, *Galatians*, 130–31.
25. A. Katherine Grieb, *The Story of Romans: A Narrative Defense of God's Righteousness* (Louisville: Westminster John Knox Press, 2002), 11.
26. Sally B. Purvis, *The Power of the Cross: Foundations for a Christian Feminist Ethic of Community* (Nashville: Abingdon Press, 1993).
27. Paul's most common description of God is "the one who raised Jesus from the dead." See, e.g., Romans 4:24; 6:4, 9; 7:4; 8:11; 1 Corinthians 6:14; 15:15; 2 Corinthians 4:14; 1 Thessalonians 1:10; Ephesians 1:20; Colossians 2:12.

28. Beverly R. Gaventa, "Galatians 1 and 2: Autobiography as Paradigm," *Novum Testamentum* 28, no. 4 (October 1986), 326, https://doi.org/10.2307/1560586.

29. See L. Johnson, *Reading Romans*, 27–28. See also, Romans 1:16–17; 1 Corinthians 15:1–2; 1 Thessalonians 1:5.

30. Luke Timothy Johnson, *Constructing Paul* (Grand Rapids: Wm. B. Eerdmans, 2020), 223.

31. See 1 Corinthians 2:1–5; 2 Corinthians 1:9.

32. See Romans 1:15; 10:15; 15:20; 1 Corinthians 1:17; 9:16, 18; 15:1; 2 Corinthians 10:16; 11:7; Galatians 1:8, 9, 16, 23; 4:13; Ephesians 2:17; 3:8; 1 Thessalonians 3:6. Paul's other primary verb for proclaiming the gospel is *kērussō*. According to Geoffrey William Bromiley, Gerhard Friedrich, Gerhard Kittel, eds., *Theological Dictionary of the New Testament* (TDNT), vol. TKTKTK (Wm. B. Eerdmans, 1964), 718, *euanggelizomai* and *kērussō* are synonymous.

33. See TDNT, vol. 2, 712.

34. See TDNT, vol. 2, 710–11; Martyn, *Galatians*, 127.

35. Several Pauline interpreters have emphasized Paul's gospel proclamation in *word and deed* without connecting this activity to the verb *euanggelizomai*. See Susan Grove Eastman, *Recovering Paul's Mother Tongue: Language and Theology in Galatians* (Grand Rapids: Wm. B. Eerdmans, 2007), 6; Jerry L. Sumney, "Paul's Weakness: An Integral Part of His Conception of Apostleship," *Journal for the Study of the New Testament* 16, no. 52 (October 1993): 89; Hooker, "A Partner in the Gospel," 92.

36. Hooker observes that the "Gospel was to be proclaimed both by Paul and by the community, not simply through preaching of the word, but in every believer's life. . . . The inhibition about recognizing Christ as an example has led many to ignore Paul's emphasis on Christ as a pattern to which they should be conformed." Hooker, "A Partner in the Gospel," 100.

37. See Matthew 3:17; 12:18; 17:5; Mark 1:11; Luke 3:22; 12:32; Romans 15:26, 27; 1 Corinthians 1:21; 10:5; 2 Corinthians 5:8; 12:10; Galatians 1:15; Colossians 1:19; 1 Thessalonians 2:8; 3:1; 2 Thessalonians 2:12; Hebrews 10:6, 8, 38; 2 Peter 1:17.

38. Matthew 3:17; Mark 1:11; Luke 3:22.

39. Matthew 17:5.

40. See 2 Corinthians 12:1–7.

41. The word "apocalypse" also characterizes a literary genre in Judaism. The word is used to describe prophetic, visionary Jewish literature such as Ezekiel

(chapter 1), Daniel, 1 Enoch, as well as the New Testament writing called Revelation (*Apokalypsis*).

42. N. T. Wright, *Galatians*, Commentaries for Christian Formation (Grand Rapids: Wm. B. Eerdmans, 2021), 72.

43. Cf. Wright, *Galatians*, 13.

44. As noted by Charles H. Cosgrove, *The Cross and the Spirit: A Study in the Argument and Theology of Galatians* (Macon, GA: Mercer University Press, 1988), 177–78, 183.

45. Cf. Gordon D. Fee, *The First Epistle to the Corinthians* (Grand Rapids: Wm. B. Eerdmans, 1987), 768–69; Anthony C. Thiselton, *The First Epistle to the Corinthians* (Grand Rapids: Wm. B. Eerdmans, 2000), 1249–51.

46. We will explore this partnership in the next chapter at our stop in Philippi.

47. See Philippians 1:29.

48. R. W. L. Moberly, *Prophecy and Discernment* (Cambridge: Cambridge University Press, 2006), 176.

49. See, e.g., Galatians 3:22–28; 5:24; Romans 6:1–11.

50. See 1 Thessalonians 1:9.

51. L. Johnson, *Constructing Paul*, 194.

52. Ibid., 193–94.

53. Ibid., 194.

54. Ibid., 195–96.

55. Ibid., 198.

56. See Lewis, *Looking for Life*.

57. See L. Johnson, *Constructing Paul*, 196.

58. See, e.g., 1 Thessalonians 5:20–22; 1 Corinthians 14:29; Romans 12:1–8.

59. Luke Timothy Johnson, *The Revelatory Body: Theology as Inductive Art* (Grand Rapids: Wm. B. Eerdmans, 2015), 2. This powerful conclusion is part of Johnson's enduring legacy that promotes new life in the church today. See also his *Scripture and Discernment: Decision-Making in the Church*; *Religious Experience in Earliest Christianity: A Missing Dimension in New Testament Studies* (Minneapolis: Fortress, 1998); *Miracles*.

60. L. Johnson, *The Revelatory Body*, 5.

61. L. Johnson, *Scripture and Discernment*, 112.

62. L. Johnson, *The Revelatory Body*, 46.

63. Ibid., 233.

64. Ulla Schmidt, "Practicing as Knowing: The Epistemological Significance of Practices, Exemplified with Funerary Practices," *Studia Theologica: Nordic*

Journal of Theology 75, no. 1 (April 2021): 32, http://dx.doi.org/10.1080/0039338X.2021.1916289.

65. Dorothy C. Bass et al., *Christian Practical Wisdom: What Is It, Why It Matters* (Grand Rapids: Wm. B. Eerdmans, 2016), 5.

66. A recent group of New Testament scholars have shown that moral formation in the image of Jesus Christ was Paul's principal goal for community building and pastoral ministry. See Lewis, *Looking for Life*; James W. Thompson, *Pastoral Ministry According to Paul: A Biblical Vision*, (Grand Rapids: Baker Academic, 2006); *Apostle of Persuasion: Theology and Rhetoric in the Pauline Letters* (Baker Academic, 2020); Timothy G. Gombis, *Power in Weakness: Paul's Transformed Vision for Ministry* (Grand Rapids: Wm. B. Eerdmans, 2021); Scot McNight, *Pastor Paul: Nurturing A Culture of Christoformity in the Church* (Grand Rapids: Brazos Press, 2019).

67. See Gorman, *Apostle of the Crucified Lord*, 82; Lewis, *Looking for Life*, 37–38; Wayne A. Meeks, *The Origins of Christian Morality* (New Haven: Yale University Press, 1993), 45; Robert Banks, *Paul's Idea of Community*, 2d ed. (Peabody, MA: Hendrickson, 1994), 27.

68. Gorman, *Apostle of the Crucified Lord*, 82.

69. Meeks, *Origins*, 45.

70. Michael J. Gorman, *Cruciformity: Paul's Narrative Spirituality of the Cross* (Grand Rapids: Wm. B. Eerdmans, 2001), 367.

71. L. Johnson, *Reading Romans*, 117. Johnson's analysis of Paul's encounter informs these next two paragraphs.

72. Timothy Gombis highlights a variety of temptations that lure contemporary pastors away from their primary calling to pastoral ministry. See Gombis, *Power in Weakness*.

73. Paula Fredriksen, "Paul and Augustine: Conversion Narratives, Orthodox Traditions, and the Retrospective Self," *Journal of Theological Studies* 37, no. 1 (April 1986): 16, https://doi.org/10.1093/jts/37.1.3. See also Krister Stendahl, "The Apostle Paul and the Introspective Conscience of the West," *Harvard Theological Review* 56, no. 3 (July 1963): 199–215, http://www.jstor.org/stable/1508631.

74. See Fredriksen, "Paul and Augustine," 15; Hans Dieter Betz, *Galatians* (Minneapolis: Fortress Press, 1979), 64.

75. Betz, *Galatians*, 70.

Chapter 2 Christ-Patterned Moral Reasoning in Philippi

1. Stephen E. Fowl, *Philippians*, The Two Horizons New Testament Commentary Series (Grand Rapids: Wm. B. Eerdmans, 2005), 12.
2. Gorman, *Apostle of the Crucified Lord*, 17.
3. Ibid., 17–20.
4. Ibid., 483. This paragraph draws on several points made by Gorman.
5. Fowl, *Philippians*, 12.
6. Gorman, *Apostle of the Crucified Lord*, 485.
7. For the possibility that Epaphroditus is delivering and reading Paul's letter, see Gorman, *Apostle of the Crucified Lord*, 487.
8. For this description of slavery in the Greco-Roman world, see Gorman, *Apostle of the Crucified Lord*, 16.
9. See Romans 1:7; 1 Corinthians 1:2; 2 Corinthians 1:1; Ephesians 1:1; Philippians 1:1; Colossians 1:2; Philemon 5, 7). The only exception is Galatians.
10. See Kent E. Brower and Andy Johnson, "Introduction: Holiness and the *Ekklēsia* of God," in Brower and Johnson, *Holiness and Ecclesiology*, xxii.
11. Fee, *First Corinthians*, 33. Cf. Brower and Johnson, "Introduction: Holiness," xxi.
12. Fowl, *Philippians*, 18, quoting Gerhard Lohfink, *Jesus and Community*, trans. J. P. Galvin (Philadelphia: Fortress Press, 1084), 131.
13. 1 Corinthians 1:30.
14. Thiselton, *First Corinthians*, 76.
15. Fee, *First Corinthians*, 32; cf. Luke Timothy Johnson, *Interpreting Paul: The Canonical Paul*, vol. 2 (Grand Rapids: Wm. B. Eerdmans, 2021), 370.
16. Thiselton, *First Corinthians*, 76 (original emphasis).
17. Brower and Johnson, "Introduction: Holiness," xxi–xxii.
18. Paul regularly uses the Greek phrase *en humin* (the second person, plural form of "you") to indicate something that takes place *in* individuals and *among* members of the group.
19. See, e.g., Thiselton, *First Corinthians*, 76; Teresa Morgan, *Being "In Christ" in the Letters of Paul: Saved Through Christ and in His Hands* (Tübingen: Mohr Siebeck, 2020); Fowl, *Philippians*, 18; Fee, *First Corinthians*, 65.
20. Fowl, *Philippians*, 18.
21. Ibid., 18.
22. Ibid., 19.
23. L. Johnson, *Interpreting Paul*, 93–94 (referring to the Christ-community in Corinth).

24. Fowl, *Philippians*, 83.
25. See also 1 Corinthians 1:4–8.
26. See Fowl, *Philippians*, 33. As we will see in Corinth, Paul characterizes love as the "more excellent way" of Christlike living (1 Corinthians 12:31–13:13).
27. This is the only use of the Greek word *aisthēsis* in the New Testament. I have translated it as "full moral understanding," which fits with its secular Greek usage. See Fowl, *Philippians*, 32, n. 28.
28. Robert Jewett, *Romans: A Commentary*, Hermeneia Series (Minneapolis: Fortress Press, 2006), 733.
29. See Thiselton, *First Corinthians*, 313.
30. In addition to Philippians 1:10, see Romans 1:28; 2:18; 12:2; 14:22; 1 Corinthians 3:13; 11:28; 16:3; 2 Corinthians 8:8, 22; 13:5; Galatians 6:4; Ephesians 5:10; 1 Thessalonians 2:4; 5:21; 1 Timothy 3:10.
31. See Romans 12:2.
32. Schmidt, "Practicing as Knowing," 32.
33. Fowl, *Philippians*, 54.
34. The NRSV translates *sōtērian* in 1:19 as "deliverance" rather than its usual translation as "salvation." Paul's deliverance will be, in fact, an experience of God's saving power and, thus, an experience of salvation.
35. Fowl, *Philippians*, 48.
36. Ibid.
37. See Philippians 2:17, 18, 28; 3:1; 4:4, 10.
38. In this and other ways, Paul and his colleagues serve as "spiritual directors" for the Philippians and their life in Christ. See Victor Copan, *Saint Paul as Spiritual Director* (Colorado Springs: Paternoster Press, 2007).
39. Paul alludes here to baptism *into* Christ. See Galatians 3:27; Romans 6:3. For a thorough study of trusting/believing into Christ in the Gospel of John, see Natalya A. Cherry, *Believing Into Christ: Relational Faith and Human Flourishing* (Waco: Baylor University Press, 2021).
40. See Philippians 1:19–20; 1 Corinthians 15:45; Galatians 4:6; Romans 8:9–10.
41. J. Ross Wagner, "Working Out Salvation: Holiness and Community in Philippians," in Brower and Johnson, *Holiness and Ecclesiology*, 270 (original emphasis).
42. See Philippians 4:7, 9.
43. See 1 Corinthians 12:26.
44. The Greek noun *splanchna* refers to human entrails and, along with its related verb *splanchnizomai*, is often translated as compassion/having compassion; what we might also call "gut-wrenching compassion." In addition to Philippians 1:8

and 2:1, see also Matthew 9:36; 14:14; 15:32; 18:27; 20:34; Mark 1:41; 6:34; 8:2; 9:22; Luke 1:78; 7:13; 10:33; 15:20; Acts 1:18; 2 Corinthians 6:12; 7:15; Colossians 3:12; Philemon 7, 12, 20; 1 John 3:17.

45. See Philippians 1:7; 2:2 (2x), 5; 3:15 (2x), 19; 4:2, 10 (2x).

46. Fowl, *Philippians*, 82.

47. See Fowl, *Philippians*, 28–29.

48. Fowl, Philippians, 28.

49. Bass et al., *Christian Practical Wisdom*, 5.

50. Wayne A. Meeks, "The Man from Heaven in Paul's Letter to the Philippians," in *In Search of the Early Christians: Selected Essays*, Allen R. Hilton and H. Gregory Snyder, eds. (New Haven: Yale University Press, 2002), 110 (emphasis added).

51. Stephen E. Fowl, *The Story of Christ in the Ethics of Paul* (Sheffield: JSOT Press [JSNTS 36], 1990).

52. Fowl, *Philippians*, 83.

53. The phrase is from A. Katherine Grieb, "'The One Who Called You...': Vocation and Leadership in the Pauline Literature," *Interpretation* 59, no. 2 (April 2005): 154–65, 159, https://doi.org/10.1177/002096430505900205.

54. Fowl, *Philippians*, 28.

55. Stephen E. Fowl, *Engaging Scripture: A Model for Theological Interpretation* (Eugene, OR: Wipf & Stock Publishers, 1998), 190–91.

56. Translators erroneously designate Paul as the person to be obeyed in 2:12. There is no Greek word in the text to suggest this. Following Paul's line of reasoning in 2:6–8, it is clear Paul is praising the Philippians' obedience to God, just as Christ was obedient to God (2:8). *Pace* Fowl, *Philippians*, 120.

57. Jane Lancaster Patterson, *Keeping the Feast: Metaphors of Sacrifice in 1 Corinthians and Philippians* (Atlanta: SBL Press, 2015), 125, including n. 15 (emphasis added). Patterson is describing the "logic of the cross" in 1 Corinthians 1:18.

58. L. Johnson, *Reading Romans*, 27–28.

59. Ibid.

60. Thus, when urging the reconciliation of broken relationships in Corinth, Paul tells the Corinthians that "See...now is a day of salvation!" (2 Corinthians 6:2). He refers to Christ-followers as those who are "being saved" (see 1 Corinthians 1:18; 2 Corinthians 2:15).

61. Wagner puts it this way, "The story of Christ is played out again and again in the lives of others whom the Philippians are called to imitate." Wagner, "Working Out Salvation," 266.

62. In 3:4–14 "Paul manifests a Christ-focused form of practical reasoning in the way he speaks about his past, his present aspirations, and his future hopes." Fowl, *Philippians*, 163.
63. See Fowl, *Philippians*, 168.
64. For a more thorough discussion of analogical imagination and catching the rhyme between a passage of Scripture and a contemporary situation, see William C. Spohn, *Go and Do Likewise: Jesus and Ethics* (New York: Continuum, 2007), 50–74.

Chapter 3 Pastoral Care as Formation in Holiness at Thessalonica

1. Abraham J. Malherbe, *The Letters to the Thessalonians*, The Anchor Yale Bible Commentaries, vol. 32B (New York: Doubleday, 2000), 14.
2. Charles A. Wanamaker, *The Epistles to the Thessalonians* (Grand Rapids: Wm. B. Eerdmans, 1990), 4.
3. This summary of first-century Thessalonica comes mostly from Gorman, *Apostle of the Crucified Lord*, 188–89.
4. The phrase "Jewish Diaspora" refers to the centuries-long dispersion of Jewish people to places outside of Israel/Palestine. This dispersion resulted from historical events such as the Assyrian conquest of Israel in the eighth century BCE, the Babylonian exile in the sixth century BCE, and the destruction of Jerusalem and the Second Temple by Rome in 70 CE.
5. Malherbe, *Thessalonians*, 92. See also, Molly T. Marshall, *1 & 2 Thessalonians*, Belief: A Theological Commentary on the Bible Series (Louisville: Westminster John Knox Press, 2022), 3.
6. See Gorman, *Apostle of the Crucified Lord*, 38.
7. Malherbe, *Thessalonians*, 65.
8. See 2 Corinthians 8:2; Romans 15:26.
9. Malherbe, *Thessalonians*, 66.
10. See Malherbe, *Thessalonians*, 65, 324. The *Rule of St. Benedict*, chapter 4, embraces Paul's vision of the Christian community as a workshop where people toil faithfully to learn and use the tools of the spiritual craft. The contemporary nonprofit ministry called St. Benedict's Workshop incorporates this same vision. We create settings where participants toil faithfully with the tools of the spiritual craft. These tools include the Bible and moral deliberations to discern acts of Christlike faithfulness and to recognize experiences of resurrection power.
11. Gorman, *Apostle of the Crucified Lord*, 196.
12. Wanamaker, *Thessalonians*, 15.

13. See Marshall, *1 & 2 Thessalonians*, 2.
14. Andy Johnson, *1 & 2 Thessalonians* (Grand Rapids: Wm. B. Eerdmans, 2016), 245 (original emphasis).
15. See 1 Thessalonians 2:17–20; Wanamaker, *Thessalonians*, 16.
16. See 1 Thessalonians 2:14–16.
17. I am using historical imagination to suggest Silvanus as the letter reader.
18. See A. Johnson, *Thessalonians*, 39, including n. 40.
19. A. Johnson, *Thessalonians*, 39, including n. 38.
20. Malherbe, *Thessalonians*, 289.
21. The source of the Holy Spirit is the resurrected Lord. See 1 Corinthians 15:45; L. Johnson, *Scripture & Discernment*, 121.
22. See A. Johnson, *Thessalonians*, 245.
23. Sumney, "Paul's Weakness," 89.
24. Ibid., 79–80.
25. Philippians 2:7.
26. Philippians 2:8.
27. Gorman, *Apostle of the Crucified Lord*, 196.
28. We will see this more clearly at our next stop in Corinth. Revelation happens in the course of deliberations in discernment (1 Corinthians 14:29–31).
29. See 1 Thessalonians 2:12; Galatians 1:4.
30. Cf. A. Johnson, *Thessalonians*, 55, 265.
31. Ibid., 265. We will see a clear example of this at our next stop in Corinth (1 Corinthians 11:27–34).
32. Ibid., 246.
33. Ibid., 59, n. 134.
34. See ibid., 92.
35. Philippians 1:10; see also 1 Corinthians 3:13; 11:28; 16:3; Romans 14:22; 2 Corinthians 8:8, 22; 13:5; Galatians 6:4; Ephesians 5:10; Philippians 1:10; 1 Thessalonians 5:21.
36. See Romans 14:18; 16:10; 1 Corinthians 11:19; 2 Corinthians 10:18; 13:7.
37. See Romans 1:28; 1 Corinthians 9:27; 2 Corinthians 13:5, 6, 7. *Pace* A. Johnson, *Thessalonians*, 62.
38. In the ancient world, a father was generally responsible for teaching the moral life to his children. Paul metaphorically depicts himself in that role with the Thessalonians. See also 1 Corinthians 4:15.
39. See Galatians 1:22–23.
40. Galatians 1:15–16.

41. L. Johnson, *Interpreting Paul*, 362. See also, L. Ann Jervis, "The Spirit Brings Life to Life," in *Reading Paul's Letter to the Romans*, Jerry L. Sumney, ed. (Atlanta: Society of Biblical Literature, 2012), 148, including n. 21 ("The idea of sanctification emphasizes a moral life in accordance with God's will").

42. 1 Corinthians 1:30.

43. See L. Johnson, *Scripture & Discernment*, 121.

44. L. Johnson, *Interpreting Paul*, 362.

45. According to Malherbe, "the communal perspective of the advice...is already part of the introduction." Malherbe, *Thessalonians*, 219. A. Johnson puts it this way: "we're asking and encouraging you all in the sphere of the Lord Jesus." A. Johnson, *Thessalonians*, 104.

46. Thiselton, *First Corinthians*, 76.

47. A. Johnson, *Thessalonians*, 243.

48. A. Johnson, *Thessalonians*, 103–04.

49. See also Galatians 1:6, 15–16. The author of Ephesians (probably someone formed by Paul's circle of colleagues) puts it this way: "For we are God's workmanship, having been created in Christ Jesus upon good works, which God prepared in advance for us to walk in them" (Ephesians 2:10).

50. Suggested by his opening words in 5:1, "Now concerning..."

51. A. Johnson, *Thessalonians*, 136.

52. As noted earlier, Paul frequently emphasizes the role of experience in this letter. See 1:4, 5, 9; 2:1, 2, 5, 9, 10, 11, 12; 3:3, 4; 4:2, 4, 5; 5:2.

53. The sudden and unexpected arrival of "the day of the Lord" is a common theme in the early Christian tradition, including the Gospels. See Matthew 24:42–44/Luke 12:39–40. The theme using similar language is also addressed in 2 Peter 3:10 and Revelation 3:3; 15:15.

54. Malherbe, *Thessalonians*, 291.

55. Ibid., 292.

56. See Galatians 3:27; Romans 13:12, 14; Ephesians 4:24; 6:11, 14; Colossians 3:10, 12.

57. Wayne A. Meeks, *The First Urban Christians: The Social World of the Apostle Paul* (New Haven: Yale University Press, 1983), 238, n. 68.

58. Barclay, "Under Grace," 68–69.

59. For Paul's emphasis on the significance of encouraging one another "one to one," see Malherbe, *Thessalonians*.

60. See 1 Corinthians 14:1–5, 29–30.

61. For Paul's use of the verb beyond 1 Thessalonians 5:11, see Romans 15:20; 1 Corinthians 8:1, 10; 10:23; 14:4, 17; and Galatians 2:18. For various uses of the noun *oikodomē*, see Romans 14:19; 15:2; 1 Corinthians 3:9; 14;3, 5, 12, 26; 2 Corinthians 5:1; 10:8; 12:19; 13:10; Ephesians 2:21; 4:12, 16, 29.
62. Luke Timothy Johnson, "Edification as a Formal Criterion of Discernment in the Church," *Sewanee Theological Review* 39, no. 4 (1996): 367.
63. L. Johnson, *Interpreting Paul*, 365.
64. See also Galatians 6:1.
65. Cf. Malherbe, *Thessalonians*, 326.
66. See also Romans 12:17–20; Matthew 5:44–48; Luke 6:27–36.
67. According to Malherbe: "[t]he final section of this letter is (5:16–28) is shot through with liturgical elements. Paul visualizes his letter being read while the church is gathered for worship, and these elements will contribute to the use of the letter in the assembly." Malherbe, *Thessalonians*, 327.
68. A. Johnson, *Thessalonians*, 147. These actions are "practices through which God continues sanctifying the audience's imagination."
69. A. Johnson, *Thessalonians*, 148 (original emphasis).
70. See Philippians 3:10–11.
71. As noted by A. Johnson, *Thessalonians*, 153.
72. 1 Corinthians 14:31.
73. 1 Corinthians 14:3.
74. See Malherbe, *Thessalonians*.
75. Cf. Malherbe, *Thessalonians*, 333.
76. A. Johnson, *Thessalonians*, 243.
77. See A. Johnson, *Thessalonians*, 243.

Chapter 4 Formation and Discernment Gone Awry in Corinth

1. The designation of First Corinthians is a misnomer, as Paul refers to an earlier, long-lost letter to them in 1 Corinthians 5:9.
2. Gorman, *Apostle of the Crucified Lord*, 275.
3. See Meeks, *The First Urban Christians*, 47.
4. Ibid., 48.
5. Gorman, *Apostle of the Crucified Lord*, 274.
6. Ibid.
7. Ibid.
8. See Andrew B. McGowan, *Ancient Christian Worship: Early Church Practices in Social and Historical Perspective* (Grand Rapids: Baker Academic, 2014), 22.

9. L. Michael White, "Regulating Fellowship in the Communal Meal: Early Jewish and Christian Evidence," in *Meals in a Social Context*, Inge Nielsen and Hanna Sigismund Nielsen, eds. (Aarhus: Aarhus University Press, 2001), 179; Matthias Klinghardt, "A Typology of the Communal Meal," in *Meals in the Earthly Christian World: Social Formation, Experimentation, and Conflict at the Table*, Dennis E. Smith and Hal E. Taussig, eds. (New York: Palgrave MacMillan, 2012), 9–22; Dennis E. Smith, "The Greco-Roman Banquet as a Social Institution," in *Meals in the Earthly Christian World*, 23–33.

10. See Smith, *From Symposium to Eucharist*; Andrew B. McGowan, "Rethinking Eucharistic Origins," *Pacifica: Australasian Theological Studies* 23, no. 2 (June 2010): 179, https://doi.org/10.1177/1030570X1002300204.

11. White, "Regulating Fellowship," 179; Klinghardt, "Communal Meal," 10.

12. Klinghardt, "Communal Meal," 10; Smith, "The Greco-Roman Banquet," 24.

13. See Klinghardt, "Communal Meal," 18.

14. Smith, *From Symposium to Eucharist*, 267.

15. See 1 Corinthians 1:26–31.

16. See Smith, *From Symposium to Eucharist*, 185.

17. See ibid.

18. Plutarch, *Quaestiones Convivales*, 612d, quoted by Smith, *From Symposium to Eucharist*, 268.

19. Smith, *From Symposium to Eucharist*, 54, citing Plutarch, *Quaestiones Convivales*, 614d.

20. Smith, *From Symposium to Eucharist*, 179.

21. See 1 Corinthians 14:26–33.

22. See Hal Taussig, *In the Beginning Was the Meal: Social Experimentation and Early Christian Identity* (Minneapolis: Fortress Press, 2009), 36–37.

23. See McGowan, *Ancient Christian Worship*, 81.

24. Ibid., 74–75.

25. Ibid., 75.

26. Ibid.

27. Ibid., 83–84.

28. Ibid., 83.

29. Taussig, *In the Beginning*, 39.

30. Gorman, *Apostle of the Crucified Lord*, 273.

31. Ibid.

32. Boykin Sanders, "Imitating Paul: 1 Cor 4:16," *Harvard Theological Review* 74, no. 4 (October 1981): 363, https://www.jstor.org/stable/1509566.
33. Gorman, *Apostle of the Crucified Lord*, 281.
34. See 8:1–13; 10:24, 33; 11:17–34.
35. Engberg-Pedersen, "The Gospel and Social Practice," 582–83.
36. See 1 Corinthians 4:6, 18, 19; 5:2; 8:1; 13:4.
37. Lewis, *Looking for Life*, 37.
38. L. Johnson, *Interpreting Paul*, 371.
39. Cf. L. Johnson, *Interpreting Paul*, 371.
40. David G. Horrell, "Restructuring Human Relationships: Paul's Corinthian Letters and Habermas's Discourse Ethics," *The Expository Times* 110, no. 10 (July 1999): 321–325, at 321–22, https://doi.org/10.1177/0014524699 11001004.
41. See Wayne A. Meeks, "The Polyphonic Ethics of the Apostle Paul," in *In Search of the Early Christians: Selected Essays*, Allen R. Hilton and H. Gregory Snyder, eds. (New Haven: Yale University Press, 2002).
42. See L. Johnson, *Interpreting Paul*, 371; Margaret M. Mitchell, *Paul and the Rhetoric of Reconciliation: An Exegetical Investigation of the Language and Composition of 1 Corinthians* (Louisville: Westminster John Knox Press, 1991), 257, including n. 396.
43. The one exception occurs in 1 Corinthians 5:5 and 13. Paul demands that the church expel the brother who Paul deems to be practicing sexual immorality. He issues this order for the sake of preserving the presence of the spirit of Christ that guides the church's practice of discernment.
44. See 1 Corinthians 10:15; 11:13; cf. 11:31.
45. Meeks, "The Polyphonic Ethics of the Apostle Paul," 204.
46. See 1:2; 6:11; 7:14.
47. See 1:18.
48. See 2:7, 8; 10:31; 11:7, 15; 15:40, 41, 43.
49. See 2:2; 4:5; 5:3, 12, 13; 6:1, 2, 3, 6; 7:37; 10:15, 29; 11:13, 31, 32.
50. See 1:3, 4; 3:10; 10:30; 15:10, 57; 16:3, 23.
51. See 3:13; 11:28.
52. See 1:18, 21; 3:15; 5:5; 7:16; 9:22; 10:33; 15:2.
53. See 1:9; 9:23; 10:16, 18, 20.
54. See 8;1, 10; 10:23; 14:4, 17.
55. See 4:21; 8:1; 13:1, 2, 3, 4, 8, 13; 14:1; 16:14, 24.
56. See 1:7; 14:6, 26, and the related verb *apokalyptō* in 14:30.

57. Romans 16:23 and 1 Corinthians 1:11–17 strongly support this conclusion.
58. For this and other insights on the epistolary genre in antiquity, see Gorman, *Apostle of the Crucified Lord*, 99.
59. Meeks, *The First Urban Christians*, 143, including n. 16 at 235.
60. See Brower and Johnson, "Introduction: Holiness," xxii.
61. Fowl, *Philippians*, 18, quoting Gerhard Lohfink, *Jesus and Community*, trans. J. P. Galvin (Philadelphia: Fortress Press, 1084), 131.
62. See Thiselton, *First Corinthians*, 76 (original emphasis).
63. Andy Johnson, "The Sanctification of the Imagination," 285.
64. See, e.g., Fee, *First Corinthians*, 32, n. 20.
65. See, e.g., Thiselton, *First Corinthians*, 76.
66. Richard B. Hays, *First Corinthians* (Louisville: John Knox Press [Interpretation], 1997), 17.
67. See Romans 5:12–21. We will closely examine this passage at our last stop on this pilgrimage in Rome.
68. I am anachronistically including chapter and verse designations for readers. These markers were not included in the original texts.
69. See 1 Corinthians 14:26, 30.
70. Patterson, *Keeping the Feast*, 125, including n. 15 (emphasis added).
71. Ibid.
72. Ibid.
73. Carey Newman, *Paul's Glory-Christology: Tradition and Rhetoric*, Supplements to Novum Testamentum, vol. 69 (Leiden: E. J. Brill, 1992), 245.
74. Alexandra R. Brown, *The Cross and Human Transformation* (Minneapolis: Fortress Press, 1995), 112.
75. A gift of grace empowers some members of the community to distinguish which spirit/Spirit is influencing particular human actions and experiences (see 12:10).
76. 1 Corinthians 3:9, 10 (2x), 12, 14; 8:1, 10; 10:23; 14:3, 4, 5, 12, 17, 26.
77. L. Johnson, "Edification as a Formal Criterion of Discernment," 367.
78. We explored "The Day of the Lord" at our stop in Thessalonica. It is the future day of God's intervention to judge the world, set things right, and then reign eternally for life in God's kingdom.
79. Paul uses the Greek noun *paidagōgos* to describe some of their leaders. The *paidagōgos* was often employed to teach the moral life to children in affluent families.

80. For the translation of the verb *exestin* in 6:12 as "permissible," see Fee, *First Corinthians*, 249, 252.
81. Fee, *First Corinthians*, 252.
82. See 1 Corinthians 12:7, where the same verb is translated in the NRSV as an action that serves the common good.
83. The NRSV translates this verb in 6:12 as "beneficial."
84. See 1 Corinthians 13:8–12.
85. See Meeks, "The Polyphonic Ethics of the Apostle Paul."
86. See David G. Horrell, "Theological Principle or Christological Praxis? Pauline Ethics in 1 Corinthians 8.1—11:1," *Journal for the Study of the New Testament;* 67 (1997): 83–114, at 106.
87. 1 Corinthians 11:17, 18, 20, 33, 34; 14:23, 26.
88. Mitchell, *Paul and the Rhetoric of Reconciliation*, 154–55.
89. Lewis, *Looking for Life*, 102.
90. See also, Romans 14:18; 16:10; 2 Corinthians 10:18; 13:7.
91. The NRSV translation of this verse ignores the phrase "in the same place" in the original Greek text.
92. 1 Corinthians 1:26–31 establishes the minority status (speaking numerically) of these elite members of the congregation.
93. Thiselton, *First Corinthians*, 886–87.
94. This is the meaning of the words of Jesus in Matthew 18:20: "where two or three are gathered in my name, I am in your midst."
95. *Diakonia* can be translated as "service" or "ministry." It is the basis for the church office of a "deacon"—one who serves others.
96. Just as Paul and Plutarch both imagined.
97. Paul uses the same analogy in Romans 6:13, 19 and 12:3–8.
98. L. Johnson, *Interpreting Paul*, 378.
99. See Romans 12:6.
100. L. Johnson, *Interpreting Paul*, 114.
101. For parts of this translation, see Thiselton, *First Corinthians*, 1258.
102. Luke Timothy Johnson, *Imitating Christ: The Disputed Character of Christian Discipleship* (Grand Rapids: Wm. B. Eerdmans, 2024), 185.
103. L. Johnson, *Imitating Christ*, 184.

Chapter 5 Discernment in Rome: Under Grace, Not Under Torah

1. Jewett, *Romans*, 60; see also Mark D. Nanos, "To The Churches Within The Synagogues of Rome," in *Reading Paul's Letter to the Romans*, Jerry L. Sumney, ed. (Atlanta: Society of Biblical Literature, 2012), 11–28, at 14.

2. Brendan Byrne, *Romans*, Sacra Pagina Series, vol. 6 (Collegeville, MN: Liturgical Press, 1996), 10.
3. Quoted by Jewett, *Romans*, 59–60.
4. McGowan, *Ancient Christian Worship*, 4.
5. See ibid., 2.
6. Ibid., 6.
7. Ibid., 184.
8. See, e.g., Matthew 14:33; 28:9, 17; John 4:20, 21, 22, 24; 12:20; Acts 7:43; 8:27; 24:11; 1 Corinthians 14:25; Hebrews 1:6; 11:21; Revelation 4:10; 5:14; 7:11; 11:1, 16; 13:4, 12, 15; 14:7, 9, 11; 19:10; 22:8. In the NRSV, *proskyneō* is occasionally translated as "paying homage to" (see, e.g., Matthew 2:2, 8, 11) or "kneeling down" before Christ (see, e.g., Matthew 8:2; 9:18; 15:25; 18:26; 20:20).
9. See, e.g., Matthew 4:10 (Luke 4:8); Luke 1:74; 2:37; John 16:2; Acts 7:7; Romans 1:9, 25; 12:1.
10. Michael J. Gorman, *Romans: A Theological and Pastoral Commentary* (Grand Rapids: Wm. B. Eerdmans, 2022), 21.
11. Johnson, *Reading Romans*, 2.
12. Ibid.
13. See Grieb, *The Story of Romans*, 1 (Paul's letter "almost certainly presupposes an actual historical situation").
14. Romans 1:5; 16:26.
15. Romans 12:1. For the verb *latreuō* see 1:9, 25.
16. Romans 4:24, 25; 6:4, 9; 7:4; 8:11, 34; 10:9.
17. See Romans 1:1; 6:6, 16 (2x), 17, 18, 19 (2x), 20, 22; 7:6, 25 (2x); 8:15, 21; 9:12; 12:11; 14:18; 16:18.
18. The Greek word *dikaiosynē* has two inseparable dimensions, like two sides of the same coin. See Patterson, *Keeping the Feast*, 168.
19. See Mark D. Nanos, *The Mystery of Romans: The Jewish Context of Paul's Letter* (Minneapolis: Fortress Press, 1996), 226.
20. See Brower and Johnson, "Introduction: Holiness," xxii.
21. See 1 Corinthians 1:2; 2 Corinthians 1:1; Galatians 1:2; Ephesians 1:1; Philippians 1:1; 1 Thessalonians 1:1; 2 Thessalonians 1:1; Philemon 2. In Colossians 1:2 Paul addresses them as "in Christ" rather than "in Christ Jesus."
22. See 1 Corinthians 16:19, where Paul sends greetings to the church in Corinth from Prisca and Aquila, who are now with Paul in Ephesus.
23. See 3:21–26; 12:1–2; 15:16.

24. See Ernst Käsemann, "Ministry and Community in the New Testament," in *Essays on New Testament Themes*, W. J. Montague, trans. (London: SCM Press, 1964), 67; James D. G. Dunn, *The Theology of the Apostle Paul* (Grand Rapids: Wm. B. Eerdmans, 1998), 556. Dunn defines *charism* as "divine grace come to effect and expression in word and deed...the contribution which the individual member makes to the whole."

25. For understanding *charisma* as a "trusteeship" for others given by God to each member of the Body of Christ in Rome, see John K. Goodrich, "'Standard of Faith' or 'Measure of a Trusteeship'? A Study in Romans 12:3," *Catholic Biblical Quarterly*, 74 (2012): 753–72. See now, 1 Peter 4:10.

26. See 15:18–21.

27. See 1 Corinthians 1:18–25.

28. Galatians 1:15–16.

29. Grieb, *The Story of Romans*, 11.

30. L. Johnson, *Reading Romans*, 27.

31. Recall 1 Corinthians 12:6.

32. 1 Corinthians 4:20.

33. Gorman, *Apostle of the Crucified Lord*, 37–38.

34. For understanding Paul's use of the verb *pisteuō* in 1:16 as "trust," see the discussion in Grieb, *The Story of Romans*, 11; see also Morgan, *Theology of Trust*, 42–43.

35. Morgan, *Theology of Trust*, 43.

36. See Martyn, *Galatians*, 130–31.

37. See Patterson, *Keeping the Feast*, 168.

38. L. Johnson, *Reading Romans*, 28.

39. See 1 Corinthians 1:9; 10:13; 2 Corinthians 1:18; 1 Thessalonians 5:24.

40. See Romans 3:21–26.

41. Galatians 2:20.

42. See 1 Thessalonians 1:1–10.

43. Grieb provides a helpful, comprehensive list of five things Paul probably intends to suggest by this single quotation.

44. For an in-depth and illuminating discussion of these words and the theme of the "righteousness of God" in Romans, see Grieb, *The Story of Romans*, especially at 12–13 and 21–25.

45. I am borrowing the phrase "two-pronged approach" from Patterson, who writes, "[w]hen one hears (or reads) the letter for the first time, 3:21–26 comes after Paul's two-pronged approach to express the common predicament of both the Jews and other nations." Patterson, *Keeping the Feast*, 163.

46. Victor Paul Furnish, "Living to God, Walking in Love: Theology and Ethics in Romans," in *Reading Paul's Letter to the Romans*, Jerry L. Sumney, ed. (Atlanta: Society of Biblical Literature, 2012), 188.

47. This is the same verb Paul applied to his own "worship" of God in 1:9.

48. Patterson, *Keeping the Feast*, 166–67.

49. Ibid., 164.

50. Furnish, "Living to God, Walking in Love," 189.

51. John M. G. Barclay, "Under Grace: The Christ-Gift and the Construction of a Christian *Habitus*," in *Apocalyptic Paul: Cosmos and Anthropos in Romans 5–8*, Beverly Roberts Gaventa, ed. (Waco: Baylor University Press, 2013), 64.

52. See Jervis, "The Spirit Brings Life to Life," 140, including n. 4.

53. Barclay, "Under Grace," 69.

54. Engberg-Pedersen, "Justice, Love, and the Gift," 14–17.

55. The Greek preposition *en* can denote location or instrumentality. In this case, Paul intends both uses.

56. For Paul's use of *dikaiōma* in Romans, see 1:28; 2:26; 5:16, 18; 8:4. For my translation of *dikaiōma* as God's just decree for life, see N. T. Wright, "Putting Paul Together Again," in *Pauline Theology, Vol 1: Thessalonians, Philippians, Galatians, Philemon*, Jouette Bassler, ed. (Minneapolis: Fortress Press, 1991), 203.

57. See Barclay, "Under Grace," 64.

58. See John M. G. Barclay, *Paul and the Power of Grace* (Grand Rapids: Wm. B. Eerdmans, 2020), 133.

59. See Jervis, "The Spirit Brings Life to Life," 141.

60. L. Johnson, *Reading Romans*, 102.

61. Grieb, *The Story of Romans*, 66.

62. See 1 Corinthians 1:2.

63. Cf. Barclay, "Under Grace," 74.

64. L. Johnson, *Reading Romans*, 104.

65. See Ephesians 4:21–22: "You were taught to put away your old way of life, your old self"; Colossians 3:9: "having taken off your old self with its practices."

66. Barclay, "Under Grace," 73.

67. See L. Johnson, *Reading Romans*, 115–16.

68. I am using this lengthy phrase to translate the Greek word *sarx*. See Grieb, *The Story of Romans*, 76.

69. The Greek verb *oikeō* can mean "inhabit," "colonize," "settle in," "dwell in," or "manage or direct a household."

70. Jervis, "The Spirit Brings Life to Life," 140.
71. Ibid.
72. See ibid., 141.
73. Grieb, *The Story of Romans*, 77.
74. Ibid.
75. Leander Keck, *Romans* (Nashville: Abingdon Press, 2005), 200.
76. According to L. Ann Jervis, the Spirit "sets up house among them," reflecting her translation of the Greek verb *oikeō* in Romans 8:9. Jervis, "The Spirit Brings Life to Life," 142. The Greek verb *oikeō* can also be translated as "manage or direct a household," which even more accurately describes the Spirit's role in the moral deliberations of the community.
77. Paul consistently uses the verb *zōopoieō* to refer to God's power to create new life. See Romans 4:17; 8:11; 1 Corinthians 15:22, 36, 45; 2 Corinthians 3:6; Galatians 3:21.
78. The spatial metaphors are from Grieb, *The Story of Romans*, 77.
79. For the creation of this relational experience of sonship through the Spirit of God's Son in Galatians, see Ramsaran, "'In Christ,'" 174.
80. See L. Johnson, *Reading Romans*, 139.
81. See Jewett, *Romans*, 729.
82. Jewett, *Romans*, 729.
83. Ernst Käsemann, "Worship in Everyday Life: A Note on Romans 12," in *Essays on New Testament Themes*, W. J. Montague, trans. (London: SCM Press, 1964), 191, 194; Grieb, *The Story of Romans*, 119. *Contra* Jewett, who complains that sacrifice is "hardly an appropriate metaphor for mopping the floor." Jewett, *Romans*, 728.
84. Romans 12:1, 2; 14:18; 2 Corinthians 5:9; Ephesians 5:10; Philippians 4:18; Colossians 3:20.
85. Romans 8:8; 1 Corinthians 7:32; 2 Corinthians 5:9; Galatians 1:10; 1 Thessalonians 2:14; 4:1.
86. Romans 15:1, 2, 3; 1 Corinthians 7:33, 34; 10:33; Ephesians 6:6; Colossians 3:22.
87. See also Romans 9:4.
88. Ian W. Scott, "'Your Reasoning Worship': ΛΟΓΙΚΟΣ [LOGIKOS] in Romans 12:1 and Paul's Ethics of Rational Deliberation," *Journal of Theological Studies* 69, no. 2 (October 2018): 525, https://www.jstor.org/stable/48548543.
89. Scott, "Your Reasoning Worship," 531.
90. See ibid., 525.
91. Eastman, "What Did Paul Think God is Doing," 215.

92. *The Book of Common Prayer* (New York: Church Publishing Company, 1979), 857.
93. Furnish, "Living to God, Walking in Love," 194.
94. Cf. Jewett, *Romans*, 734.
95. Furnish, Living to God, Walking in Love," 195.
96. Ibid.
97. Cf. ibid.
98. See Lewis, *Looking for Life*, 41, n. 31, summarizing Käsemann, "Ministry and Community," 64–65.
99. Paul uses the same Greek noun *melos* to characterize an individual's bodily limbs in 6:13 and 6:19, and the members of Christ's body in 12:4 and 12:5.
100. Cf. L. Johnson, *Reading Romans*, 205.
101. Romans 4:24, 25; 6:4, 9; 7:4; 8:11, 34; 10:9.
102. A problem Paul also identified in 1 Corinthians 3:1–4.
103. L. Johnson, *Reading Romans*, 212.
104. Grieb, *The Story of Romans*, 127–28.
105. For this analysis and that of the following paragraph, see L. Johnson, *Reading Romans*, 212–13.
106. Johnson acknowledges that Paul reached this conclusion "in Christ Jesus." But he doesn't connect the conviction to the moral deliberations and discernment of Paul's community. He does characterize this conviction as one of the "most radical positions taken by the first Christians against virtually every form of contemporary Judaism." L. Johnson, *Reading Romans*, 215.
107. Cf. L. Johnson, *Reading Romans*, 215.
108. The Greek adjectives *dynatos* ("powerful") and *adynatos* ("powerless") have the same root as *dynamis*, which I have consistently translated as "power."
109. This is the same verb Paul used in 14:1 to open this section of the letter.

Chapter 6 Discernment in Christ Jesus Today

1. Collect For Guidance, as revised, *The Book of Common Prayer* (New York: Church Publishing, 1979), 832.
2. Collect, Proper 28, as revised, *The Book of Common Prayer* (New York: Church Publishing, 1979), 236.

Epilogue: Where Have We Been? Where Are We Going?

1. L. Johnson, *Miracles*, 279.
2. See, e.g., Thompson, *Pastoral Ministry According to Paul*, and *Apostle of Persuasion*; Gombis, *Power in Weakness*; McNight, *Pastor Paul*.

INDEX

Index of words, phrases, and authors for *Discernment in the Early Church and Today*
Note: Pages followed by "n" refer to notes.

accountability, 92–94, 100, 111, 116, 210, 227, 230, 231, 233, 246
agapē, 46, 52, 78, 86, 94, 113, 131, 142–44, 148, 173, 185
anakrinō, 124, 127, 132, 134, 145
analogy, 21, 28, 31, 32, 48, 60, 62, 67, 78, 80–82, 84, 100, 103, 132, 144, 162, 176, 178, 192, 211, 212, 218
apocalyptic, 8, 9, 18, 27–29, 40, 50, 69, 76, 81, 82, 85, 90, 92, 93, 100, 109, 110, 121, 122, 148, 162–202, 204, 216
Aristotle, 58, 63, 135, 206

baptism into Christ, 21, 49, 66, 115, 130, 175, 176, 178
Barclay, John, 260n58, 268n51, 268n53, 268n57, 268n58, 268n63, 268n66
body of Christ, 1, 2, 4, 11, 36, 49, 88, 89, 107, 115, 130, 133, 141, 142, 166, 175, 176, 179, 210, 225, 229, 233
build up, 35, 57, 60, 76, 86, 90, 93, 95, 111, 113, 123, 126, 131, 134, 143, 145–47, 152, 159, 177, 198, 213

charis, 51, 56, 113, 116, 117, 123, 125, 140, 162, 163, 166, 173, 174, 179, 190, 192

charisma/charismata, 117, 118, 123–25, 130, 140–42, 166, 174, 175, 178, 181, 182, 185, 186, 190–92, 194, 204, 229
citizenship, 29, 44–46, 50, 55–57, 66, 69

deliberative assembly, 17, 19, 35–36, 41, 52, 77, 88, 90, 94, 97, 103, 114, 115, 131, 134, 136, 143, 145, 147–49, 151, 160, 164, 165, 189, 203, 209–26
diakrinō, 129, 138, 146
discernment
  communal discernment, 4, 10, 12, 13, 34, 92, 97, 112, 138, 149, 178, 188, 193, 194, 229–32, 234, 235
  defined, v, 41
  practice of discernment,, 2–6, 8, 9, 12, 13, 32, 34, 35, 41, 48, 52, 53, 56, 58–60, 64, 65, 68, 74, 81, 82, 84, 90, 92, 96, 99, 101, 111, 116, 118, 119, 122, 126, 143, 147–50, 152, 159, 165, 173, 175, 183, 185, 186, 188, 194, 198, 199, 201, 206, 224, 225, 227, 228, 230, 232–35
  spirit-led discernment, 122–24, 139–41, 179–85, 228

dokimazō, 46, 52, 53, 76, 83, 95, 96, 113, 126, 136, 138, 186, 188, 189, 200

dynamis, 24

Eastman, Susan, 249n3, 252n35, 269n91

egeirō, 161, 196

ekklēsia, 17, 19, 35–37, 50, 77, 84, 85, 94, 109, 114, 115, 128, 134–36, 139, 142, 145, 149, 151, 160–62, 164, 165, 189, 195, 201, 227

embodiment, 3, 25, 49, 79, 117, 118, 123, 124, 130, 132, 134, 140–42, 166, 167, 174, 175, 181, 182, 186, 190–92, 229

embody Christ, 20, 22, 27, 31, 39, 41, 53, 59, 62, 63, 68, 77, 82, 96, 100, 111, 117, 121, 125, 133, 134, 147, 151, 160, 188, 227, 228, 233

encourage/encouragement, 9, 10, 16, 26, 29, 54–57, 61, 63, 64, 71, 75, 76, 78, 79, 81, 83–87, 89, 90, 93–96, 101, 132, 144, 145, 147, 152, 160, 166, 178, 188, 191, 194–97, 199–201, 204, 212, 213, 217, 218, 224, 225, 233, 234

Engberg-Pedersen, Troels, 250n5, 250n7, 251n17, 263n35, 268n54

entrust, 3, 20, 22, 24, 39, 83, 121, 122, 124, 151, 164, 167–69, 172, 202, 210, 228

euanggelion, 17, 19, 22–24, 44, 45, 51, 147, 162, 163

euanggelizomai, 17, 19, 25–27, 85, 120, 121, 147, 159, 166, 167, 202

faithfulness, 2, 3, 6, 9, 18, 20–22, 24, 25, 27, 28, 30–32, 34, 37, 39–41, 49, 50, 52, 55, 56, 58, 65, 66, 75, 76, 78–86, 88, 92, 94–97, 99, 102, 107, 126, 132, 142, 143, 144, 153, 157, 160–69, 171, 172, 174, 175, 181–84, 190–93, 196, 199, 200, 202–4, 210, 213, 228, 231

Fee, Gordon, 130, 253n45, 255n11, 255n15, 255n19, 264n64, 265n80, 265n81

Fowl, Stephen, 57, 58, 60, 255n1, 255n5, 255n12, 255n19, 255n20, 256n24, 256n26, 256n27, 256n33, 256n35, 257n46–257n48, 257n51, 257n52, 257n54–257n56, 258n62, 258n63, 264n61

Furnish, Victor, 189, 268n46, 268n50, 270n93, 270n95

Gombis, Timothy, 249n5, 254n66

Gorman, Michael, 109, 158, 250n7, 254n67, 254n68, 254n70, 255n2, 255n4, 255n6–255n8, 258n3, 258n6, 258n11, 259n27, 261n2, 261n5, 262n30, 263n33, 264n58, 266n10, 267n33

gospel-event(s), 22–26, 29, 40, 61, 63, 64, 78–80, 85–86, 98, 99, 120, 133, 152, 167–69, 214, 220, 223, 228

grace, 7–9, 19, 51–52, 56, 59, 63, 112, 113, 116–18, 123–27, 130, 140–42, 144, 147, 148, 155–207, 209, 210, 213, 214, 227, 229

Grieb, Katherine, 167, 245, 251n25, 257n53, 266n13, 267n29, 269n34, 267n43, 267n44, 268n61, 268n68,

269n73, 269n78, 269n78, 269n83, 270n104

holiness, 7, 9, 17, 32, 37, 48, 49, 71–103, 121, 162, 163, 178
Hooker, Morna, 21, 250n8, 252n35, 252n36
Horrell, David, 263n40, 265n86
human experience, 33, 34, 78–80

imagination, 6, 8, 16, 41, 49, 62, 67, 74, 82, 95–98, 103, 115, 143, 159, 177, 206, 211, 212, 230, 233, 234
imitation, 89, 147, 149
in Christ Jesus, 49–50, 84–85, 115–16, 160, 164–65, 175, 179–85, 189–90, 194–95, 198–201, 210–13, 227–30

Jervis, L. Ann, 260n41, 268n52, 268n59, 269n70, 269n76
Jewett, Robert, 256n28, 265n1, 266n3, 269n81–269n83, 270n94
Johnson, Andy (A. Johnson), 95, 250n6, 255n10, 255n11, 259n14, 259n18, 259n19, 259n22, 259n30, 260n45, 260n47, 260n48, 260n51, 261n68, 261n69, 261n71, 261n76, 261n77, 264n63
Johnson, Luke (L. Johnson), 4, 33, 34, 111, 149, 159, 231, 234, 245, 249n1, 251n22, 251n23, 252n29, 252n30, 253n51, 253n57, 253n59–253n62, 254n71, 255n10, 255n11, 255n15, 255n17, 255n23, 256n41, 257n58, 259n21, 260n41, 260n43, 261n62, 261n63, 263n38, 263n39, 263n42, 264n60, 264n77, 265n98,

265n100, 265n102, 265n103, 266n11, 266n20, 267n30, 266n38, 268n60, 266n64, 266n67, 269n80, 270n100, 270n103, 270n105, 270n106, 270n107, 271n1

Käsemann, Ernst, 267n24, 269n83, 270n98
koinōneō, 64
koinōnia, 31, 46, 51, 52, 57, 107, 113, 117–19, 133
krinō, 112, 121, 122, 127, 129, 130

logic of the cross, 9, 111, 112, 119–22, 125, 127–35, 147, 151, 197, 210, 211, 229
love, 2, 17, 20–22, 25, 32, 39, 40, 42, 46, 52, 53, 58, 65, 74, 78, 85–89, 92, 94, 97, 99, 113, 121, 131, 132, 142–44, 146, 148, 149, 151, 153, 167, 173, 174, 181, 182, 185, 188, 194–96, 206, 210, 211, 215, 219, 223, 225, 228

Malherbe, Abraham, 258n1, 258n5, 258n7, 258n9, 258n10, 259n20, 260n45, 260n54, 260n59, 261n65, 261n67, 261n74, 261n75
Martyn, J. Louis, 23, 251n19, 251n20, 251n24, 252n34, 267n36
McGowan, Andrew, 108, 158, 261n8, 262n10, 262n23, 266n4
McNight, Scot, 254n66
Meeks, Wayne, 58, 112, 254n66, 257n50, 260n57, 261n3, 263n41, 263n45, 264n59, 265n85
mind of Christ, 111, 120, 124, 129, 144, 147, 151, 188, 195, 197, 211

moral deliberations, 3, 5, 9, 12, 53, 55, 56, 57, 58, 61, 62, 63, 64, 65, 86, 92, 107, 108, 109, 110, 111, 116, 119, 129, 130, 133, 135, 136, 138, 146, 147, 148, 149, 150, 151, 177, 183, 186, 187, 191, 193, 194, 198, 199, 200, 227

moral reasoning, 3, 8, 43–69, 92, 111, 120, 132, 170, 188, 197, 198, 201, 223, 229

Moberly, R. W. L., 32, 253n48

Morgan, Teresa, 21, 250n10, 251n12, 251n16, 255n19, 267n34, 267n35

Nanos, Mark, 265n1, 266n19

obedience of faithfulness, 161, 162, 163

oikodomeō, 76, 93, 113, 125, 126, 131, 134, 142, 143, 145

partnership, 8, 30, 31, 46, 51, 52, 54, 64, 95, 107, 113, 117, 118, 119, 133, 135, 140

Patterson, Jane, 4, 120, 246, 247, 257n57, 264n70, 266n18, 267n37, 267n45, 268n48

phroneō, 46, 57, 58, 63, 182, 188, 190, 194, 200

phronēsis, 58, 63

pistis, 18, 20, 21, 55, 76, 78, 95, 97, 122, 167, 197

Plutarch, 107, 135, 144

power of God, 3, 4, 15, 20, 22, 24, 25, 32, 33, 39, 79, 97, 120, 121, 122, 124, 127, 133, 147, 160, 164, 167, 169, 172, 174, 176, 185, 193, 196, 201, 202, 228

practical wisdom, 2, 13, 34, 58, 87, 153, 192, 193, 210, 225, 232

proof through testing, 9, 34, 53, 54, 73, 83, 96, 97, 126, 153, 186, 189, 192, 193, 194, 200, 201, 206, 229

prophets/prophecy, 92, 93, 96, 108, 144, 145, 146, 147, 152, 162, 163, 190, 191

reasoned worship, 161, 178, 184

resurrection power, 1, 2, 3, 4, 5, 8, 12, 13, 15–42, 50, 51, 53, 61, 78, 79, 84, 86, 96, 97, 99, 102, 110, 112, 118, 119, 120, 121, 122, 123, 125, 128, 135, 141, 143, 146, 147, 148, 150, 151, 152, 159, 160, 166, 167, 168, 176, 178, 181, 182, 183, 185, 186, 189, 193, 194, 196, 197, 198, 201, 202, 210, 220, 223, 228, 229, 230, 235

save/salvation, 3, 7, 22, 23, 25, 45, 46, 54, 55, 56, 60, 61, 63, 67, 91, 92, 93, 113, 120, 121, 133, 147, 167, 168, 174, 183, 196, 201, 214, 235

Schmidt, Ulla, 34, 253n64, 256n32

slave, 30, 46, 48, 59, 62, 81, 105, 141, 156, 162, 163, 177, 203

Smith, Dennis, 249n2, 262n9, 262n10, 262n12, 262n14, 262n16, 262n18, 262n20

St. Benedict's Workshop (Workshop), 4, 9, 12, 101, 206, 207, 209, 235

suffering, 8, 28, 30, 31, 43, 45, 51, 52, 54–55, 56, 57, 62, 63, 64, 67, 71, 74, 80, 81, 83, 85, 94, 95, 101, 102, 143

Sumney, Jerry, 79, 250n8, 252n35, 259n23, 259n24, 260n41, 265n1, 268n46
synerchomai, 135, 136, 139

Taussig, Hal, 262n9
Thiselton, Anthony, 253n45, 255, 256n29, 260n46, 264n62, 264n65, 265n93, 265n101

Thompson, James, 254n66
two-stage dinner party, 2, 10, 106, 107, 109, 116, 119, 135, 147

worship, 1, 2, 3, 7, 9, 10, 11, 40, 44, 46, 53, 66, 74, 100, 106, 107, 116, 135, 136, 145, 149, 150, 156, 157–58, 161, 165, 178, 184 186, 187, 206, 227, 230, 231, 233, 234

www.ingramcontent.com/pod-product-compliance
Lightning Source LLC
Chambersburg PA
CBHW050210240426
43671CB00013B/2287